Black / Gay

Black / Gay

THE HARLEM RENAISSANCE, THE PROTEST ERA,
AND CONSTRUCTIONS OF BLACK GAY IDENTITY
IN THE 1980S AND 90S

Simon Dickel

MICHIGAN STATE UNIVERSITY PRESS | *East Lansing* ■ LIT VERLAG | *Münster*

Copyright © 2011 by LIT Verlag

⊗ The paper used in this publication meets the minimum requirements of ANSI/NISO Z39.48-1992 (R 1997) (Permanence of Paper).

LIT Verlag
Münster

Michigan State University Press
East Lansing, Michigan 48823-5245

Printed and bound in the United States of America.

19 18 17 16 15 14 13 12   1 2 3 4 5 6 7 8 9 10

LIBRARY OF CONGRESS CATALOGING-IN-PUBLICATION DATA
Dickel, Simon.
Black/gay: the harlem renaissance, the protest era, and constructions of black gay identity in the 1980s and 90s / Simon Dickel.
p. cm.
Includes bibliographical references.
ISBN 978-1-61186-009-2 (pbk. : alk. paper) 1. Gays' writings, American—History and criticism. 2. American literature—20th century—History and criticism. 3. African Americans in literature. 4. Homosexuality in literature. 5. African Americans in motion pictures. 6. African American men—Race identity. 7. Homosexuality in motion pictures. 8. Homosexuality and literature—United States. I. Title.
PS153.G38D53 2012
810.9'9206642—dc22
2010054070

Cover design by Sharp Des!gns, Inc.
Cover art: Richard Bruce Nugent, "Mr. Brooklyn" © Thomas H. Wirth. Used by permission.

g green press initiative Michigan State University Press is a member of the Green Press Initiative and is committed to developing and encouraging ecologically responsible publishing practices. For more information about the Green Press Initiative and the use of recycled paper in book publishing, please visit www.greenpressinitiative.org.

■ Visit Michigan State University Press at www.msupress.org

For my parents
Egilde Dickel and Winfried Dickel

Acknowledgements

My work on this book would have been impossible without the support of colleagues, friends, and loved ones. I want to thank my teacher Maria I. Diedrich for her inspiration and support, Sylvia Mayer and Helma Lutz for their encouragement and feedback, Jeffery Allen Tucker for a long discussion about his work on Delany and for a guided tour of Rochester, Charles I. Nero for his encouragement to carry on with my project and for taking Martin and me to the Chi Chiz bar on Christopher Street, Steven G. Fullwood for his helpful assistance at the Schomburg Center for Research in Black Culture and for introducing me to Charles I. Nero, and Samuel R. Delany for a challenging conversation, a meal at the Silk Road Palace, and his permission to research his collection at the Howard Gotlieb Archival Research Center in Boston. I want to thank Ransom Bradford for proofreading and for sharing his personal experiences of growing up gay in the USA in the 1950s, Michael Bucher for detailed feedback on each chapter of the manuscript, Thomas Behm for a private surprise screening of *Looking for Langston* on 16mm, a magical experience that was to become one of the starting points for this book, and Philipp Offermann for keeping morale up in our shared office and for technical assistance. I want to thank Hanna Wallinger for her feedback at the final stages of the book's production, Thomas H. Wirth for his permission to use Bruce Nugent's painting *Mr. Brooklyn* for the book cover, the Rosa-Luxemburg-Stiftung for a grant, and the Collegium for African American Research (CAAR) for being a supportive network of political and charming intellectuals. I want to thank my parents Egilde Dickel and Winfried Dickel for their love, care, and confidence. My partner Martin Pleitz has supported me and my work on this book in more ways than I can name here. I want to thank him for allowing me to sometimes regard him as a tower of strength and for everything else.

Contents

1 Introduction

Perry Williams, the protagonist of Rodney Evans's 2004 film *Brother to Brother*, is a young black gay artist who is trying to come to terms with racism, homophobia and the way his blackness and gayness affect his life and art.[1] Set in the 1980s, the film focuses on Perry's friendship with the character depicting the elderly Harlem Renaissance poet Bruce Nugent.[2] Perry inhabits a hostile world; he experiences his white boyfriend's racism and his father's homophobia. As his personal guide, Nugent helps Perry to come to terms with his life as a black gay man and artist. Evans's film shows Perry's interest in the work and persona of James Baldwin, and it focuses on Perry's personal affiliations with Nugent, who raises his awareness of a rich heritage of African American "gay" literature and art that goes as far back as the 1920s. Consequently, the film illustrates a strategy that has been firmly established by black gay writers, artists, filmmakers, and activists since the 1980s: the construction of a cultural tradition that constitutes black gay identity.

The circumstances of the fictional character Perry, his strategy of survival, and his subsequent emancipation as a black gay man mirror the state of affairs and the political strategies of black gay men in the 1980s. Confronted with racism in the white-dominated gay community and homophobia in the black community, they looked at the work of those homosexual men in black cultural history who did not see their race and their sexuality as two separate or even antagonistic aspects of their identities. For this reason, many black gay cultural activists, like Perry, focused their attention on two historical periods, the Harlem Renaissance of the 1920s and 1930s and the Protest Era of the 1950s and 1960s. In my study, I will analyze the different strategies that black gay texts of the 1980s and 1990s employ in referring to these two constitutive periods of the African American cultural tradition.

In the 1980s, black gay men were marginalized within hegemonic culture as well as within the black and the gay liberation movement. Since the early

---

1 Rodney Evans, dir., *Brother to Brother*, San Jose CA: Wolfe, 2004, DVD.

2 It is obvious that the film does not aim at historical accuracy. Bruce Nugent, who died in 1987, is still alive in the film, in which the LA riots of 1992 are mentioned.

1980s, they have organized independently from these movements and started to base their politics and artistic strategies on the categories blackness and gayness. They have produced a large number of periodicals, anthologies, plays, novels, and films, which have resulted in a growing visibility of black gay men. Consequently, the 1980s were the first decade of a consciously black gay literature and art. In the earliest anthologies of writings by black gay men in the mid-1980s, the authors frequently referred to the Harlem Renaissance and the Protest Era, and they established literary forefathers who served as role models, most notably Richard Bruce Nugent, Langston Hughes, and James Baldwin.

The scope of my study is limited to the first decade of a consciously black gay culture. It focuses on four anthologies, four novels, one film, and one autobiographical memoir, all of which were published between 1984 and 1995. To set the stage, I initially focus on the four literary anthologies *In the Life: A Black Gay Anthology* (1986) edited by Joseph Beam, *Brother to Brother: New Writings by Black Gay Men* (1991) edited by Essex Hemphill, and the Other Countries Collective's two volumes *Black Gay Voices* (1988) and *Sojourner: Black Gay Voices in the Age of Aids* (1992). As paradigmatic texts of black gay cultural activism, I analyze six longer texts: Isaac Julien's film *Looking for Langston* (1989), Steven Corbin's novel *No Easy Place to Be* (1989), Samuel R. Delany's short novel "Atlantis: Model 1924" (1994), and his autobiographical memoir *The Motion of Light in Water* (1988), Randall Kenan's novel *A Visitation of Spirits* (1989), and Melvin Dixon's novel *Vanishing Rooms* (1991).

Four of these five writers and filmmakers were personally affiliated with the four anthologies. Dixon's writings appeared in *In the Life* and *Brother to Brother*. At the time, he was also working as an associate editor on the journal staff of the first volume of *Black Gay Voices*, and his text "I'll be Somewhere Listening for My Name" appeared posthumously in *Sojourner: Black Gay Voices in the Age of Aids*. The anthology *In the Life* contains an interview with Delany conducted by Joseph Beam with the title "The Possibility of Possibilities," and there are blurbs by Delany on the covers of the first volume of *Black Gay Voices* as well as in *Brother to Brother*. Hemphill, who also worked with Julien on the film *Looking for Langston*, made an interview with Julien for *Brother to Brother*. This anthology also contains Julien and Kobena Mercer's essay "True Confessions: A

Discourse on Images of Black Male Sexuality." Kenan's writings are not included in any of the anthologies, but there is a blurb by Kenan on the cover of *Sojourner*. Steven Corbin is the only writer central to my study who is not affiliated in any way with these black gay anthologies. As he is the only writer who was living in Los Angeles rather than on the East Coast, there might be geographical reasons for his absence. Owing to the personal affiliations and friendships in the community of black gay activists, it is safe to say that at least Dixon, Delany, Julien and Kenan were aware of the topics and discussions that were central to the 1980s and early 1990s black gay discourse.

Apart from Delany, who was born in 1942 and has been an established writer of Science Fiction and non-fictional texts since the 1960s, all of the other authors started to produce their work in the 1980s and 90s. The professional affiliations with academic life show in the texts of all five writers and filmmakers. The AIDS crisis had devastating consequences for the group of authors, activists and editors on which my study focuses. Most of the members of the "Other Countries Collective" and many of the contributors of the early black gay anthologies died of AIDS-related complications. Beam died from AIDS in 1987. Hemphill, Corbin, and Dixon died from AIDS in the early 1990s.

This study is an interdisciplinary analysis of texts that belong to a variety of genres: essay, fiction, experimental fiction, autobiographical memoir, as well as film. My use of the term "text" is not limited to written texts. The concept of text changed because of Roland Barthes's semiotic approach explained in his book *Mythologies* (1973). According to the semiotic approach, text refers to "a pan-disciplinary concept that encompasse[s] any cultural object of investigation, including the full range of media (visual, aural, and corporeal), ritual spectacles and social activities (from presidential inaugurations and wars to sports and shopping), commodities, and spaces (from shopping centers to cities)."[3] All of these cultural objects can be read as semiotic systems, and because of their interactions with other texts, their meaning is open and subject to change:

3 Terry Threadgold, "Text," *New Keywords: A Revised Vocabulary of Culture and Society*, eds. Tony Bennett, Lawrence Grossberg, and Meaghan Morris, Malden, MA and Oxford, 2005, 346.

> Any text is always quite literally a weaving together of other, similarly interconnected, texts. Thus, rather than having a single or stable meaning somehow embodied in the structure or the 'words on the page,' the text is engaged in a continuous play of meaning across the field of intertextuality.[4]

One consequence of this view of texts and textuality is the idea that there is no such thing as a reality that could be perceived independently from language, but that texts construct and structure our notions of reality. Of course, "the continuous play of meaning across the field of intertextuality" is present in any given text and does not have to be intended by the writer of a novel or the director of a film. Drawing on Mikhail Bakhtin's idea of a dialogic relation between texts, Julia Kristeva uses the term "intertextuality" to refer to the ways texts refer to one another. Still, I will put emphasis on those instances of intertextuality that are intended by the writers/directors and discuss the texts in relation to their pretexts. Thus, I will look for re-writings of earlier texts and analyze references to literary traditions.

Even though the texts investigated belong to different genres and media, they still form a relatively homogeneous body of work. What the texts have in common is the fact that they were produced by men who have referred to their own subject position as black and gay, even if they have done so in different ways and for different reasons. The texts engage in discussions about identity and identity politics and they do so by referring to earlier texts addressing issues of race, gender, and sexuality (including for example writings by Harlem Renaissance authors, the novels and essays of James Baldwin, photos by James Van der Zee and Robert Mapplethorpe, and the films of Oscar Micheaux). In this respect, I regard the written texts and Julien's film as texts that signify on earlier texts, mirror the political context of the 1980s and 1990s, and engage in the political discourse surrounding race, sexuality, and gender.

Of course, a director has other means of expression than a novelist or essayist, and I will reflect on the possibilities and limitations of the different genres and media when discussing the films, novels, essays, etc. But all of the texts are concerned with the ways in which black gay and queer identities at

---

4 Threadgold, 346.

the end of the twentieth century relate to African American literary traditions. Consequently, Julien's film *Looking for Langston* is comparable to the written texts in the way it refers to earlier writers and adapts earlier texts.

There are three reasons that led black gay men to work independently and distance themselves from the Black Power and the gay liberation movement: the success of the political movements of the 1960s and 70s that based their politics on a common identity, the shortcomings of these movements in addressing the intersections of multiple lines of difference, and the threat of the AIDS-crisis.[5] As the authors of these texts refer to their own subject positions with the term "black gay man" and as the texts negotiate and politicize the categories blackness and gayness, I discuss the texts as expressions of black gay cultural activism.

Whereas I contend that the texts I analyze are representative of the 1980s and 1990s black gay cultural movement, I do not suggest that they comprise a complete list of the important texts by black gay men stemming from that period. Black gay men worked in all fields of cultural production, including poetry, theater, performance, and visual art. For example, the novels of Larry Duplechan, the poetry of Assotto Saint, the performance art of the groups Cinque and PomoAfroHomos, the photographs of Rotimi-Fani-Kayode, and the films by Marlon Riggs are also constitutive of the black gay culture of the 1980s and 1990s. However, I have focused on those texts from the 1980s and 1990s that assert a specific literary lineage starting with the literature of the Harlem Renaissance, rather than aiming at a complete overview of 1980s and 1990s black gay culture.

The strategy of referring to former periods, historical persons, and aesthetic traditions is not unusual for marginalized groups. Members of such groups often try to legitimize themselves by emphasizing the trans-historical validity of a collective identity. For example, Black Nationalists have often

---

5 Black gay activists followed the example set by black feminists who distanced themselves from the women's movement and the black movement in the 1970s. Joseph Beam, Essex Hemphill, Charles I. Nero, and other black gay men have emphasized the impact the work of black (lesbian) feminists had on their own work, and they have repeatedly expressed their affiliations and solidarity with black feminist thought.

emphasized the African roots of African Americans, and early historians who worked in the field of gay studies argued in favor of the essentialist belief that homosexual men had always existed throughout history and frequently referred to ancient Greece to give evidence for their argument.[6] Even after the constructionist paradigm shift within gay and lesbian studies that led to a differentiated analysis of sexuality in earlier historical periods, members of gay and lesbian communities frequently refer to the Stonewall riots as one important origin of their political agenda. Nowadays Stonewall is taken as a myth of origin for gay and lesbian communities symbolized by the annual pride parades. Within the black gay community, however, the status of the Stonewall riots is controversial. Whereas some black gay men have tried to reclaim the Stonewall riots by emphasizing the central role of black persons in the rebellion,[7] others have distanced themselves from the Stonewall riots.[8] Regardless of their attitudes towards the historical significance or insignificance of the Stonewall riots, since the 1980s, black gay writers, artists, and filmmakers have established two other important points of reference. They refer to the Harlem Renaissance and the Protest Era of the 1950s and 1960s and especially to the work and personae of Bruce Nugent, James Baldwin and Langston Hughes as origins for black gay identity.

For black gay activists and artists of the 1980s and 1990s, the reference to the Harlem Renaissance and the Protest Era serves a threefold function. First, the

---

6 Jonathan Katz's 1976 book *Gay American History* is an example of this approach. In his second book *Gay/Lesbian Almanac* (1983), Katz differentiates between modern homosexual *identity* and (homo-)sexual *behavior* in former periods. See also Stefan Micheler and Jakob Michelsen, "Von der 'Schwulen Ahnengalerie' zur Queer Theory. Geschichtsforschung und Identitätsstiftung," *Jenseits der Geschlechtergrenzen: Sexualitäten, Identitäten und Körper in Perspektiven von Queer Studies*, ed. Ulf Heidel, Hamburg: MännerschwarmSkript, 2001, 127–143.

7 See, for example, the black drag queen Francine in Assotto Saint's play *Risin' to the Love We Need*. Assotto Saint, "Risin' to the Love We Need," *Spells of a Voodoo Doll*, New York: Masquerade, 1996, 321–380.

8 One example is Lonnie McGill of New York's Committee of Black Gay Men, who argues against the significance of Stonewall for black gay men and lesbians: "Most Black homosexuals should realize that Stonewall has no significance for us. The white homosexual community has not allowed its legend to create any advantages for us, and it has prostituted Stonewall to death, giving no support to the memory or lives of those black backs that were first beaten in that so-called historic event." Charley Shively, "Smoke, Lilies, and Jade: Black Gay Poetry as an Act of Revolution," *Gay Community News* (1987): 7–10, 7.

emphasis on these black cultural traditions is a strategy of self-empowerment. Second, it is a way to separate black gay identity from the white dominance within the gay community. Third, via the connection to periods and writers that are firmly rooted in and helped to establish the black literary and cultural tradition, black gay artists and activists aim to legitimize the existence of the black gay community in the eyes of the black community as a whole: it is a strategy of legitimization that reacts to the heteronormativity found in some segments of the black community.

In this introduction I have so far used the terms "black," "gay," and "black gay" as a matter of course. However, a study that covers a period of time comprising seventy years has to be sensitive to discursive changes. This is particularly true for political terms whose usage is often the result of controversies over their legitimacy. The current usage of the two terms "black" and "gay" is the result of their appropriation by the political movements of the 1960s. In the late 1960s "black" replaced the earlier terms "colored" and "Negro," and "gay" is a term devoid of the negative aspects of the earlier and derogatory term "queer" as well as of the pathological connotations of the more medical 1950s term "homosexual." The idea of gay identity and the concomitant political strategy to come out of the closet as a way of affirming this identity are fairly recent developments dating from the 1960s. As homosexuality has not always been conceptualized in terms of an identity, I will use two terms in my study: "homosexuality," a term that signifies homosexual behavior, and "gay," a term I use when I refer to homosexuality as an identity. As the concept of gay identity was unknown in the Harlem Renaissance, and as Baldwin remained skeptical of gay identity during his lifetime, I use the terms "homosexuality" and "homosexual" when I deal with the Harlem Renaissance and Baldwin. As most black gay cultural activists in the 1980s and 1990s wanted to emphasize the similarities and sameness of writers such as Nugent, Baldwin and themselves, they use the term "gay" when they refer to these periods.

Since the mid-1990s the term "queer" is used in academic contexts as well as by many political activists. Queer politics are a reaction to the critique directed at the exclusionary effects of identity politics by gay and lesbian groups, and queer theory evolved as a consequence of poststructuralist approaches towards concepts of identity. Even though black gay cultural activism was one important factor that led to the emergence of "queer" as a term of reference, I have decided to use the term "black gay" because it denotes a specific subject position that grows out of a negotiation of the sometimes antagonistic constructions of blackness and gayness. In addition, scholars who work to establish a distinct black queer theory have argued recently that the term "queer" makes black subjects invisible.[9]

Research Report

The recent publication of two literary anthologies indicates the growing interest in black queer literature. The anthology *Black Like Us: A Century of Lesbian, Gay, and Bisexual African American Fiction* (2002), edited by Devon W. Carbado, Dwight McBride, and Don Weise, collects black queer literature from the Harlem Renaissance to the end of the twentieth century. The introductory essay to the third part of this anthology, "1980–2000: Coming Out Black Like Us," provides an extensive overview of gay, lesbian, bisexual, and transgender literature published after 1980. E. Lynn Harris's anthology *Freedom in This Village: Twenty-Five Years of Black Gay Men's Writings* (2004) focuses on black gay literature since 1979 and collects many texts from the early black gay anthologies. Despite this recent interest in black gay and black queer literature, there is yet no book-length critical study focusing solely on black gay literature, film, and art of the 1980s and 1990s. My study aims at throwing light upon this period of black gay cultural activism. It is written with a specific research interest connecting the 1980s and 1990s to earlier periods of African American culture.

To understand the political debates among black gay men at the beginning of the 1980s, I have examined the unpublished papers of Joseph Beam, Melvin Dixon, and Assotto Saint, as well as rare materials, such as small magazines, reviews, photocopied leaflets, and posters announcing meetings of black gay groups. These materials are collected at the *Black Gay and Lesbian Archive Project*

---

9 E. Patrick Johnson, "'Quare' Studies, or (Almost) Everything I Know About Queer Studies I Learned from My Grandmother." *Black Queer Studies: A Critical Anthology*, eds. E. Patrick Johnson and Mae G. Henderson, Durham: Duke UP, 2005, 124–157.

housed at the *Schomburg Center for Research in Black Culture* in Harlem. The *Black Gay and Lesbian Archive Project* was initiated by the *Schomburg Center*'s librarian Steven G. Fullwood, a black gay cultural activist himself. His black gay and lesbian collection is an invaluable resource for future research in black queer culture. My research at the Schomburg Center was of seminal importance for the critical perspective of my study. The collected materials demonstrate the precarious position of black gay men during the 1980s and their need to be validated and recognized in a larger scheme. For example, Dixon's personal diaries are a sign of the difficulties he faced in finding a publisher for the manuscript of *Vanishing Rooms*. Throughout the 1980s, Dixon unsuccessfully tried to get his black gay narrative published. Saint's and Dixon's papers reveal the devastating consequences the AIDS epidemic had for them as well as for this whole generation of black gay men. Beam's papers clarify the central importance of the publication of *In the Life* for his self-image as a black gay man. His papers include the correspondence with those writers who contributed their writings to *In the Life*. The urgency expressed in the personal papers of Dixon, Saint, and Beam was one reason leading to my focus on how black gay men validate their identity by referring to earlier periods of African American culture.

The overall approach of this study is influenced by two essays. In her essay "Looking for Harlem: (Re)Konstruktionen Harlems als 'queer Mecca', 1925–1995" (2001), Dorothea Löbbermann analyzes the way Delany's short novel "Atlantis: Model 1924" refers to constructions of Harlem as a "queer mecca" in criticism as well as fiction. In analyzing the ways black gay texts refer to African American culture, I am also indebted to Charles I. Nero's essay "Toward a Black Gay Aesthetic: Signifying in Black Gay Literature" (1991). It is the first essay to provide a systematic critical framework for the analysis of contemporary black gay texts. Referring to Henry Louis Gates's theory of African American literature put forward in *The Signifying Monkey* (1988), Nero analyzes the signifying strategies of black gay writers, among them Hemphill, Duplechan, and Delany.

Taking a new historicist approach, I have paid special attention to specific sociopolitical and historical contexts, not only with regard to the 1980s and 1990s but also concerning those periods the texts refer to. At the beginning of chapters four and five, I concentrate on the sociopolitical, aesthetic, and historical dimensions of the Harlem Renaissance and the Protest Era of the 1950s and 1960s. Moreover, I give an overview of traditional and more recent queer approaches to the literature of the Harlem Renaissance, the Protest Era, and James Baldwin. The contexts given at the beginning of these chapters provide a precondition for understanding the differences between these periods and the 1980s and 1990s, the era of black gay cultural activism. In this introductory research report, I concentrate on those recent books and essays concerning these periods that are most important for my argument.

In her study *Gay Voices of the Harlem Renaissance* (2003), A.B. Christa Schwarz analyzes the key male Harlem Renaissance writers. In doing so, she pays special attention to the writers' homosexuality and the ways sexual orientation is depicted in their texts. George Chauncey's *Gay New York* (1994) includes a chapter on Harlem as a gay neighborhood. His study is important for an understanding of the way the homosexual subculture was organized in the early twentieth century. Chauncey discusses the transitions of concepts of sexual identities and considers the transformation of the terms denoting homosexual practices. Thomas H. Wirth's book *Gay Rebel of the Harlem Renaissance: Selections from the Work of Richard Bruce Nugent* (2002) includes a long introductory essay partly based on interviews Wirth conducted with his friend Nugent. Consequently, Wirth's book is an important resource for an account of the queer dimensions of the period. Seth Clark Silberman's essay "Lighting the Harlem Renaissance AFire!!: Embodying Richard Bruce Nugent's Bohemian Politic" (2000) is a queer approach towards Nugent's work. Joseph Allen Boone's literary study *Libidinal Currents* (1998) contains a chapter on Harlem as a queer site of modernism in which he argues that Nugent's story "Smoke, Lilies and Jade" is a modernist text containing queer elements. The historical context of the 1950s and 1960s, the political debates surrounding Baldwin's work, and the queer perspective on Baldwin are provided by Dwight A. McBride's anthology *James Baldwin Now* (1999), a collection of essays by scholars such as Marlon B. Ross, Michelle Wright, Roderick Ferguson, and others. Robert F. Reid-Pharr's essay "Tearing the Goat's Flesh: Homosexuality, Abjection, and the Production of a Late Twentieth-Century Black Masculinity" (1997), as well as his chapter "Alas Poor Jimmy" in his most recent book *Once You Go Black: Choice, Desire, and the Black American Intellectual* (2007), belong to the same paradigm. Dwight McBride's essays "Can the Queen Speak? Sexuality, Racial Essentialism, and the Problem of Authority" (2005) and "Straight Black Studies: On African American Studies, James Baldwin, and Black Queer Studies" (2005) re-evaluate Baldwin's work from a black queer perspective. The 2007 conference "James Baldwin: Work, Life, Legacies," held in London (with McBride as a keynote speaker), put special emphasis on a queer-studies perspective in approaching Baldwin's work. The volume *Black Queer Studies* (2005) contains McBride's "Straight Black Studies" and two further essays directly focused on Baldwin's work. These studies indicate the central importance Baldwin's work has for the formulation of a distinct black queer theory.

With the exception of Arthur Flannigan Saint-Aubin's critical evaluation of *Brother to Brother* in his essay "Black Gay Male Discourse: Reading Race and Sexuality Between the Lines," published in the *Journal of the History of Sexuality* in 1993, the four black gay anthologies *In the Life*, *Brother to Brother*, *Black Gay Voices*, and *Sojourner: Black Gay Voices in the Age of Aids* have been disregarded by literary critics. In my analysis of these volumes, I largely refer to contemporary reviews published in small (black) gay magazines and newspapers.

There are no book-length studies on the films and writings of Julien, Corbin, Kenan, and Dixon. In my reading of *Looking for Langston* I mainly refer to the work of film theorist Manthia Diawara. In his essay "The Absent One: The Avant-Garde and the Black Imaginary in *Looking for Langston*," he discusses Julien's avant-gardist film language and its function in the attempt to construct a trans-temporal filmic space which combines disparate elements specific to black gay culture. In his essay "The Films of Isaac Julien: Look Back and Talk Black" (1991), José Arroyo analyzes the historical references in Julien's films from a film studies point of view. There are numerous essays discussing *Looking for Langston* from a cultural studies perspective, such as Kobena Mercer's "Dark and Lovely: Black Gay Image-Making" (1994), bell hooks's "Seductive Sexualities: Representing Blackness in Poetry and on Screen" (1990), and Henry Louis Gates's "Looking for Modernism" (1993) and "The Black Man's Burden" (1993). These writers argue that *Looking for Langston* is an example of an alternative black gay aesthetics, and they pay special attention to postmodern debates about identities.

The Film Art of Isaac Julien (2000) is the catalogue of the eponymous exhibition shown in the U.S., Australia, Sweden, and Norway during the years 2000–2002. It gives an overview of Julien's work and contains critical essays, interviews, filmography, and a detailed bibliography of secondary sources covering the years 1987–1999. The last chapter of Maria Balshaw's study *Looking for Harlem: Urban Aesthetics in African American Literature* (2000), entitled "Elegies to Harlem," considers the way *Looking for Langston*, as well as Toni Morrison's *Jazz* (1992), refer to the Harlem Renaissance. Löbbermann's essay "Looking for Harlem" and her study *Memories of Harlem: Literarische (Re)Konstruktionen eines Mythos der Zwanziger Jahre* (2000) are focused on Harlem Renaissance texts and on 1980s and 1990s reconstructions of Harlem, among them *Looking for Langston*, "Atlantis: Model 1924," and *No Easy Place to Be*. With the exception of Löbbermann's study, Corbin's *No Easy Place to Be* has largely been ignored by literary critics.

The intertextual references between Baldwin's *Go Tell It on the Mountain* and Kenan's *A Visitation of Spirits* are discussed in Robert McRuer's study *The Queer Renaissance* (1997). The chapter "Queer Locations/Queer Transformations" focuses solely on Kenan's novel. Like Nero, McRuer refers to Gates's theory of Signifying. Sheila Smith McKoy's essay "Rescuing the Black Homosexual Lambs: Randall Kenan and the Reconstruction of Southern Gay Masculinity" follows McRuer's line of argument. In her essay "(Pro)Creating Imaginative Spaces and Other Queer Acts: Randall Kenan's *A Visitation of Spirits* and Its Revival of James Baldwin's Absent Black Gay Man in *Giovanni's Room*" (1999), Sharon P. Holland focuses on the intertextuality of *A Visitation of Spirits* and *Giovanni's Room*. Lindsey Tucker's essay "Gay Identity, Conjure, and the Uses of Postmodern Ethnography in the Fictions of Randall Kenan" (2003) focuses more closely on Kenan's ethnographic style of writing, a style that is continued in his book *Let the Dead Bury Their Dead* (1992). Trudier Harris discusses Kenan as a Southern writer in her study *The Power of the Porch: The Storyteller's Craft in Zora Neale Hurston, Gloria Naylor, and Randall Kenan* (1996).

There are two essays focussing on Dixon's *Vanishing Rooms* from an intersectional perspective: Darieck Scott's "Jungle Fever? Black Gay Identity Politics, White Dick, and the Utopian Bedroom" (1994) and Vivian M. May's "Reading Melvin Dixon's *Vanishing Rooms* – Experiencing 'the ordinary rope that can change in a second to a lyncher's noose or a rescue line'" (2000). Both essays deal with the construction of gay whiteness. In his essay "The Autochoreography of an Ex-Snow Queen: Dance, Desire, and the Black Masculine in Melvin Dixon's *Vanishing Rooms*" (1997), Maurice Wallace analyses the role dance plays for the development of the novel's protagonist Jesse.

Delany's writings have been more broadly acknowledged in criticism. There are four book-length studies on his work, Douglas Barbour's *Worlds Out of Words: The SF Novels of Samuel R. Delany* (1979), Jane Branham Weedman's *Samuel R. Delany* (1982), Seth Mc Evoy's *Samuel Delany* (1984), and more recently, Jeffrey Allen Tucker's *A Sense of Wonder: Samuel R. Delany, Race, Identity, and Difference* (2004). A special issue of the *Review of Contemporary Fiction* (1996) is dedicated to Delany and Edmund White. The essays on Delany's texts collected in this volume are first and foremost focused on Delany's science fiction writings. David Lunde's essay "Black Man/Gay Man/Writer... Prodigy: The Quest for Identity in Delany's Early Work" contained in this volume is a discussion of the topic of identity formation with regard to Delany's early 1960s novels. James Sallis, the editor of the Delany-section in this edition of the *Review of Contemporary Fiction*, also edited the volume *Ash of Stars: On the Writing of Samuel R. Delany* (1996), which focuses on Delany's Science Fiction writings, too. Michael W. Peplow and Robert S. Bravard's authorized bibliography *Samuel R. Delany: A Primary and Secondary Bibliography: 1962–1979* (1980) provides resources dealing with the early criticism on Delany's work.

Robert Elliot Fox discusses Delany's writings, together with those of Amiri Baraka and Ishmael Reed, as an example of black postmodernist fiction in his study *Conscientious Sorcerers: The Black Postmodernist Fiction of LeRoi Jones/Amiri Baraka, Ishmael Reed, and Samuel R. Delany* (1987). In his book *A Sense of Wonder* (2004), Tucker analyzes Delany's writings asking for its affiliations with African American cultural traditions, and he pays special attention to debates about identity and difference. Ross Posnock's study *Color and Culture* (1998) and Hazel Carby's *Race Men* (1998) each contain a chapter on Delany. In discussing Delany's *The Motion of Light in Water*, Carby analyzes constructions of African American masculinities. In analyzing *The Motion of Light in Water* and "Atlantis: Model 1924," Posnock argues for Delany's position as an American intellectual rather than as a representative of African American culture. Tucker's and Posnock's readings of Delany's work are contradictory. Whereas Tucker takes Delany's work as an example of strategic essentialism and argues in favor of its rootedness in African American traditions, Posnock states that Delany's work is an example of the end of the era of identity politics. My own reading of Delany's texts takes both approaches into account. The *Howard Gotlieb Archival Research Center* at the University of Boston houses Delany's unpublished papers, notebooks, letters, and emails. In a personal conversation, Delany suggested that I read the letters he exchanged with Tucker prior to the publication of *A Sense of Wonder*. In these letters, Delany and Tucker debate questions of identity and identity politics, Delany's affiliations with African American traditions, as well as Posnock's position in *Color and Culture*. My conversation with Delany, my reading of his mail communication with Tucker, and a subsequent conversation with Tucker have influenced my own reading of Delany's texts. The first conference to solely focus on Delany's writings was held at the University of Buffalo in the spring of 2006. The proceedings of this conference will be published in a forthcoming volume.

My study is the first extensive account of the first generation of black gay writers and filmmakers. It takes a trans-temporal perspective by combining three epochs, the Harlem Renaissance, the Protest Era, and the black gay era of the 1980s and 1990s. Hence, my analysis emphasizes intertextual references between the texts stemming from these three periods. Considering poems, songs, short plays, novels, experimental fiction, an autobiographical memoir, and a film, my study takes an inter-generic and inter-medial approach. Considering the intersections of the categories race, gender, sexuality, and class, it goes beyond more traditional concepts of textual analysis.

Structure

I will distinguish two ways in which black gay texts evoke black cultural traditions. They explicitly refer to historical persons, particularly Richard Bruce Nugent, Langston Hughes, and James Baldwin, all three of whom are frequently seen as black gay forebears. They also signify on earlier texts by Nugent, Hughes, and Baldwin. I begin my study by analyzing four anthologies that are paradigmatic of the black gay political discourse of the 1980s and

90s: Joseph Beam's *In the Life: A Black Gay Anthology* (1986), *Brother to Brother: New Writings by Black Gay Men* (1991) edited by Essex Hemphill, and *Black Gay Voices* (1988), and *Sojourner: Black Gay Voices in the Age of Aids* (1992) edited by the "Other Countries Collective." My study starts with these anthologies for two reasons. First, the anthologies are collections of texts by the key figures of 1980s black gay culture. Second, the anthologies are collections of texts that belong to different genres and thereby give an overview of the different forms of black gay cultural expression in the 1980s. The more controversial texts, many of which were first published in smaller magazines, for example Beam's "Black Men Loving Black Men: The Revolutionary Act of the 1980s," were reprinted in these anthologies. Consequently, the four volumes give an overview of the important political debates among black gay men that started in the 1980s. These discussions deal with white gay racism, homophobia in the black community, interracial love and sexuality, and HIV/AIDS. My second chapter shows that the political debates central to the longer texts covered in my study are rooted in 1980s black gay activism.

I develop the theoretical outline for my study in chapter three. The key concepts I use for the analysis of the longer texts were themselves strongly influenced by black gay cultural activism as well as by black feminist thought. Examples from black gay and black (lesbian) feminist literature and art have often been taken to show the limitations of traditional and monolithic concepts of identities and identity politics. I will argue in the second chapter that, far from being monolithic approaches, black gay texts make visible the contradictory constructions of black heterosexual and white gay masculinities. Theoretical concepts that focus on the intersections of various lines of difference emerged for two reasons: the formulation of the political critique of traditional identity politics, and poststructuralist developments in the academy.

As there is no canonized theory with which to approach texts by black gay men, I have combined different theoretical approaches in order to develop a critical framework for my study. The concepts I refer to stem from disciplines such as literary criticism, cultural studies, African American studies, queer studies, history, sociology, philosophy, performance studies, and studies in visual culture. Kobena Mercer has argued that a black gay subject position points at the limitations of earlier concepts of gay and black identities and thereby reveals the constructed character of any identity. Starting from this assumption in the second chapter, I refer to Kimberlé Crenshaw's concept of representational intersectionality as a means of theorizing how the categories race, gender, and sexuality intersect in stereotypical images of black men. The theoretical approaches by Stuart Hall, first outlined in his influential essay "New Ethnicities" (1988) and Cornel West's formulation of "The New Cultural Politics of Difference" (1999) pay particular attention to those differences concealed by a monolithic understanding of the category of blackness.

The critical reflection on contemporary black gay literature began simultaneously with the publication of the early black gay anthologies. Continuing the work begun by Nero, I draw on theories that particularly focus on black gay strategies of resistance. I refer to two theoretical approaches that have grown out of the field of performance studies: José Esteban Muñoz's concept of disidentification (based on Louis Althusser's concept of interpellation) and E. Patrick Johnson's concept of quare. Their black queer approaches take up earlier modes of resistance that Lawrence W. Levine has analyzed with regard to the black oral tradition. The combination of their approaches with Gates's critical theory of Signifying is the theoretical framework with which I analyze how black gay texts counter the racist and homophobic hegemonic discourse, homophobia in black communities, as well as racism in the white-dominated gay community. I will particularly consider the indebtedness of the strategy of constructing a black gay heritage to Alice Walker's womanist aesthetics and her project of referring to Zora Neale Hurston as a role model.

One critical approach underlying my study is the recent formulation of Critical Whiteness Studies. In addition to the general approach put forward by Ruth Frankenberg, I rely specifically on those studies analyzing constructions of gay identity from a critical whiteness studies point of view.[10] In her essay

---

10 Allan Bérubé, "How Gay Stays White and What Kind of White It Stays," *The Making and Unmaking of Whiteness*, ed. Birgit Brander Rasmussen, Durham: Duke UP, 2001, 234–256; Keith Boykin, *One More River to Cross: Black and Gay in America*, New York: Doubleday, 1996; Charles I. Nero, "Why are Gay Ghettoes White?," *Black Queer Studies: A Critical Anthology*, eds. E. Patrick Johnson and Mae G. Henderson, Durham: Duke UP, 2005, 228–245.

"Representing Whiteness in the Black Imagination" (1997), bell hooks specifically regards the construction of whiteness in texts by black writers and argues that whiteness is represented as terror. Taking her perspective, I frequently ask whether gay whiteness is represented in similar ways when the authors are black gay men.

In the fourth chapter, I analyze three texts and focus on their references to the Harlem Renaissance. Steven Corbin's novel *No Easy Place to Be*, the first text I analyze, is a historical novel set in the Harlem Renaissance. Pursuing the didactic aim of raising tolerance and acceptance of black gay men and lesbians, it depicts the conflicts of two black homosexual characters, one male and one female. In showing Rudy's successful emancipation as a black homosexual man, the novel takes up the traditional form of the quest narrative that is an important element of African American literature and applies it to a black gay topic.

The second text I analyze is Julien's film *Looking for Langston*. Julien's experimental film opens a trans-temporal and trans-cultural space that connects different epochs and artists as a way of negotiating black gay identity. Made by a black British filmmaker who collaborates with intellectuals and artists throughout the black diaspora, the film is an example of Paul Gilroy's concept of the Black Atlantic. It refers to the Harlem Renaissance and to Baldwin, and it features poems and songs by black gay men of the 1980s like Essex Hemphill and Blackberri. I particularly focus on how the film refers to political debates among black gay men concerning the question of representation.

In the fifth chapter, I analyze three texts and focus on the references to the Protest Era and the work and person of James Baldwin. Both Randall Kenan's *A Visitation of Spirits* and Melvin Dixon's *Vanishing Rooms* refer to two of Baldwin's novels, particularly to *Go Tell It on the Mountain* and *Giovanni's Room*. Both writers locate their narratives in the 1980s. The novel *A Visitation of Spirits* is the only text among the six longer texts that does not have a metropolitan setting. Set in the rural South and containing magical realist elements, it alludes to the womanist writings of Alice Walker. *Vanishing Rooms* transfers the Parisian setting of *Giovanni's Room* to New York. While sensitive of the intersectionality of differences, Dixon's *Vanishing Rooms* tells the story of Jesse's quest and his emancipation as a black gay man.

Baldwin's novels contain many elements contradicting the political agenda of most black gay activists in the 1980s and 90s, such as bisexuality, love between two white men, and inter-racial love. I will argue that Kenan's and Dixon's novels alter these elements from a perspective rooted in the political context of the 1980s. Against the background of recent approaches in the field of critical whiteness studies, I will consider the ways in which both novels formulate a critique of the normative construction of gayness as a white identity.

Not all of the references to the Harlem Renaissance and the Protest Era by black gay authors of the 1980s and 1990s are political appropriations which aim at legitimizing and empowering black gay men: the texts of Samuel R. Delany are exceptional regarding the way he refers to historical periods and aesthetic traditions. I will therefore discuss two of his texts at the end of chapter four and chapter five, "Atlantis: Model 1924" and the autobiographical memoir *The Motion of Light in Water*.

"Atlantis: Model 1924" is set in New York during the Harlem Renaissance, and *The Motion of Light in Water* describes Delany's life during the time of the Protest Era. In discussing "Atlantis: Model 1924" as an experimental text exploring the postmodern literary genre of historiographic metafiction, I will read it as a humorous and sometimes ironic comment on the 1980s and 90s project of inventing black gay forefathers. The last text I analyze is Delany's autobiographical memoir *The Motion of Light in Water: Sex and Science Fiction Writing in the East Village*. Delany's memoir focuses on his experiences as a black gay man in New York during the 1960s. The text evokes two reader expectations: an involvement with the African American autobiographical tradition and with the coming out narrative. Reflecting on these genres on the level of content and employing experimental devices as well as irony, the text uses metafictional elements to deconstruct such expectations. Near the end of the memoir, where James Baldwin makes a brief appearance, he exemplifies the ironic way in which Delany refers to the strategy of establishing black gay forefathers.

On the most recent CD of the Oakland-based black gay hip hop group Deepdickollective *On Some Other* (2007), there is a song called "For Colored Boys." This title and the refrain about "chocolate colored rainbows" refer to black feminist traditions by alluding directly to Ntozake Shange's 1975 play *For Colored Girls Who Have Considered Suicide/When the Rainbow Is Enuf*. The "chocolate colored rainbow" also refers to the rainbow flag symbolizing the lesbian, gay, bisexual, and transgendered community. The song's lyrics create a cultural history specific to contemporary black gay men. Let me quote one verse:

> The point of this colored noise
> This joint is for colored boys
> This is for Essex, Asoto, Donald and Marlon Troy
> This is for Aimee, for Melvin, Claude, and for Countee C.
> This is for Larry Duckette, for Joseph and Jimmy B.[11]

I have quoted this verse because it shows that the strategy of referring to the Harlem Renaissance (Claude McKay and Countee Cullen) and to James Baldwin (Jimmy B) is still employed in contemporary black gay cultural activism. Moreover, those cultural activists that are the subject of my study, such as Essex Hemphill, Assotto Saint,[12] Melvin Dixon, and Joseph Beam, are also part of this contemporary list of black gay forebears.

But I have quoted this verse for another reason, too. The song is clearly addressed to "colored boys whose rainbows forgot how to bloom." This verse and many black gay texts of the 1980s and 90s are not addressed at white gay men like myself. Their main purpose is the empowerment of black gay men. Therefore, it would be naïve if I tried to read black gay texts or listen to the music of Deepdickollective for my own empowerment. But there is another important aspect in these texts, and that is the way gay whiteness is marked as a privileged position. Black gay cultural activists have repeatedly demanded that white gay men become aware of the importance of black cultural traditions for the project of gay liberation. One motivation for my study was to de-center gay whiteness and recognize the importance of black gay literature, film, and art within queer contexts.

---

11 Deepdickollective, "For Colored Boys," *On Some Other*, Oakland: Sugartruck, 2007, CD.

12 As a reaction to the low number of t-cells resulting from AIDS, Saint added a second letter "t" to his first name.

2 Debates of the 1980s

The early writings of black gay cultural activists are collected in four major black gay anthologies published between 1986 and 1993: *In the Life: A Black Gay Anthology* (1986), *Brother to Brother: New Writings by Black Gay Men* (1991), *Black Gay Voices* (1988), and *Sojourner: Black Gay Voices in the Age of Aids* (1993). They are the defining texts of the black gay sub-cultural discourse from the mid-1980s to the early 1990s. These anthologies contain the key texts that led to controversial debates within the black gay movement. The editors of the anthologies, Joseph Beam, Essex Hemphill, and the members of the Other Countries Collective, were central figures of the black gay activism of the 1980s and early 1990s.

There are two reasons why I focus on the early writings of black gay men. First, I want to establish a context for the theoretical outline in the third chapter by considering the politics of the early black gay activists. Just as black (lesbian) feminists criticized male dominance within the black movement and criticized white feminists for ignoring race as a line of difference, so black gay men criticized the exclusionary politics of both the black movement and the white-dominated gay movement. This critique was one prerequisite for approaches that considered the intersection of various axes of difference such as race, gender, sexuality, and class (see 3.1). Second, I want to focus on the politics and aesthetics of the texts. By considering the political debates that evolved from the texts collected in these anthologies and by throwing light upon the publishing policies of the editors involved, I want to establish a context for the analysis of the longer texts that will be central to the argument in the main part of my study. Analyzing the anthologies, I will focus on debates concerning the way black men are depicted, white gay racism, and black gay identity politics. In the last part, I will focus on the strategy these writers used in constructing myths of the origin of black gayness by referring to black literary traditions, a strategy that can already be found in the four anthologies. As will be shown in the following chapters, subsequent black gay writers, filmmakers and activists employed this very strategy, and they repeatedly referred to the debates started in the four anthologies.

The themes found in the early writings by black gay men were strongly influenced by the social and political conditions of the 1980s. In this decade, the circumstances of black gay men were determined by racism, homophobia, the construction of gayness as a white identity, and the threat of HIV/AIDS (see 3.1). In his article "African American Literature: Gay Male," the literary critic Emmanuel S. Nelson identifies four major themes which are prominent within texts written by black gay writers: "the complex relationship between the individual black gay self and the larger African American community, the devastating consequences of racism, the pain and the possibilities of interracial love, and the tragedy of AIDS."[13] These topics are also central in the four anthologies.

There are three reasons for the argument that the first wave of black gay activism evolved between 1984 and 1994 and came to an end in the mid-1990s. It is more difficult to identify a distinct group of black gay writers, filmmakers, and activists with their own body of work and political agenda for the time since the mid-1990s. The main reason lies in the devastating consequences of the AIDS crisis. In the late 1980s and early 1990s, many of the early black gay activists, writers and filmmakers died from AIDS. Many writers simply did not live long enough to publish more than one or two novels. For that reason alone, the knowledge and achievements of these men could not be actively passed on to the next generation of black gay men. In addition, the rise of queer theory and queer politics led to new political coalitions. In contrast to the autonomous publishing policy of the 1980s, there have been a variety of anthologies that feature texts by black gay men, black lesbians, black bisexuals and black transgendered persons since the mid-1990s.[14] Finally, once black gay topics became acceptable to

---

13 Emmanuel S. Nelson, "African-American Literature: Gay Male," *GLBTQ: An Encyclopledia of Gay, Lesbian, and Queer Culture*, <www.glbtq.com/literature/African_am_ lit_gay.html>, accessed June 26, 2005.

14 See for example Shawn Stewart Ruff, ed., *Go the Way Your Blood Beats: An Anthology of Lesbian and Gay Fiction by African-American Writers*, New York: H. Holt, 1996; Delroy Constantine-Simms, ed., *The Greatest Taboo: Homosexuality in Black* Los Angeles: Alyson, 2001; Devon W. Carbado, Dwight A. McBride, Donald Weise, and Evelyn C. White, eds., *Black Like Us: A Century of Lesbian, Gay, and Bisexual African American Fiction*, San Francisco: Cleis, 2002.

larger publishing houses and mainstream audiences, black gay writers did not have to organize separately to get their texts published.[15]

2.1 Political Strategies and Debates

In the late 1970s and early 1980s, the first black gay and lesbian newspapers and magazines were published. *Moja*, the first newspaper for black gays and lesbians, was founded in 1978 by Calvin Lowery. The first black gay and lesbian magazine *Blacklight* was founded one year later, in 1979. *Blackheart* was edited by the Blackheart Collective, consisting of Daniel Garret, Isaac Jackson, and Colin Robinson, who produced three issues starting in 1981. In the late 1980s, Garret and Robinson were also members of the Other Countries Collective, a group of black gay writers who worked in New York City. There were also other black gay newspapers and magazines such as *Habari-Daftari, Yemonja, B, BGM, Diplomat,* and *Brothers*.[16] The first issue of the quarterly *Black/Out* was published in the summer of 1986 by the National Coalition of Black Lesbians and Gays (NCBLG),[17] and its Board of Directors included such notables as Audre Lorde, Barbara Smith, Michelle Parkerson, and Joseph Beam, who also worked as the magazine's editor. Since the mid-1980s, black gay editors and writers'

---

15 Two successful authors are E. Lynn Harris and James Earl Hardy. From 1991 onwards, both of them have published serialized novels featuring black gay protagonists. Harris's novels are published by Doubleday and attain a large circulation. On Harris, see Craig Seymour, "Envisioning Lives: Homosexuality and Black Popular Literature," *The Greatest Taboo: Homosexuality in Black Communities*, ed. Delroy Constantine-Simms, Los Angeles: Alyson, 2001, 362–383.

16 For a list of magazines for black gay men and lesbians of color that existed in 1984 see Noel Parks, "Magazines for Gays of Color," <www.blacklightonline.com/gcn.html>, accessed October 7, 2006, and for a list solely focusing on work by black gay men, including books, journals and periodicals, see Robert Reid-Pharr, "Books, Journals, and Periodicals by Black Gay Authors and Publishers," *Brother to Brother: New Writings by Black Gay Men*, ed. Essex Hemphill, Boston: Alyson, 1991, 263–269. Many of these magazines are collected at Steven G. Fullwood's black gay and lesbian archive project at the Schomburg Center in Harlem.

17 For the history of the NCBLG see SidneyBrinkley, *Making History: NCBLG – 25 Years Ago a Small Group of Black Lesbians and Gay Men Formed the First National Black Gay Organization.* <http://www.blacklightonline.com/ncblg.html>, accessed Oct. 7, 2006.

collectives started to publish anthologies of writings by black gay men. The most influential of these anthologies are Joseph Beam's *In the Life: A Black Gay Anthology* (1986), Essex Hemphill's *Brother to Brother: New Writings by Black Gay Men* (1991), the two volumes of the journal of the Other Countries Collective named *Black Gay Voices* (1988) and *Sojourner: Black Gay Voices in the Age of Aids* (1993), a collection of poetry called *Tongues Untied* (1987) that was published with Gay Men's Press in London, and two collections of poetry edited by Assotto Saint, *The Road Before Us: 100 Black Gay Poets* (1991) and *Here to Dare. 10 Black Gay Poets* (1992). These black gay anthologies contain texts by black gay writers who later published novels, made films or pursued academic careers, among them Essex Hemphill, Melvin Dixon, Marlon Riggs, Thomas Glave, and Charles I. Nero.

It is not uncommon for a marginalized group denied a public voice to start the process of self-actualization by the publication of anthologies. Anthologies are a comparably cheap way to publish texts of a variety of writers. In addition to these economic reasons, Assotto Saint stresses the symbolic power of black gay anthologies. Asked by Robert Reid-Pharr in a symposium on contemporary gay male literature why a lot of black gay writing has been published in anthologies, he states that "an anthology is, first, a symbol of community, and as gay black writers we have had to be published together in that way." [18] In his essay "Why I Write," Saint has also argued in favor of an autonomous black gay aesthetics and infrastructure to counter the marginal position black gay men and black gay artists inhabited in the 1980s:

> American [sic] is a capitalist society. Let us save, beg, and borrow money to keep building our autonomous publications and other cultural institutions. Let us make sure that these institutions outlast us and do not become self-serving. Let us live beyond the here and now by nurturing each other and supporting one another's works. [19]

---

18 Martin B. Duberman, "On Contemporary Gay Male Literature in the United States: A Symposium with Christopher Bram, Dennis Cooper, Michael Cunningham, Dale Peck, Robert Reid-Pharr, and Assotto Saint," *Queer Representations: Reading Lives, Reading Cultures: A Center for Gay and Lesbian Studies Book*, ed. Martin B. Duberman, New York: New York UP, 1997, 371–377, 374.

19 Assotto Saint, "Why I Write," *Spells of a Voodoo Doll*, ed. Assotto Saint, New York: Masquerade, 1996. 3–8, 5.

In his statement, Saint implies that he considers black gay men to be the intended addressees of texts by black gay artists. Likewise, Beam states in the introduction to the anthology *In The Life* that the volume is aimed at a black gay male readership. Examples of a similar publication policy can be found in the anthologies and presses of black and Chicana (lesbian) feminist writers, such as the influential anthologies *This Bridge Called My Back* and *Home Girls* and the publishing company Kitchen Table – Women of Color Press.[20]

Saint published two anthologies of poetry by black gay writers with Galien's Press, his own independent press. The Other Countries Collective published their two anthologies *Black Gay Voices* and *Sojourner. Black Gay Voices in the Age of Aids* themselves. Just as *In the Life, Brother to Brother* was published by Alyson Publications, which had been an independent white gay press from 1980 to 1992. Even if in the introduction to *Brother to Brother*, Hemphill gives Sasha Alyson, the owner of Alyson Publications, credit for publishing *Brother to Brother*, he, like Saint, expresses the importance of autonomous black gay publishing houses when he writes in the introduction that he hopes black gay men "will see a day when black gay men will bring forth anthologies and literature published and distributed by companies we have created and own."[21]

However, as Arthur Flannigan Saint-Aubin argues in a critical essay on *Brother to Brother*, the aim of financial and artistic autonomy was sometimes contradicted by the reality of the market, and this reality had consequences for the style of writing, too. In his analysis, Saint-Aubin examines the consequences of the marginalized position of black gay literature. He states that because black gay men were a minority within the gay movement, their texts had at least partly to appeal to a white readership in order to be published and argues that it is a

---

20 Barbara Smith, ed. *Home Girls: A Black Feminist Anthology*, New York: Kitchen Table Women of Color Press, 1983; Cherríe Moraga and Gloria Anzaldúa, eds., *This Bridge Called My Back: Writings by Radical Women of Color*, New York: Kitchen Table Women of Color Press, 1983.

21 Essex Hemphill, "Introduction," *Brother to Brother: New Writings by Black Gay Men*, ed. Essex Hemphill, Boston: Alyson, 1991, xv-xxxi, xxx.

characteristic of any and every attempt at blackgaymale textuality – indeed a minority inflection within a minority literary corpus – given the particular modes of literary production and dissemination and the particular patterns of literary consumption in this culture: Who publishes? What gets published? Who reads? In order for this collection [*Brother to Brother*] to constitute a commercial and political success, it must engage the white gay male reader even if it does not explicitly or consciously attempt to do so.[22]

Saint Aubin considers the different ways in which white gay male readers are addressed in black gay texts to be one characteristic of what he calls "blackgaymale textuality."

2.2 The Critique of White Gay Racism

In 1983, Michael J. Smith published the anthology *Black Men/White Men* with Gay Sunshine Press. The sleeve of *Black Men/White Men* announces that it addresses "[f]or the first time, the Black and interracial gay experience in White America."[23] The editor Michael J. Smith was a white gay man and the founder of the group "Black and White Men Together." Mirroring the politics of this group, the anthology contains texts by black and white men. Smith has been criticized for his decision to publish the volume without a black gay man as co-publisher.[24] The book was severely criticized by some black gay men because of Smith's publishing policy and because of the photographs of black men contained in the volume. Nearly all of the photographs in *Black Men/White Men* show erotic images of nude black men. Calvin Anderson, a white photographer and founder of Sierra Domino, a company that publishes books of photographs of nude black men, took the photos. The bibliographical notes of *Black Men/White Men*

---

22 Arthur Flannigan Saint-Aubin, "Black Gay Male Discourse: Reading Race and Sexuality between the Lines," *Journal of the History of Sexuality* 3.3 (1993): 468–490, 480.

23 Michael J. Smith, ed. *Black Men/White Men: A Gay Anthology*, San Francisco: Gay Sunshine Press, 1983.

24 Isaac Jackson, "Review of Black Men/White Men," *Blackheart* 2 (1984): 48–50, 48.

contend that Sierra Domino Publishing House is "the major U.S. firm dealing with the positive imagery of the nude Black male."[25] However, in the second volume of the black gay periodical *Blackheart* (1984), there is a review of the anthology by Isaac Jackson, who criticizes the images because they confirm the racist stereotype of the hypersexual black man (see 3.1.2), whereas the book does not include any images of nude white men. He is also critical of most of the texts by black and white writers. Jackson comes to the conclusion that the anthology does a "disservice" to the political aims of black and white gay men who want to fight racism.[26] The confirmation of racist stereotypes within the white dominated gay subculture is repeatedly criticized within the black gay anthologies, and it is one reason that led to an autonomous organization of black gay men. For example, in the introduction of *Brother to Brother* Essex Hemphill writes that the failure of white gay men to address issues of race and racism is one reason for the impossibility of a meaningful coalitional politics between white gay men and other oppressed groups:

> It has not fully dawned on white gay men that racist conditioning has rendered many of them no different from their heterosexual brothers in the eyes of black gays and lesbians. Coming out of the closet to confront sexual oppression has not necessarily given white males the motivation or insight to transcend their racist conditioning. This failure (or reluctance) is costing the gay and lesbian community the opportunity to become a powerful force for creating real social changes that reach beyond issues of sexuality. It has fostered much of the distrust that permeates the relations between the black and white communities. And finally, it erodes the possibility of forming meaningful, powerful coalitions.[27]

Despite these shortcomings of *Black Men/White Men*, the volume does in some ways already point in the same direction as the later black gay anthologies. The decision to start the anthology with Eric Garber's essay "T'aint Nobody's Bizness (Homosexuality in 1920s Harlem)" and to follow it by reprints of Bruce Nugent's experimental story "Smoke, Lilies and Jade" and Langston Hughes's

---

25 Michael J. Smith, 232.

26 Jackson, 50.

27 Hemphill, "Introduction," xviii-xix.

poems "I Loved My Friend" and "Café: 3 A.M." anticipates one of the main strategies pursued by later black gay writers and filmmakers. They intended to consolidate the newly emergent black gay identity by referring to the Harlem Renaissance. In addition, the volume contains two reprints of poems by Adrian Stanford from his 1977 book of poetry *Black and Queer*, which had not been widely circulated up to that time. Stanford was murdered in 1981, and Smith's anthology makes at least two of his poems available to a larger public.[28]

If one compares *Black Men/White Men* to the black gay anthology *In the Life* (1986), it is striking that there is hardly any overlap in the contributing writers. There are only two writers whose texts appear in both volumes, Richard Bruce Nugent and the theologian James S. Tinney. There might be geographical reasons for this fact. *Black Men/White Men* was published in San Francisco, whereas *In the Life* was published in Boston. However, another reason may be more important: whereas the contributors of *Black Men/White Men* consider themselves members of the gay community, those of *In the Life* consider themselves men being rooted in the black community. Moreover, whereas *Black Men/White Men* is clearly addressed to white and black gay men, *In the Life* and the follow-up anthology *Brother to Brother* are mainly addressed to black gay men and the black community. [29]

2.3 The Debate about Black Gay Identity

The importance of Beam's anthology *In the Life* was emphasized in the 2002 anthology *Black Like Us: A Century of Lesbian, Gay and Bisexual African American Fiction*, where Beam's anthology is called "groundbreaking."[30] What is more, the editors state that *In the Life* "launched the first post-Stonewall movement

---

28 Adrian Stanford, *Black and Queer*, Boston: Good Gay Poets Press, 1977. Six years later, Essex Hemphill published more poems by Stanford in *Brother to Brother*.

29 Joseph Beam, *In the Life: A Black Gay Anthology*. Boston: Alyson, 1986, 17.

30 Carbado, McBride, 282.

of openly gay work by black men."[31] The title of Beam's anthology, as well as the way the content is structured, already hints at the intended connection to the larger black community and the black gay agenda of the volume. The expression "to be in the life" comes from the African American vernacular and denotes a person who is sexually interested in persons of the same gender. The expression was already used at the beginning of the twentieth century for same-gender loving persons within the black community.[32] Today, the expression is used within black gay and lesbian culture. For example, the film company that published the biographical film about the black lesbian feminist Ruth Ellis *Living with Pride. Ruth Ellis@100* is called "sisters in the life," and the black gay and lesbian archive project which is housed at Harlem's Schomburg Center holds material by the "black LGBT/SGL/Q/Q/inthelife community."[33]

When one reads Beam's anthology 20 years after it was first published, it is striking that there seems to be no unified political agenda to combine the texts included. In fact, the volume is very heterogeneous, and in some cases the political positions are even contradictory. The topic of gay men in the military serves as an example to illustrate this heterogeneity: Oye Apeji Ajanaku's poem "Discharge USN '63" is about a soldier's memories of his time in the military 1961–1963. When the soldier remembers his discharge and his black military comrades, and he states that

> on departing, I know
> every moment of true happiness
> I may ever find,
> Will be a tender moment,
> Somewhat akin,
> To being together with you all again.[34]

---

31 Carbado, McBride, 282.

32 George Chauncey, *Gay New York: Gender, Urban Culture, and the Making of the Gay World, 1890–1940*, New York: Basic Books, 1994, 15.

33 LGBT = lesbian, gay, bisexual, transgender; SGL = same gender loving; Q = queer/questioning (Steven G. Fullwood, *Black Gay and Lesbian Archive*, <http://bgla.stevenfullwood.org>, accessed September 2, 2005).

34 Oye Apeji Ajanaku, "Discharge USN '63," *In the Life: A Black Gay Anthology*, ed. Joseph Beam, Boston: Alyson, 1986, 114–115, 115.

In the poem, there are no markers of irony. Instead, male bonding within the military is uncritically connected to homosexual desire. As many social movements of the 1980s adopted the non-violent politics of the Civil Rights movement, the tone of this poem is surprising. The fact that in the 1980s male homosexuality was a reason to be discharged from the military makes the inclusion of the poem in the anthology all the more surprising. This piece of writing is directly followed by Brad Jonson's "Protest Poem," which ends with the words "fuck the war"[35] and takes a deliberate and radical stand against the military.

Even if Beam states in the introduction that "by the final deadline, [he] had been inundated with over 100 manuscripts and portfolios from as far away as London,"[36] some of the texts included were not exclusively written for the anthology. Given this large number of original manuscripts, Beam's publishing decision regarding the reprint of Sydney Brinkley's "Passion" is surprising. Brinkley's erotic text was first published in a 1981 issue of the black gay periodical *Blacklight*, the first black gay periodical. One of Beam's reasons for reprinting a text by Brinkley might have been to emphasize Brinkley's role as the editor of *Blacklight*. "Passion" contains a detailed description of anal sex without the use of condoms, an unsafe sexual practice. The publication of such a text might have been emancipating in 1981, the first year of the AIDS crisis, when the virus was still unknown. However, the decision to publish the text in the year 1986 without further comments or guidelines regarding safer sex is striking. Nowhere in the anthology is there a comment on the risks of sexually transmitted diseases, especially of HIV/AIDS, and there is no discussion of safer sex practices. As Craig G. Harris's text "Cut off from among their people,"[37] another text included in *In the Life*, directly addresses problems connected

---

35 Brad Johnson, "Protest Poem," *In the Life: A Black Gay Anthology*, ed. Joseph Beam, Boston: Alyson, 1986, 116.

36 Joseph Beam, "Introduction," *In the Life: A Black Gay Anthology*, ed. Joseph Beam. Boston: Alyson, 1986, 13–18, 15.

37 In "Cut off from among their people," the family of a black gay man who has died of AIDS rejects his black lover and treats him in a disrespectful way during the funeral. In the end, the undertaker who is also a black gay man familiar with AIDS comforts the rejected lover (Craig G. Harris, "Cut Off From Among Their People," *In the Life: A Black Gay Anthology*, ed. Joseph Beam, Boston: Alyson, 1986, 63–69).

with AIDS and as Samuel R. Delany's "The Tale of Plagues and Carnival," one of the first fictional accounts of AIDS had already been published in 1985, it can be said that AIDS was already an issue among black gay men at the time the anthology was published. The lack of a unified political agenda in the volume might have led Charles I. Nero to be reluctant in his praise for *In the Life*. He calls it "pathfinding" rather than groundbreaking, and in describing it as a "brainchild" of Joseph Beam, he possibly indicates a lack of political support from other black gay men.[38]

Two essays included in *In the Life* triggered two debates among black gay men that are still prevalent. The first debate concerns the question of one's primary identity. In his essay "By the Year 2000," Max C. Smith distinguishes between black gay men and gay black men:

> Gay Blacks are people who identify first as being gay and who usually live outside the closet in predominately white gay communities. I would estimate that they amount to roughly ten per cent of all Black homosexuals. Black gays, on the other hand, view our racial heritage as primary and frequently live 'bisexual front lives' within black neighborhoods.[39]

Smith does not consider the grammar of the two expressions. Grammatically, the adjective "black" in the expression "black gay man" modifies the phrase "gay man." Consequently and contradictory to Smith, one could argue that the term "black gay man" emphasizes the centrality of gayness rather than blackness.

Most writers, filmmakers and artists whose subject positions are determined by the categories blackness and gayness have referred to their own identity as that of a black gay man. This expression became common during the 1980s, but it does not necessarily refer to the afrocentric meaning suggested by Smith.

---

38 Charles I. Nero, "Black Gay Men and White Gay Men: A Less Than Perfect Union," *Out in the South*, ed. Carlos L. Dews and Carolyn Leste Law, Philadelphia: Temple UP, 2001, 115–126, 124.

39 Max C. Smith, "By the Year 2000," *In the Life: A Black Gay Anthology*, ed. Joseph Beam, Boston: Alyson, 1986, 224–229, 226.

2.4 The Debate about Gay Interracial Love and Sexuality

In his essay "Brother to Brother: Words from the Heart," the editor Joseph Beam coins the slogan "black men loving black men is the revolutionary act of the 1980s."[40] This slogan has led to controversial debates among black gay men arguing about the political dimensions of interracial sexuality and relationships. In his essay, in which Beam addresses all black men, he includes but does not limit his plea to black gay men. He wants his political demand to be understood as a strategy for all black men to survive in a racist society, an agenda "which is not rooted in any particular sexual, political, or class affiliation, but in our mutual survival."[41] At the end of Marlon Riggs's film *Tongues Untied*, Beam's slogan appears on the screen, but it is reduced to the sentence "Black Men Loving Black Men is the Revolutionary Act" and omits the reference to the 1980s. *Tongues Untied* was released in 1989. In a key scene, Riggs recites his poem of the same title, which is included in the anthology *Brother to Brother*, and speaks of a black man's adolescence in a homophobic and racist society. The black gay narrator recounts his first love for a white boy, his experiences in the racist, white-dominated gay sub-culture, his desire for white men, his growing awareness of racist images of black men that are popular in white gay publications, "joke fetish cartoon caricature or disco diva adored from a distance."[42] He decides to leave this sub-culture, "in search of something better,"[43] an autonomous black gay culture. He at first depicts his love for a white boy as innocent and even liberating, but he then calls it "a curse." At the end of the poem, he rejects the white-dominated gay sub-culture altogether because of white gay racism. Both debates – "gay black vs. black gay" and "black men loving black men" – support the tendency in *In the Life* of establishing a black gay identity with an afrocentric agenda.

---

40 Joseph Beam, "Black Men Loving Black Men: The Revoulutionary Act of the 1980s," *Gay Community News* (1985): 5. Reprinted as "Brother to Brother: Words From the Heart," *Brother to Brother: New Writings by Black Gay Men*, ed. Essex Hemphill, Boston: Alyson, 1991, 230–242.

41 Beam, "Brother to Brother," 242.

42 Marlon Riggs, "Tongues Untied," *Brother to Brother: New Writings by Black Gay Men*, ed. Essex Hemphill, Boston: Alyson, 1991, 200–205, 202.

43 Riggs, 202.

As he was rather skeptical of this project, the novelist and literary critic Darieck Scott formulated a critique eight years after the anthology was first published. In contrast to most contemporary reviewers of *In the Life*, Scott stated that *In the Life* should be critically regarded against the background of the specific historical context in which it was produced rather than be taken as still valid. Scott's critical view of Beam's anthology was put forward in his essay "Jungle Fever? Black Gay Identity Politics, White Dick, and the Utopian Bedroom?" In the essay, he refers to both discussions "black gay vs. gay black," and "black men loving black men is the revolutionary act."

In his essay, Scott explains the two sides of Beam's slogan "black men loving black men is the revolutionary act." On the one hand, it can be understood, as it was originally intended in Beam's essay, as a demand for "mutual nurturing," but Scott also shows that, on the other hand it has become a "directive against interracial dating."[44] He praises Beam's anthology because it aims at ending the invisibility of black gay identities, and he values the fact that it has given black gay men the terms they can use to speak of their subject positions. However, with respect to the new identity category *black gay*, Scott sees the danger of hierarchies and exclusions that are connected with categorization:

> Black gay identity positions challenge the essential whiteness of what we call gay sexuality and gay desire, and in doing so, create an aporia through which what it means for men to have sex with men could be usefully interrogated. But the promise of such a position remains largely unfullfilled. The creators of black gay identity, while explicitly criticizing the hierarchy of desirability constructed in white gay social and political life, implicitly reinscribe that hierarchy's static concept of desire.[45]

According to Scott, both discussions tend to have exclusionary results. Even if it was not initially intended by Beam, his slogan "black men loving black men is the revolutionary act" has often been used to criticize interracial gay relationships. According to Scott, the concentration on the discussion about "black gay vs. gay black" forecloses discussions about other differences like class

44 Darieck Scott, "Jungle Fever? Black Gay Identity Politics, White Dick, and the Utopian Bedroom," *GLQ* 1 (1994): 299–321, 304.

45 Scott, 303.

or age and their intersections with blackness and gayness[46] (see 3.1). Rather than clinging to these discussions, Scott, like Stuart Hall and Cornel West (see 3.1.1), proposes an anti-essentialist way of dealing with identity categories in order to emphasize "the strategic quality of identity, indeed of all political positions."[47]

In his 1993 essay "Confessions of a Snow Queen," Julien also criticizes both the slogan "black men loving black men is the revolutionary act" and the ending of Rigg's film *Tongues Untied* by deliberateley calling himself a snow queen. "Snow queen" is a slang term designating black men who prefer white men as sexual partners, and "dinge queens" is a term for white men who have a sexual desire for black men. Historically, these terms had a derogatory meaning and were mostly used among homosexual men, but recently these terms have been re-appropriated to theorize the connections between racial difference and desire.[48] Julien states that "the out black snow queen draws attention to the fact of black desire for the white subject and contests pathologised racial identities, the products of afrocentric readings."[49] He insists "on the fact of interracial desire, its very transgression of racial boundaries."[50] By calling himself a "snow queen," Julien opposes the view of a black person's sexual desire for a white person as pathological. In "Toward a Black Gay Aesthetic," Nero looks at the origins of this view and states that it has been prevalent in both the black middle classes and the gay subculture since the 1960s, and he argues that "the black middle class and the mental health professions have conspired together to label a black person's sexual attraction to a white as pathology."[51] The tendency to regard interracial sexual desire as pathological affected the attitudes of gay men as well. Referring to the terms "dinge queen"

---

46 Scott, 303.

47 Scott, 307.

48 See for example Isaac Julien, "Confessions of a Snow Queen: Notes on Making The Attendant," *The Film Art of Isaac Julien*, ed. Amada Cruz, Annandale-on-Hudson: Center for Curatorial Studies, 2000, 79–83. See also Robert Reid-Pharr, "Dinge," *Black Gay Man*, New York: New York UP, 2001, 85–98.

49 Julien, "Confessions of a Snow Queen," 82.

50 Julien, "Confessions of a Snow Queen," 82.

51 Charles I. Nero, "Toward a Black Gay Aesthetic: Signifying in Contemporary Black Gay Literature," *Brother to Brother: New Writings by Black Gay Men*, ed. Essex Hemphill, Boston: Alyson, 1991, 229–252, 237.

and "snow queen" Nero argues that they were created by gay men "to denigrate participants in black/white sexual relationships."[52] In coming out as snow queens, Julien and others employ a strategy of resignificaction. This strategy is similar to the way other derogatory terms such as "queer" have been taken up and re-defined by political activists. Julien takes the denigrating term "snow queen" and uses it to describe himself in order to criticize normative ideas about sexuality and desire. Since Scott formulated his critque in 1994, a number of black gay men have started to dismantle this hierarchy of desirability within the black gay community. In addition to Scott and Julien, Robert Reid-Pharr's and Samuel R. Delany's work can be read in these terms.[53] As will be shown later, the two debates about black gay identity, on the one hand, and gay interracial love and sexuality, on the other, are important prerequisites for my analyses of the longer texts in the following chapters, especially for my readings of Julien's *Looking for Langston* and Dixon's *Vanishing Rooms*.

In 1991, Essex Hemphill edited *Brother to Brother: New Writings by Black Gay Men*. The book was originally conceived and planned by Beam as a companion anthology to *In the Life*, but he was not able to complete the work before he died in 1988. Beam's friend Hemphill completed the work with the support of Beam's parents Dorothy and Sun Beam in their home in Philadelphia. Like *In the Life*, the anthology includes texts by important black gay artists of the 1980s, among them Assotto Saint, Craig G. Harris, and Melvin Dixon. It was awarded the Lambda Literary Award. As the title of the volume is taken from Beam's essay "Brother to Brother: Words from the Heart," Hemphill posits the anthology in a political tradition inspired by Beam's gay afrocentrism.[54] In his poem "When My Brother Fell," with its sub-heading "For Joseph Beam," Hemphill reflects on the task of completing the work and continuing the political program that Beam had begun. In the first stanza, he says:

---

52 Nero, "Toward a Black Gay Aesthetic," 237.

53 See for example Reid-Pharr, "Dinge," and Samuel R. Delany, *Times Square Red, Times Square Blue*, New York: New York UP, 1999.

54 Beam, "Brother to Brother."

When my brother fellI picked up his weapons
and never once questioned
whether I could carry
the weight and grief,
the responsibility
he shouldered.
I never questioned whether I could aim
or be as precise as he.
I only knew he had fallen
and the passing ceremonies
marking his death
did not stop the war.[55]

Hemphill, the editor of the anthology, was a well-known and politically-outspoken black gay activist, performance artist, and writer. Together with Wayson R. Jones and Larry Duckette, he formed the Washington-based poetry performance group Cinque in 1983, and in 1985 and 1986 he self-published his first two books of poems *Earth Life* and *Conditions*. In 1987, his poetry was included in *Tongues Untied*, an anthology of poems by five black gay poets published in England. The title refers to Michael Harper's poem "Tongue-Tied in Black and White" and was chosen because Harper "expounds on how the mores and language of a dominant culture can stifle the creativity of peoples within that culture."[56] Two years later, the filmmaker Marlon Riggs chose the same term as the title for his influential documentary on black gay identity. He combines poetry, performances, and personal testimony to reflect on the situation of black gay men in the United States. It is one of three films in which Hemphill and his poetry appear. He also performed his poetry for the soundtrack of *Looking for Langston* (1989) and Riggs's *Black Is ... Black Ain't* (1994), a personal examination of black gay experiences in the age of AIDS.

Owing to these films, Hemphill became an internationally-known black gay cultural activist. After the publication of *Brother to Brother*, he was invited to England to launch the anthology and to read his own work during

---

55 Essex Hemphill, "When My Brother Fell," *Brother to Brother: New Writings by Black Gay Men*, ed. Essex Hemphill, Boston: Alyson, 1991, 110–112, 110.

56 Martin Humphries, "Introduction," *Tongues Untied*, ed. Martin Humphries, London: Gay Men's Press, 1987, 5–10, 5.

a tour across the country.[57] Hemphill's poetry collection *Ceremonies: Prose and Poetry* was also published in 1992. Its poems and essays cover a wide range of topics concerning the situation of black gay men in the United States: the intersections of the categories blackness and gayness, white gay racism, homophobia among some Black Nationalists, and AIDS. Hemphill's pointed critique of racist representations of black men in the work of the white gay photographer Robert Mapplethorpe in his essay "Does Your Mama Know About Me" led to controversial debates within the gay community.[58]

Brother to Brother differs from *In the Life* in that its political agenda is more focused. Furthermore, the last two parts directly address problems specific to black gay men. Part III "Hold Tight Gently" consists of fourteen texts dealing with AIDS, and the last part "The Absence of Fear" contains texts that try to develop a theoretical framework to deal with black gay masculinities. One of these theoretical texts is Isaac Julien and Kobena Mercer's "True Confessions: A Discourse on Images of Black Male Sexuality."[59] Another is Ron Simmons's "Some Thoughts on the Challenges Facing Black Gay Intellectuals,"[60] which deals with relationships between black gay men, on the one hand, and the black community and its spokespersons, on the other. A third is Nero's "Toward a Black Gay Aesthetic: Signifying in Black Gay Literature," which I will deal with in the following chapter (see 3.5). When treating Simmons's and Nero's essays, Don Belton states in a review that "to read these two essays is to glimpse the first yield of a legacy that has been long buried by lies, omission and fear. They make up a rough draft for the rewriting of black social and literary history."[61]

---

57 The UK-poetry tour took place between March 10 and 27, 1992.

58 *Ceremonies* was awarded the National Library Association's Gay, Lesbian, and Bisexual New Author Award. – I will discuss Hemphill's critique of Mapplethorpe in the sub-chapter on Julien's *Looking for Langston* (see 4.3.4).

59 Isaac Julien and Kobena Mercer, "True Confessions: A Discourse on Images of Black Male Sexuality," *Brother to Brother: New Writings by Black Gay Men*, ed. Essex Hemphill. Boston: Alyson Publications, 1991, 167–173.

60 Ron Simmons, "Some Thoughts on the Challenges Facing Black Gay Intellectuals," *Brother to Brother: New Writings by Black Gay Men*, ed. Essex Hemphill, Boston: Alyson, 1991, 211–228.

61 Don Belton, "Gay Voices, Gay Lives: Black Gay Men Speak Out in an Anthology – Celebrating and Defining Their World," *The Philadelphia Inquirer* Aug. 25 (1991): 1c-2c, 2c.

Whereas Hemphill's anthology was reviewed positively in black gay periodicals, the reaction of white gay reviewers was divergent. For instance, in his review of *Brother to Brother*, the white gay critic Michael Bronski calls the anthology "an intense experience for white readers." He states that "it becomes apparent page after page how large a gap there is between the cultural experience of white and black gay men."[62] Rick Whitaker, another white critic, is of a different opinion. Apart from one poem, Whitaker claims that "the remainder of the book, however – that is, the other 260 pages – is, I'm afraid, with some incidental and brief exceptions throughout, full of complaint, bitchiness, simplemindedness, and sentimentality."[63] In his review, he does not distinguish between the different genres of the texts contained in the volume, and he does not even mention Simmons's, Nero's or Julien and Mercer's theoretical texts. In contrast to Bronski, he does not reflect on his own position as a white critic, and he fails to reflect on the criticism directed at white gay men formulated in the pages of *Brother to Brother*. In 1993, Arthur Flannigan Saint-Aubin formulated an extensive critique of *Brother to Brother* in the *Journal of the History of Sexuality*. Being basically sympathetic to the anthology, he also elaborates on the shortcomings of the volume. His main argument is that, in criticizing homophobia in the black community and racism in the white gay community, the texts in the volume do not go far enough. He states that, in contrast to the claim made in Hemphill's introduction, they are implicitly addressed to black heterosexual male and white gay male readers[64] and thus fail in creating an "exclusive, safe place for the black gay male reader."[65]

Saint-Aubin illustrates his argument with an analysis of Charles Henry Fuller's short story "The Jazz Singer,"[66] which is about an encounter between a

---

62 Michael Bronski, "Reading Through *Brother to Brother: New Writings By Black Gay Men* (Between the Lines with Michael Bronski: Books in Review)," *The Guide* July (1991): n.p.

63 Rick Whitaker, "Telling Politics," *City Pages* Dec. 6 (1991): 50–51, 51.

64 Saint-Aubin, 479.

65 Saint-Aubin, 470.

66 Charles Henry Fuller, "The Jazz Singer," *Brother to Brother: New Writings by Black Gay Men*, ed. Essex Hemphill, Boston: Alyson, 1991, 3–61.

father who walks in on his black gay son who is crossdressed and imagines himself as an impersonator of a female jazz singer. The father is furious, and beats his son, but apologizes in the end. Saint-Aubin argues that the intended reader of this story is the father of a gay son. His strong thesis is formulated as follows:

> The texts create a heterosexual space for the reader to enter, a heterosexual readerly position from which meaning can be produced. The reader [...] must play the role of a black heterosexual reader because he is the one who is encoded and dramatized within the text and he is the one, therefore, who gives the text coherence.[67]

His argument supports the more general thesis that a lot of black gay texts are addressed to the larger black community in order to raise acceptance for the newly emerging identity category "black gay," which, in 1989, was used as a political category for only a decade. I agree with Saint-Aubin that this strategy is employed in "The Jazz Singer," too. However, since the story is narrated from the perspective of the black gay son, it addresses black gay readers and implicitly asks them for their solidarity with the narrator. For this reason, the argument put forward by Saint-Aubin that meaning is produced from a heterosexual perspective is not convincing. On the contrary, the narrative initially evokes the reader's sympathy with and solidarity for the black gay protagonist. In a second step, the heterosexual father is depicted as a threatening force intruding from the outside.

Saint-Aubin's further objection concerns the intersections of differences (see 3.1). He argues that the texts in the anthology are not sensitive to differences other than race and sexual orientation. Addressing the fact that the anthology features no texts written by black women and that black women are neither addressed as readers nor as subject matter in the texts of *Brother to Brother*, he claims that the anthology is "complicitous with the machinations of patriarchal culture."[68] In reducing the focus to the categories black and gay, the anthology ignores the fact that black gay men, though oppressed because of their blackness and gayness, can at the same time be oppressors because of their male gender.[69]

---

67 Saint-Aubin, 473.

68 Saint-Aubin, 473.

69 Saint-Aubin, 474–475.

According to Saint-Aubin, the texts in the anthology imply that blackness and gayness are separate systems of oppression because the white homosexual reader and the black heterosexual reader are addressed in two distinct voices. One effect is the impression that these oppressions are symmetrical and that blackness and gayness have no connection to maleness.[70] Saint-Aubin coins the term "blackgaymale" and outlines the most important guiding questions for future research in the field of black gay literature that are similar to the program of West's "new cultural politics of difference" (see 3.1.1). Saint-Aubin asks "how do different forms of oppression connect and intermingle and yet remain distinct? And how can one complex identity (which I call blackgaymale) be both oppressed (black/gay) and oppressor (male/middle-class)?"[71] He poses a number of questions as a guideline for research in blackgaymale textuality and suggests that the category blackgaymale should be applied to texts because of the way black gay men structure their texts. The points he raises concern the question whether a black gay male standpoint determines "a distinct conception of the world" which is expressed through concepts such as, for instance, a blackgaymale imagination, a distinct discourse, a way of knowledge production, a distinct historical consciousness, or a particular way of speaking and writing.[72]

2.5 Constructing Black Gay Myths of Origin

Other Countries was a New York-based collective of black gay writers. The collective's name refers back to James Baldwin's novel *Another Country* (1962). After establishing the group in 1986, they published two anthologies called *Black Gay Voices* (1988) and *Sojourner: Black Gay Voices in the Age of Aids* (1993). The latter received a Lambda award. In the foreword of *Black Gay Voices*, the anthology is characterized as

---

70 Saint-Aubin, 474.

71 Saint-Aubin, 474.

72 Saint-Aubin, 476.

a brave and sometimes difficult journey into new territory and the simultaneous excavation of a past that has been lost, hidden, stolen. It is a homage to our forebears – like Richard Bruce Nugent and James Baldwin – a recognition of our pioneers – like Samuel Delany, Adrian Stanford, Assotto Saint, Essex Hemphill and Joseph Beam – a pride in our immediate parentage in Blackheart.[73]

Even though the first volume of *Black Gay Voices* was published only two years after *In the Life*, Saint, Beam, and Hemphill are already canonized, together with Delany and Stanford, as "pioneers" of black gay literature. Nugent and Baldwin, those writers more firmly rooted in the black community are called "forebears." The volume is dedicated to Baldwin, Nugent, and Bayard Rustin, all of whom died one year earlier, in 1987. In outlining the aim of the volume to excavate a lost, hidden, and stolen past, the editors use a terminology which is very similar to the words José Esteban Muñoz used eleven years later in describing the works of black gay men whose writings and films have a lot more in common than the fact that the artists' subject positions are determined by the categories blackness and gayness. Muñoz argues that these black gay artists have a common aim, "the (re)telling of elided histories that need to be excavated and (re)imagined, over and above the task of bearing the burden of representing an identity that is challenged and contested by various forces."[74]

Like *In the Life*, *Black Gay Voices* emphasizes the connections between black gay men and black traditions. The first volume contains texts that construct a black gay lineage, such as an interview with Bayard Rustin connecting black gay identity with the Civil Rights movement,[75] and the didactic play "Morning After Blues" that shows the different relations and attitudes of two black gay men to the larger black community, as well as to black history. "Morning After Blues" is set in an apartment in New York's West Village in the autumn of 1982. At the

---

73 Other Countries Collective, "Introduction," *Other Countries: Black Gay Voices*, ed. Other Countries, New York: Other Countries, 1988. 1.

74 José Esteban Muñoz, *Disidentifications: Queers of Color and the Performance of Politics*, Minneapolis: U of Minnesota P, 1999, 57.

75 Redvers Jeanmarie, "An Interview with Bayard Rustin." *Other Countries: Black Gay Voices.* Ed. Other Countries, New York: Other Countries, 1988, 3–16.

center of the play are the two black men, Juney and Mike. Mike is a 29-year-old professor of English and Juney is a 30-year-old advertising executive. Whereas Juney is shown as an openly gay man who is living in a gay neighborhood, Mike is represented as a closeted black man from Harlem with an afrocentric political agenda. Their relationship is depicted as rather tense because Mike wants it to remain secret. At one point they discuss the effectiveness of coming out as a gay man with regard to the Harlem Renaissance poets. The topic comes up because Mike is teaching a class on the Harlem Renaissance at Harlem's City College:

> Juney. You know, I've heard that a lot of the writers of that period were Gay.
> Mike. What are you talking about?
> Juney. My Sister. She was telling me about Langston Hughes and Nora Hurston. I don't know where she read it.
> Mike. Zora. Zora Neale Hurston is the name. *Their Eyes Were Watching God*? Have you heard of it? No? Anyway, what difference does it make? They were great writers. They'll influence Black art for generations. What difference does it make who they went to bed with?
> Juney. I don't know. It shouldn't make any difference, I suppose. So if the boys went to bed with the boys and the girls with the girls and a good time was had by all, up and down 125th Street that's all the more reason –
> Mike. To keep quiet about it.
> Juney. No, to be proud of who we are. Of who we were.[76]

This quotation is exemplary of the didacticism of the play. Directed at the black community, it tries to raise acceptance for black gay men within the larger black community, and it also aims at politicizing black gay men. The passage quoted above is an example of the black gay movement's strategy of referring to the gay dimensions of earlier epochs of black culture. At first, it emphasizes the significance of the Harlem Renaissance for black art in general, in saying "they'll influence Black art for generations." In a second step, the sexual orientation of the Harlem Renaissance poets is taken as a legitimization of pride in one's own homosexuality. And in a third step, the quotation constructs a direct heritage between the Harlem Renaissance and 1980s black gay men when Juney uses the pronoun "we" to include the Harlem

---

76 Cary Alan Johnson, "Morning After Blues," *Other Countries: Black Gay Voices*, ed. Other Countries, New York: Other Countries, 1988, 63–82, 67.

Renaissance poets as well as black gay men and lesbians in the 1980s: "that's all the more reason (...) to be proud of who we are. Of who we were."

Another illustration of a direct reference to black literary and cultural traditions is the short essay "Don't Turn Your Back On Me," by the then 19-year-old writer Stephen Lee Dais, which is included in *In the Life*. In a key passage that directly refers to Langston Hughes and James Baldwin, he states that rejecting black gayness has negative effects for the black community: "By dismissing black gays, the black community denies a considerable portion of its identity. Does the sexual orientation of James Baldwin or Langston Hughes invalidate their insightful writings?"[77] The answer to this question given in the later writings by black gay men goes beyond the answer expected of this rhetorical question: the sexual orientation of James Baldwin and Langston Hughes does not invalidate their own writings. It is strategically referred to in order to validate the existence and the writings of black gay men who wrote at the end of the twentieth century.

In a 1991 review of *Brother to Brother*, Don Belton states that "*In the Life* was welcome evidence that the meaning of the often-lone witness of James Baldwin, who died in 1987, had not been lost on a new generation."[78] As Baldwin was a spokesperson of the Civil Rights movement and as he is the best-known African American homosexual writer, many black gay and lesbian artists refer to Baldwin as a role model. In 1992, the D.C. Coalition of Black Lesbians and Gay Men published a volume on James Baldwin called "The Fire This Time." The title refers to a volume of essays by James Baldwin with the title *The Fire Next Time*, published in 1963. Likewise, in "Not a Bad Legacy, Brother," Beam describes how reverently he listened to Baldwin at a reading. In his text, Beam deliberately puts himself in a tradition that follows Baldwin's work:

---

77 Stephen Lee Dais, "Don't Turn Your Back On Me," *In the Life: A Black Gay Anthology*, ed. Joseph Beam, Boston: Alyson, 1986, 60–62, 62.

78 Belton, 2c.

> The first and only time I heard James Baldwin read, I sat perched on the edge of my chair catching every syllable that dropped from his lips. In the too-crowded, too-hot room, I watched him pat beads of perspiration from his forehead with a flourish only a true diva could muster. He was a diva, yet up close he seemed quite fragile, having paid the price of the ticket for being arrogant, articulate, and black.[79]

In including the term "the price of the ticket," Beam alludes to Baldwin's essay by the same title.

"Not a Bad Legacy, Brother" is one of the essays in the section "Speaking of Baldwin" published in *Au Courant* shortly after Baldwin's death in 1987. The essay was re-published in *Brother to Brother*. The feature also includes Cheryl Clarke's vivid description of taking part in Baldwin's funeral in Harlem called "The Space in Me Where Baldwin Lives," the text "We Must Always Bury Our Dead Twice" by Barbara Smith, and a poem by Phil Robinson.[80] In *Brother to Brother*, Carlyle R. Black's poem "James Baldwin (1924–1987)" comes directly after Beam's essay. It is a homage to Baldwin's work because it mainly consists of the titles of 19 texts by Baldwin.[81] In his review, Belton criticizes both Beam's and Black's texts. Commenting on Carlyle's poem, he states that "a simple bibliography of Baldwin's magnificent oeuvre would have sufficed – or a more extended essay on Baldwin's formidable contribution to the very possibility of books such as *In the Life* or *Brother to Brother* should have been included rather than the anthology's pithy one left behind by Beam ('Not a Bad Legacy, Brother')."[82]

The strategy of constructing a black gay ancestry to validate one's own subject position can also be found in black gay texts that focus on HIV/AIDS. *Sojourner*, the second volume of the Other Countries collective, is an example of this strategy. Following the introduction, the volume starts with three pages entitled "Standing on the Shoulders of Our Ancestors." The pages are black, and the words on the pages are printed in white letters. It is a long list of names,

---

79 Joseph Beam, "James Baldwin: Not a Bad Legacy, Brother," *Brother to Brother: New Writings by Black Gay Men*, ed. Essex Hemphill, Boston: Alyson, 1991, 184–186, 186.

80 Joseph Beam, Barbara Smith, Cheryl Clarke, and Phil Robinson, "Speaking of Baldwin," *Au Courant* 6.6 (1987).

81 Carlyle R. Black, "James Baldwin (1924–1987)," *Brother to Brother: New Writings by Black Gay Men*, ed. Essex Hemphill. Boston: Alyson, 1991, 187–188.

82 Belton, 2c.

a "tribute to men [the editors] have named as ancestors. Most died of AIDS-related complications. Most of them were Gay. Most share in the legacy of the African Diaspora."[83] In the face of the threat of the AIDS epidemic, the term "ancestor" includes those who only recently died of AIDS as well as those who lived in earlier historical periods. The list names well-known writers like Dixon, the Cuban writer Reinaldo Arenas and Beam, as well as many less well-known persons. The texts collected in *Sojourner* belong to different genres such as poetry, essay, and letter, and they are very personal accounts of the HIV/AIDS crisis.[84]

Craig G. Harris's poem "State of Grace (For Lawrence Washington)." is about different generations of the narrator's biological family, and it pays tribute to different generations of black gay men and activists. It focuses on two persons, the black gay narrator and his 14-year-old nephew who share a traditional family meal together. The narrator is a self-proclaimed gay activist who explains the situation of (black) gay men to his nephew. In discussing the politics of ACT UP, whose slogan "Silence Equals Death," he refers to "Audre Lorde's axiom: 'our silence will not protect us.'"[85] The narrator and his nephew feel a strong connection and "share a secret smile." When the narrator blesses the food, he remembers "the ancestors upon whose shoulders we stand:

> James, Bayard, Bruce,
> Calu Lester, Fred Garnett, Eddie King,
> Mel Boozer,
> Joe Beam,
> And on and on,[86]

until he cries and also speaks the name of his dead lover. His prayer has a threefold meaning. First, this list of persons connects him to the experiences of Bruce Nugent, James Baldwin and Bayard Rustin and then to his own generation of black gay men and to himself because he is mourning.

---

83 Michael B. Hunter, "Introduction," *Sojourner: Black Gay Voices in the Age of Aids*, ed. Michael B. Hunter, New York: Other Countries, 1993, xiii-xiv, xiv.

84 Some of the texts have appeared in journals and other anthologies before.

85 Craig G. Harris, "State of Grace," *Sojourner: Black Gay Voices in the Age of Aids*, ed. Michael B. Hunter, New York: Other Countries, 1993, 151-152, 151.

86 Harris, "State of Grace," 152.

The last stanza explains the importance of a black gay heritage and of remembering those black gay men who have died. The narrator expresses the need to pass his knowledge on to the next generation, embodied by his nephew:

> I feel my nephew's hand comforting my shoulder
> reminding me that understanding
> comes with time and sharing and feeling
> and the passing of traditions of hope and struggle
> from generation to generation[87]

Thus, the early anthologies of black gay writings show the ways in which black gay men reacted to the oppressive situation of the 1980s. Some writers promoted a new afrocentric black gay identity. Equally important, their texts initiated debates about traditional forms of identity politics rooted in a monolithic group identity as black people or gay men. A strategy that can already be found in these texts is the construction of myths of origin of black gay identity. By explicitly referring to the Harlem Renaissance, the Civil Rights era, and the personas of Nugent, Hughes, Rustin and Baldwin, they aim at legitimizing black gayness and empowering other black gay men. In the later chapters I will show that this strategy became more elaborate because the longer texts by Corbin, Julien, Delany, Kenan and Dixon refer to the queer dimensions of earlier texts rather than to the sexual orientation of their writers.

---

87 Harris, "State of Grace," 152.

3   Queer of Color Critique –
Contemporary Theoretical Approaches

On the basis of the political debates and strategies specific to the major black gay anthologies, I will now establish a theoretical outline for the analysis of the longer black gay texts of the 1980s and 1990s that are at the center of my study. This chapter is organized in two parts. In the first step, I will develop an anti-essentialist perspective that emphasizes the simultaneous importance of socially-constructed identity categories such as race, gender, and sexual orientation. On the basis of Stuart Hall's and Cornel West's suggestions for an anti-essentialist political practice, as well as Kimberlé Crenshaw's theory of intersectionality, I will look at the intersections of the categories blackness and gayness and analyze the reasons that influenced the emergence of black gay cultural activism, that is the origins of prevailing stereotypes of black masculinity, the dominant construction of gayness as a white identity and the threat HIV/AIDS posed specifically for black homosexual men.

In the second step, I will focus on recent developments within the emerging field of black queer theory, especially Muñoz's concept of "disidentification" and E. Patrick Johnson's concept of "quare." Focusing on Muñoz and Johnson, I will consider theoretical approaches that are influenced by poststructuralism. In addition to their affiliations with poststructuralist thought, theses approaches stand in the tradition of the critique black lesbians and black gay men directed at the earlier gay and lesbian studies' focus on texts by white gay men and lesbians. Both approaches regard the work of black queer cultural activists as forms of resistance rooted in black vernacular traditions. I will argue that the project of constructing myths of origin of black gayness by referring to black cultural traditions can be considered as an act of resistance to the oppression black gay men face within the dominant culture as well as within sub-cultural contexts, and I will connect Muñoz's and Johnson's film studies and performance studies approaches with African American literary criticism, especially Henry Louis Gates Jr.'s theory of Signifying.[88] The connection

---

88   In using Gates's theory, I follow Charles I. Nero, who was the first literary critic to approach black gay texts with Gates's theory of Signifying (Nero, "Toward a Black Gay Aesthetic").

between Muñoz's and Johnson's approaches and literary criticism will allow me to approach the different media, film as well as the different literary genres, covered in my study in a theoretical way.

3.1 Intersectionality

3.1.1 Anti-essentialist Approaches towards Identities

The texts I will consider in my study were conceived from an explicitly black and gay perspective, but owing to developments within the political movements, as well as in the academic world, it is not a contradiction to analyze them in the context of an anti-essentialist approach towards identities. In doing so, I follow the British cultural-studies theorist Kobena Mercer, who is well aware of the paradox connected with the notion that a group of artists that organize around the identity categories black and gay should be the vanguard of an anti-essentialist politics and aesthetic that aims at a deconstruction of identities altogether. In his study *Welcome to the Jungle: New Positions in Black Cultural Studies*, Mercer states the following about the work of black gay artists:

> Surely there is more than a whiff of essentialism in my implicit claim that black gay men are producing some of the most innovative and challenging work on the subject of identity? Are we to assume that the works of image-makers as diverse as Rotimi Fani-Kayode, Sunil Gupta, Isaac Julien, Marlon Riggs or Lyle Ashton Harris has intrinsic value merely *because* its authors share a common identity as black gay men? No. What is at issue in the politics of identity articulated in their work is not that they constitute some wretched subaltern subculture, damned by double or triple 'disadvantage,' who therefore warrant your 'right-on' sympathies, but on the contrary: how their work interrupts commonsense essentialism in favor of a relational and dialogic view of the constructed character of any social identity.[89]

Mercer's argument is not only true for black gay men who work in the field of visual arts. Through their texts, black gay writers also question essentialist

---

89 Kobena Mercer, "Dark and Lovely: Black Gay Image Making," *Welcome to the Jungle: New Positions in Black Cultural Studies*, New York: Routledge, 1994, 221–232, 221–222.

notions of identities and thereby reveal the constructed character of any social identity.[90] In order to avoid a misunderstanding common to the reception of constructionist theories, it is important to emphasize that, in asserting that identity categories do not refer to fixed, coherent 'natural' subjects, constructionist theories do not suggest that blacks, lesbians, and gay men would not think of themselves as black, lesbian or gay. They may even experience their socially-constructed 'otherness' as if it were biologically determined. Queer theorist David Halperin explains why our intuitions about our own "natural" identities do not contradict the thesis that identity categories are cultural constructions. He calls the process that makes us accept intuitions about ourselves and about the world "acculturation." According to Halperin "acculturation consists precisely in learning to accept as natural, normal, and inevitable what is in fact conventional and arbitrary."[91]

In criticizing constructionist theory, some conservative critics and some natural scientists are misreading it. Most of the critics share a similar focus. They see no reason to take (lesbian and gay) identities seriously if these are not the effects of biological determination. They consider these identities to be trivial or argue that sexual identities are easily changeable if they are social constructions. In her essay "Social Construction Theory: Problems in the History of Sexuality," Carole S. Vance responds to this kind of criticism as follows:

> To suggest that any feature of human life, for example, national or ethnic identity, is socially constructed is not to say that it is trivial. Nor is it to say that entire cultures can transform themselves overnight, or that individuals socialized in one cultural tradition can acculturate at whim to another. This criticism of social construction confuses the individual level with the cultural level: that sexuality is constructed at the level of culture and history through complex interactions which we are now trying to understand

---

90 The turn in thinking about identities designated by the "essentialism vs. anti-essentialism-debate" was fueled by poststructuralist theories such as Jacques Lacan's psychoanalytic models of de-centered, unstable identity, Jacques Derrida's deconstruction of western metaphysics, and Michel Foucault's investigations of discourse, knowledge and power, that came after the linguistic turn. The term 'linguistic turn' designates the thesis that the rules of language not only structure our perception of reality, our way of thinking, and consequently our actions, but that reality itself is constituted by language, because reality can never be conveyed in any 'direct' way that makes no use of language.

91 David M. Halperin, *One Hundred Years of Homosexuality*, New York: Routledge, 1990, 44.

does not mean that individuals have an open-ended ability to construct themselves, or to reconstruct themselves multiple times in adulthood.[92]

In his recent book *On Sexuality and Power*, the literary theorist Alan Sinfield puts forward a similar argument when stating that "one inference from antiessentialist theory should be that we cannot simply throw off our current constructions. We are consequences of our histories – those that have been forced upon us and those that we have made ourselves."[93]

For the analysis of texts by black gay men, it is important to acknowledge the constructedness of all categories of identity without trivializing black gay men's experiences of racism and homphobia. Mercer's statement that the work of black gay men "interrupts commonsense essentialism in favor of a relational and dialogic view of the constructed character of any social identity" is enforced when one considers the ways in which black queer subject formations are contradictory to the respective dominant constructions of blackness and gayness.

Mercer's reading of the works of black gay artists belongs to the Black Britsh Cultural Studies school of thought. Another important text of Black Britsh Cultural Studies focusing on the consequences an anti-essentialist approach has for black art is Stuart Hall's "New Ethnicities," a paper delivered at the "Black Film/British Cinema" conference in 1988. Hall argues that the "end of the innocent notion of the essential black subject"[94] draws attention to the differences within the category black, which is a prerequisite for the analysis of the intersections of blackness and gayness. Hall states the following.

> The end of the essential black subject is something which people are increasingly debating, but they may not have fully reckoned with its political consequences. What is at issue here is the recognition of the extraordinary diversity of subjective positions, social experiences and

---

92 Carole S. Vance, "Social Construction Theory: Problems in the History of Sexuality," *Social Perspectives in Lesbian and Gay Studies*, eds. Peter M. Nardi, and Beth E. Schneider, London: Routledge, 1998, 160–173, 162.

93 Alan Sinfield, *On Sexuality and Power*, New York: Columbia UP, 2004, 189.

94 Stuart Hall, "New Ethnicities," *Black Film, British Cinema*, ed. ICA London: Institute of Contemporary Arts, 1988, 27–30, 28.

cultural identities which compose the category 'black'; that is the recognition that 'black' is essentially a politically and culturally *constructed* category, which cannot be grounded in a set of fixed, trans-cultural or transcendental racial categories and which therefore has no guarantees in Nature. What this brings into play is the recognition of the immense diversity and differentiation of the historical and cultural experience of black subjects. This inevitably entails a weakening or fading of the notion that 'race' or some composite notion of race around the term black will either guarantee the effectivity of any cultural practice or determine in any final sense its aesthetic value.[95]

While Hall presents a British perspective, Cornel West's program of a "new cultural politics of difference" comes out of an African American context. Similar to Hall, West is in agreement with the notion of the constructed nature of all identity categories, and he directs his attention to the intersections of various axes of difference. West particularly considers the intersections of the categories race, gender, class, and sexual orientation from an anti-essentialist perspective. From an historical distance, West disapproves of traditional forms of black politics. He criticizes the Civil Rights movement for an "*assimilationist manner* that set out to claim that Black people were really like White people and thereby eliding differences (in history and culture) between Whites and Blacks."[96] As one of their aims was to be accepted by the white society, their politics resulted in subordination to the white power structure. He also criticizes the politics of Black Nationalism for a "*homogenizing impulse* that assumed that all black people were really alike, hence obliterating differences (class, gender, religion, sexual orientation) between black people."[97] West is far from suggesting that black people should abandon these forms of politics altogether. He agrees that, although black and white people share a common humanity, *all* black people are "subject to white Supremacist abuse."[98] However, he sees the danger of an assimilationist politics and of an impulse to exclude other axes of difference in the construction of the black subject. To avoid these

---

95 Hall, 28.

96 Cornel West, "The New Cultural Politics of Difference," *The Cultural Studies Reader*, ed. Simon During, London: Routledge, 1999. 256–271, 262.

97 West, 262.

98 West, 262.

dangers, he outlines his idea of "the new cultural politics of difference" and argues that, in doing so, he is revising traditional forms of black politics:

> Black cultural workers must constitute and sustain discursive and institutional networks that deconstruct earlier modern Black strategies for identity formation, demystify power relations that incorporate class, patriarchal, and homophobic biases, and construct more multivalent and multidimensional responses that articulate the complexity and diversity of Black practices in the modern and postmodern world.[99]

In maintaining the importance of a particular black culture that includes the experiences of black women, black lesbians, and black gay men, and at the same time in addressing allies among other marginalized agents like "people of color, Jews, women, gays, lesbians, and the elderly,"[100] the new cultural politics of difference combines strategic identity politics with coalitional politics. I will show that many texts by black gay artists focus on differences within the black community while at the same time standing in a tradition of a black culture and history. They are examples of this new cultural politics of difference. What is more, the type of critique formulated by black gay and feminist artists who criticized the idea of a monolithic blackness might even have fueled Hall's and West's theoretical concepts.[101]

In order to understand the ways in which constructions of gayness and blackness are antagonistic and contradictory, I have to pay special attention to the ways in which these categories intersect in constructions of black gay masculinities. An analysis of the constructions and the intersectionality of blackness and gayness is an important prerequisite if one wants to understand the politics and aesthetics of 1980s and 1990s black gay culture.

The political interventions formulated by the early black gay writers stand in a tradition of criticism put forward by black (lesbian) feminists in

---

99 West, 264.

100 West, 257.

101 The papers presented at the conference Black Film/British Cinema held in London in 1988 indicate the influence the pro-feminist and pro-gay work of black film collectives such as Sankofa and the Black Audio Collective had on British cultural studies. The proceedings of this conference are published in ICA.

the 1970s, who criticized the women's movement because they did not want to be represented by mostly white middle-class heterosexual women. What is more, theorists and activists like Audre Lorde and Angela Davis[102] criticized the black liberation movement because black women were invisible within the movement. The Combahee River Collective was a black feminist collective that formed in the USA in 1974 against the background of black women's experiences in both the women's movement and the black liberation movement. Their text, *A Black Feminist Statement*, is an example of the criticism put forward by black women who felt invisible within these movements:

> A black feminist presence has evolved most obviously in connection with the second wave of the American women's movement beginning in the late 1960s. Black, other Third World, and working class women have been involved in the feminist movement from its start, but both outside reactionary forces and racism and elitism within the movement itself have served to obscure our participation. [...] Black feminist politics also have an obvious connection to movements for black liberation, particularly those of the 1960s and 1970s. Many of us were active in those movements (civil rights, black nationalism, the Black Panthers), and all of our lives were greatly affected and changed by their ideology, their goals, and the tactics used to achieve their goals. It was our experience and disillusionment within these liberation movements, as well as experience on the periphery of the white male left, that led to a need to develop a politics that was antiracist, unlike those of white women, and antisexist, unlike those of black and white men.[103]

Political groups like the Combahee River Collective did not limit their political analysis to a single form of oppression. As they believed that "the major systems of oppression are interlocking,"[104] they were "actively committed to struggling against racial, sexual, heterosexual, and class oppression."[105] This black feminist critique motivated Kimberlé Crenshaw's concept of

102 See for example Angela Y. Davis, "Reflection on the Black Women's Role in the Community of Slaves," *Black Scholar* 4 (1971): 2–15.

103 Combahee River Collective, "A Black Feminist Statement," *Social Perspectives in Lesbian and Gay Studies*, eds. Peter M. Nardi and Beth E. Schneider, London: Routledge, 1998, 521–522.

104 Combahee River Collective, 521.

105 Combahee River Collective, 521.

intersectionality. The volume *Words That Wound: Critical Race Theory, Assaultive Speech, and the First Amendment* contains her essay "Beyond Racism and Misogyny: Black Feminism and 2 Live Crew." Focusing on the intersections of the categories race and gender, she outlines a general theory of intersectionality. It is influential for approaches that try to go beyond monocausal frameworks when addressing systems of oppression.

Crenshaw argues that the theoretical framework of intersectionality is important for two reasons. First, it discloses the dual or multiple positioning of women of color. Second, it is helpful to explicate the "ways in which political and representational practices relating to race and gender interrelate."[106] Traditional political strategies that treat feminist, gay and lesbian, and antiracist issues separately "marginalize those who are subject to multiple systems of subordination,"[107] such as black gay men and black lesbians. Traditional political strategies might even "result in oppositionalizing race and gender discourses."[108] Therefore, the basic function of intersectionality is to answer the question: "How does the fact that women of color are simultaneously situated within at least two groups that are subjected to broad societal subordination bear upon problems traditionally viewed monocausal?"[109]

3.1.2 Representational Intersectionality: Stereotypes of Black Men

Crenshaw looks at mainstream media images of women of color in popular culture to explain a particular form of intersectionality, which she calls representational intersectionality. She comes to the conclusion that race and gender images intersect in representations of women of color and

---

106 Kimberlé Williams Crenshaw, "Beyond Racism and Misogyny: Black Feminism and 2 Live Crew" *Words that Wound: Critical Race Theory, Assaultive Speech, and the First Amendment*, ed. Mari J. Matsuda, Boulder: Westview, 1993, 111–132, 112. See also Kimberlé Williams Crenshaw, "Politics, and Violence Against Women of Color," *Stanford Law Review* 43 (1991): 1241–1299. See also the special issue of the *European Journal of Women's Studies* on Intersectionality (Ann Phoenix and Pamela Pattynama, eds., "Special Issue on Intersectionality," *European Journal of Women's Studies* 13.3 (2006)).

107 Crenshaw, "Beyond Racism," 112.

108 Crenshaw, "Beyond Racism," 113.

109 Crenshaw, "Beyond Racism," 114.

that "it is through sexuality that images of minorities and women are most sharply focused."[110] Mainstream and sub-cultural images of black men are often focused through sexuality, too, and black gay cultural activists have reacted to these sexualized images of black masculinity in their work. In dealing with the connection between sexuality and race, Isaac Julien and Kobena Mercer argue in their text "Race, Sexual Politics and Masculinity: A Dossier" that the

> essentialist view of sexuality is in fact based on the prevailing Western concept of sexuality which *already contains racism*. Historically, the European construction of sexuality coincides with the epoch of imperialism and the two inter-connect. Imperialism justified itself by claiming that it had a civilising mission – to lead the base and ignoble savages and 'inferior races' into culture and godliness. The person of the savage was developed as the Other of civilization and one of the first 'proofs' of his otherness was the nakedness of the savage, the visibility of his sex. This led Europeans to assume that the savage possessed an open, frank and uninhibited 'sexuality' – unlike the sexuality of the European which was considered to be fettered by the weight of civilization.[111]

This historical connection between sexuality and racism[112] is one of the origins of stereotypes of black men, in this case the stereotype of black men as "hypersexual."

As Lynne Segal, a professor of psychology and gender studies, has shown in her book *Slow Motion: Changing Masculinities, Changing Men*, this image of the *super-macho*, and the stereotype of the *emasculated black man*, have always been prevalent in US discourses about African American men: "Anxiety about the 'emasculation' of the

---

110 Crenshaw, "Beyond Racism," 116.

111 Isaac Julien and Kobena Mercer, "Race, Sexual Politics, and Masculinity: A Dossier," *Male Order. Unwrapping Masculinity*, eds. Rowena Chapman and Jonathan Rutherford, London: Lawrence and Wishart, 1988, 97–165, 106.

112 Siobhan B. Somerville's interest also lies in the historical and discursive connections of the categories of sexuality and race. In her study *Queering the Color Line: Race and the Invention of Homosexuality in American Culture*, she tries to combine methodologies of African American studies and queer studies, and she also states that "questions of race – in particular the formation of notions of 'whiteness' and 'blackness' – must be understood as a crucial part of the history and representation of sexual formations, including lesbian and gay identity and compulsory heterosexuality in the United States" (Siobhan B. Somerville, *Queering the Color Line: Race and the Invention of Homosexuality in American Culture*, Durham: Duke UP, 2000, 5). In her interdisciplinary study, she investigates texts and films from the late nineteenth and early twentieth century in order to support her thesis that "the structures and methodologies that drove dominant ideologies of race also fueled the pursuit of knowledge about the homosexual body" (Somerville, 17).

black man co-exists with anxiety over the super-sexual, super-macho nature of the black man. Is he not-man-enough, or is he too-masculine-by-half?"[113] At first glance, the two constructions contradict each other, and yet both stereotypes have the same racist origins. While studies that present the black man as emasculated can be "accommodated into a phallocentric narrative, which ascribes the possession of the 'phallus' to white men and its lack to the social inferiority complex of black men,"[114] the stereotype of the black man as super-macho can be traced down to colonial images that presented the black man's masculinity as that of "the subhuman animal."[115] Segal presents a wide range of literary examples that illustrate the colonial discourse, which, in turn, constructed the black man as a super-macho by combining the categories of race and sexuality. This image of black men "as mere body – primitive, sexual and violent"[116] illustrates the binary opposition of white masculinity as *mind* and black masculinity as *body*.

David Marriott follows Segal in explaining the stereotype of the black emasculated man as the result of a translation of societal power relations into sexual concepts. For him, the stereotype came into being because the

> earlier sociology of race-relations theories of black masculinity, in which kinship structures were shown to be based on socially dysfunctional gender relations, tended to view black male sexual cultures as the pathological reflection of white hegemonic masculinities.[117]

According to Marriott, the methodologies of studies like the influential *Moynihan Report on the Black Family*[118] (1965) reinforce racist stereotypes. Its approaches include the analysis of black kinship structures. Moynihan puts forward the argument that there is a crisis in black masculinity for various reasons, but that it can be traced back to the structure of the black family. He

---

113 Lynne Segal, *Slow Motion: Changing Masculinities, Changing Men*, New Brunswick, N.J: Rutgers UP, 1990, 184–185.

114 David Marriott, "Reading Black Masculinities," *Understanding Masculinities: Social Relations and Cultural Arenas*, ed. Mairtin Mac an Ghaill, Buckingham: Open UP, 1996, 185–201. 185.

115 Segal, 180–181.

116 Segal, 178.

117 Marriott, 185.

118 Daniel Moynihan, *The Negro Family: The Case for National Action*, Washington: US Department of Labor, 1965.

states, for instance, that the absence of fathers and the resulting power of black mothers over their sons leads to an "emasculation," a "symbolic castration."[119]

These racist stereotypes had consequences for black politics and for the situation of black gay men. The notion of black men as hypersexual and a confirmation of the opposites of black = body and white = mind can be found in texts by white writers, such as Norman Mailer's "The White Negro"[120] and in texts by black writers such as Eldridge Cleaver' *Soul on Ice* and Amiri Baraka's essays.[121] As I will show in more detail, Cleaver's and Baraka's texts provide evidence for Michèle Wallace's thesis that the racist stereotype of the black man as super-macho was popular in the Black Power movement (see 5.1.3). She argues that "the white man's fantasy/nightmare about the black man [...], through an Americanization process of several hundred years, had become, to a great extent, the black man's as well."[122] Julien and Mercer explain how the affirmation of the "white man's nightmare" of the black super-macho in the ways black men perceive themselves was rooted in colonialism:

> A central strand of the 'racial power' exercised by the white slave master was the denial of certain masculine attributes to black males, such as authority, dignity, and familial responsibility. Through these collective historical experiences, black men have adopted and used certain patriarchal values such as physical strength, sexual prowess, and being in control to create a system of black male gender roles in which macho tactics are used to cope with the repressive and destructive power of the plantocracy and the state.[123]

In affirming the stereotype of the hypersexual black man, revolutionary black politics supported the image some Black Nationalist (heterosexual) men had of themselves. Their attitude towards white men, whom they in turn accused of emasculation, is another result of this situation. Under the conditions of a pre-Stonewall heteronormative discourse, hypersexuality is identified with heterosexuality and emasculation with homosexuality. Thus

119 For a detailed criticism of Moynihan, see Marriott, 191–192.

120 Norman Mailer, *Advertisements for Myself*, New York: Putnam, 1959.

121 See for example Amiri Baraka (LeRoi Jones), "American Sexual Reference: Black Male," *Home: Social Essays*, New York: Morrow, 1966, 216–234, 116.

122 Michele Wallace, *Black Macho and the Myth of the Superwoman*, London: John Calder, 1978, 46.

123 Julien and Mercer, "True Confessions," 171.

the accusation of emasculation took the form of a charge of homosexuality. Marlon B. Ross states that

> black nationalists did not want to sacrifice the charge of (white) homosexuality – which had become highly visible in major cities during the 1960s – as a powerful weapon that could be lodged against white America, a charge that could easily link homosexual decadence with the irreversible decline of the (white) nation-state at the same time that it could be used as a symbol of the reproductive power and consolidation of the emerging black national family. In other words, the black nationalists took the charge that powerful white men had invented to create so much fear and anxiety among themselves during the cold war – that of an insidious, pervasive homosexual decadence and betrayal lurking within America's seats of greatest power – and aimed it back at those seats of power.[124]

However, in affirming the white racist stereotype of the black super-macho, some Black Nationalists did more than merely say that homosexuality was a white man's condition. Together with its negative counterpart, the stereotype of the emasculated black man, it had consequences for black gay men, too. They are in danger of being stereotypically reduced to their sexuality by white gay men [125] and of being regarded as emasculated sissies by Black Nationalists if they positively identify themselves as gay. Thus the connections between the constructions of race and sexuality — the sexualized stereotypes about black men — can help us understand the homophobia and misogyny of some spokespersons of Black Nationalism.

Many representatives of the black community had and still have difficulties in dealing with homosexuality in a supportive or at least unprejudiced way. Henry Louis Gates Jr. considers homophobia to be "an almost obsessive motif that runs through the major authors of the Black Aesthetic and Black Power movements."[126] Julien and Mercer comment on the fact that black women and lesbians and black gay men were excluded in Black Nationalist notions of a black self-image:

---

124 Marlon B. Ross, "White Fantasies of Desire," *James Baldwin Now*, ed. Dwight A. McBride, New York: New York UP, 1999, 13–55, 1999, 30–31.

125 For a discussion of racist depictions of black men in white gay pornography, see Julien and Mercer, "Race, Sexual Politics," 101–110.

126 Henry Louis Gates Jr., "The Black Man's Burden," *Fear of a Queer Planet: Queer Politics and Social Theory*, ed. Michael Warner, Minneapolis: U of Minnesota P, 1993, 230–238, 234.

During the Black Power revolution in the 1960s, slogans such as 'black is beautiful' cleared the ground for the cultural reconstruction of a positive black self-image, but this was done at the expense of black women, gays, and lesbians. Because of the hidden sexism and implicit homophobia of the agenda of revolutionary nationalism, as defined by figures like Eldridge Cleaver, black women organized autonomously in the 1970s.[127]

Hegemonic masculinity is constructed via an exclusion of what is considered to be its opposite, femininity and male homosexuality (seen as the effiminacy of men). Jefferey Weeks states that "masculinity or the male identity is achieved by the constant process of warding off threats to it. It is precariously achieved by the rejection of femininity and homosexuality."[128] This is also the case with a black masculinity which – while itself the object of racial oppression – excludes femininity and homosexuality. Marriott observes that

the radical forms of black masculinity that emerged in the 1960s included forms of romantic nationalism and repressive gender politics that required an internal policing and coercive consensus for black women and black gay men every bit as authoritarian as the white patriarchal structures they sought to contest.[129]

These quotations show that it is a common notion held by many black cultural critics that parts of the Black Nationalist discourse are misogynous and homophobic. Black Nationalist texts contribute to a counter-cultural discourse which contests the hegemonic discouse as a racist societal structure. Efforts to change the negative images of black people were often formulated as a re-negotiation of black masculinity. Thus the categories race and sexuality are combined in the challenge to racism. This intersection of categories is a reaction to the sexualized racism prefigured in hegemonic stereotypes about black masculinity.

---

127 Julien and Mercer, "True Confessions," 171.

128 Jefferey Weeks, qtd. in David S. Gutterman, "Postmodernism and the Interrogation of Masculinity," *Theorizing Masculinities*, eds. Harry Brod, and Michael Kaufman, vol. 5, Thousand Oaks: Sage, 1994, 219–238, 225.

129 Marriott, 190.

3.1.3 The Construction of Gayness as a White Identity

José Esteban Muñoz argues, with respect to Frantz Fanon's foundational cultural studies text *Black Skin White Mask*, that within black politics, homosexuality "is basically understood as an 'it's a white thing' dismissal of queerness."[130] But he also states that "the phenomenon of 'the queer is a white thing' fantasy is strangely reflected in reverse by the normativity of whiteness in mainstream North American gay culture."[131] The dominance of white middle-class men within the gay community since the 1950s and 1960s made it even more difficult for black gay men to create a positive image of themselves. During that time, neither the social sciences nor the early gay and lesbian groups addressed the realities of black gay men. Consequently, the idea of a gay identity was limited to white gay men. As white middle-class gay men and lesbians were not racially or economically oppressed, they did not depend on supportive family structures to the extent that black people did. Thus white gay men and lesbians could more easily leave their families and form gay and lesbian communities in the cities. Robert J. Corber states that

> insofar as class and ethnicity played an increasingly unimportant role in determining the identities of white Americans, it was easier for them to identify primarily as gay and to risk marginalization by participating in the gay subculture. Unlike men of color for whom ethnicity necessarily remained the basis of group identity and survival, white Americans did not have to depend on their families and ethnic group for protection and support.[132]

Explanations by white (gay) scholars for the white dominance in gay neighborhoods of larger North-American cities are often similar to that put forward by Corber. However, Nero criticizes explanations, such as Corber's, which claim that it is less complicated for white middle-class gay men to identify themselves as gay than for black gay men and lesbians, as "extremely weak."[133] In his essay "Black Gay Men and White Gay Men: A Less than Perfect Union,"

---

130 Muñoz, *Disidentifications*, 9.

131 Muñoz, *Disidentifications*, 9.

132 Robert J. Corber, *Homosexuality in Cold War America: Resistance and the Crisis of Masculinity*, Durham: Duke UP, 1997, 48.

133 Nero, "Black Gay Men and White Gay Men," 119.

he refers to gentrification processes in New Orleans's neighborhood Faubourg Marigny and argues that more attention should be paid to material reasons such as housing discrimination underlying the formation of gay neighborhoods and the exclusion of people of color from these neighborhoods, if one wants to analyze why the gay ghettos are white.

Recent studies have analyzed how gayness is constructed as a white identity. Allan Bérubé's essay "How Gay Stays White and What Kind of White It Stays" starts with an observation he made in college courses he taught on queer history. In approaching social categories, he usually asks his students "first to imagine the stereotypical figure associated with a certain category and then to call out the figure's race, gender, class, and sexuality."[134] Concerning the category "gay man" he writes about the students' responses:

> Whenever I get to the social category "gay man," the students' response is always the same: 'white and well to do.' In the United States today, the dominant image of the gay man is a white man who is financially better off than most everyone else.[135]

In his essay "Where Rhetoric Meets Reality: The Role of Black Lesbians and Gays in Queer Politics," Keith Boykin makes a similar point. Black lesbians and black gay men do not have significant positions in gay and lesbian political organizations. They are either excluded or they have a tokenizing function. In addition, black gays and lesbians are only represented strategically to serve a particular function. Boykin states that the predominantly white gay and lesbian community engages in racially backward practices even though its rhetoric might be inclusive.[136]

Berubé's analysis of the politics of the gay movement in the late 1990s corresponds to Boykin's observation. Bérubé concludes from his own experiences as a white gay man and from a critical evaluation of some recent political campaigns of the gay movement, for instance the discussion about gay men in the military, that gay activists employ what he calls "whitening

---

134 Bérubé, 234.

135 Bérubé, 234.

136 See Boykin's chapter on "Gay Racism."

practices" in their activism that "construct, maintain, and fortify the idea that gay male means white."[137]

As the construction of a gay *identity* was predominantly white and as black homosexual men have been excluded from participating in the political structure of the gay liberation movement after the 1970s, some afrocentric Black Nationalists who emphasized their common African heritage could easily see the notion of a gay identity as un-African even though they possibly did not object to homosexual *behavior*. With regard to the African American community, Ron Simmons states that there is a difference between homosexual behavior and homosexual identity.

> In the African American Community, 'homophobia' is not so much a fear of 'homosexuals' but a fear that homosexuality will become pervasive in the community. Thus, a homophobic person can accept a homosexual as an individual friend or family member, yet not accept homosexuality. This is the attitude that predominates in the African American Community.[138]

In the 1980s, black gay artists had to react both to the homophobic rhetoric within the black community and to the construction of gayness as a white identity which denied them a meaningful position in the struggle for gay liberation. One reaction to this situation is the way in which whiteness is constructed in black gay texts. The analysis of constructions of gay whiteness will be central in the later chapters, most prominently in my readings of Julien's *Looking for Langston* (see 4.3) and Dixon's *Vanishing Rooms* (see 5.3).

Most of the studies that belong to the field of critical whiteness studies focus on the question why, within white culture, whiteness appears as an unmarked category.[139] In revealing the constructedness of whiteness, these

---

137 Bérubé, 237. The whitening practices he identifies include racial exclusion, the selling of gay whiteness, the use of race analogies, and mirroring.

138 Simmons, 211.

139 Among these texts are Ruth Frankenberg's sociological study (Ruth Frankenberg, *White Women, Race Matters: The Social Construction of* Whiteness, Minneapolis: U of Minnesota P, 1993), David Roediger's historical study (David R. Roediger, *The Wages of Whiteness: Race and the Making of the American Working Class*, London: Verso, 2007) Toni Morrison's book of literary criticism (Toni Morrison, *Playing in the Dark: Whiteness and the Literary Imagination*, Cambridge, Mass: Harvard UP, 1992), and Richard Dyer's film studies book (Richard Dyer, *White*, London: Routledge, 1997).

theories are an important step toward changing racial hierarchies and destabilizing privileges connected with whiteness. In her essay "Representing Whiteness in the Black Imagination," bell hooks analyzes the way whiteness is represented in texts by black writers and argues that many black authors depict whiteness in ways that cannot be found in books by white writers. She contends that whiteness is frequently represented as terror.[140] Inspired by hooks's approach, I will narrow her perspective and focus on representations of gay whiteness in texts by black gay writers.

3.1.4 AIDS

The 1980s were not only the first decade of black gay art and literature. It was also the first decade of the AIDS crisis. As black gay men were affected by AIDS in disproportionally high numbers,[141] AIDS became one of the main concerns and a major topic in black gay art and literature in the second half of the 1980s.

The construction of gayness as a white identity and the fact that AIDS was presented as a gay disease[142] in most newspapers, journals, and television programs had far-reaching consequences for black people. One consequence was that most black men thought that they could not get AIDS because AIDS was believed to be the disease of white gay men. Black gay men who were interviewed by Cathy Cohen for her study *The Boundaries of Blackness: AIDS and the Breakdown of Black Politics* (1999) said that during the first half of the

---

140 bell hooks, "Representing Whiteness in the Black Imagination," *Displacing Whiteness: Essays in Social and Cultural Criticism*, ed. Ruth Frankenberg, Durham: Duke UP, 1997, 165–179.

141 The failure to address race in aids activism led to the following results: "By 1987, African Americans and Latinos represented more than forty percent of AIDS cases, even though they accounted for only about twenty percent of the U.S. population. Among women, the racial numbers were even more stark. In 1988, black women and Latinas made up more than seventy percent of all women with AIDS, with black women alone accounting for forty-nine percent of the total. Meanwhile, of children with AIDS, fifty-seven percent were black, twenty-three percent Hispanic. Despite the highly disproportionate impact of AIDS on minority communities, AIDS education and prevention funding nevertheless flowed to groups serving white gay males. Within the African American community, civil rights leaders contributed to the shortfall of services by maintaining that AIDS was not a black civil rights issue." (Carbado, McBride, 269).

142 The first newspaper articles about a new disease among gay men date from the summer of 1981. The initial news coverage was focused on the white gay male community. An early acronym for the disease was GRID which stands for Gay Related Immune Deficiency. In the initial phase of the epidemic, AIDS was sometimes referred to as "gay cancer."

1980s it was a common belief among black gay men that AIDS was a disease affecting only white gay men.[143] This attitude did not change until 1985. Even though the major black and gay organizations were established before the AIDS epidemic, the "choice, or in many cases the perceived need [of black gays and lesbians], to embrace openly a black gay or lesbian identity undoubtedly escalated with the emergence of AIDS."[144] Colin Robinson, a black gay activist says that "AIDS precipitated a lot of that [black gay] culture."[145] However, the anthology *Sojourner: Black Gay Voices in the Age of Aids*, focusing exclusively on AIDS, is just one example that demonstrates how devastating the AIDS crisis was for black gay cultural activists (see 2.5), and one could even speculate that black gay culture would have become much more influential without the many AIDS-related deaths in the black gay community.

3.2 Black Queer Studies

From the late 1990s onwards, several studies have been published that outline drafts of a distinct black queer theory.[146] The aim of this black queer theoretical intervention is to create a dialogue between African American Studies and Queer Studies that puts special emphasis on the intersections of race and sexuality, a topic that is often neglected in both fields of research. Queer theory partly resulted from the critique black lesbian feminists and black gay men formulated in response to gay and lesbian studies, and it contends to be more inclusive regarding the intersections of differences and less dominated by white gay men. However, critics such as E. Patrick Johnson and Judith Halberstam argue that queer theory – again – erases differences of race

143 Cathy J. Cohen, *The Boundaries of Blackness: AIDS and the Breakdown of Black Politics*, Chicago: U of Chicago P, 1999, 91–101.

144 Cathy Cohen, 95.

145 Cathy Cohen, 100.

146 For an overview of the emerging field of black queer studies, see Rinaldo Walcott, "Somewhere Out There: The New Black Queer Theory," *Blackness and Sexualities*, eds. Michelle M. Wright, and Antje Schuhmann, Berlin: Lit, 2007, 29–40.

and class.[147] The new black queer theory stands in a tradition which criticizes identity politics formulated by earlier black gay and lesbian writers, filmmakers and artists, and it also evolves from the academic discipline of queer theory.

The dialogue between blackness and queerness is not only theorized within an African and black British context. In her study *Becoming Black: Creating Identity in the African Diaspora* (2004), Michelle M. Wright takes a transnational perspective. She analyzes Afro-German, Afro-French, Afro-British, and African American texts and focuses on the differences between black subjects. She particularly emphasizes the central position of black feminist and queer discourses in theorizing black diasporic identities.[148] In drawing on these different locations and paying attention to the differences within the category of blackness, Wright goes beyond the scope of Paul Gilroy's book *The Black Atlantic* (1993), which is mainly concerned with dialogues between black British culture and African American and Caribbean culture and politics. Gilroy uses the term "Black Atlantic" to introduce a dynamic and anti-essentialist concept of blackness that stresses the routes black subjects and discourses took and criticizes the idea of black roots on the African continent. However, his theory has been criticized for its focus on a black male context and for the geographical limitations that the Atlantic imposes. In his essay "The Uses of Diaspora," Brent Hayes Edwards argues that "it is the fascination with the Atlantic frame, and its focus on the triangular slave trade in particular, that continually draws Gilroy back into the quagmire of origins."[149] Edwards suggests that we use the term "diaspora" instead of "Black Atlantic" because it accounts for the "difference among African-derived populations" and it forces us "to think not in terms of some closed and autonomous system of African dispersal but explicitly in terms of a complex past of forced migrations and racialization."[150]

---

147 For a discussion of the limitations of queer theory and especially the white gay male dominance in the field, see Johnson "'Quare' Studies," 128–131. See also Judith Halberstam, "Shame and White Gay Masculinity," *Social Text* 84–85.23 (2005): 219–233.

148 Michelle M. Wright, *Becoming Black: Creating Identity in the African Diaspora*, Durham: Duke UP, 2004.

149 Brent Hayes Edwards, "The Uses of Diaspora," *Social Text* 66 (2001): 45–73, 63.

150 Edwards, 64. Tina Campt discusses the concept of diaspora in chapter five of her study *Other Germans*. Tina Campt, *Other Germans: Black Germans and the Politics of Race, Gender, and Memory in the Third Reich*, Ann Arbor: U of Michigan P, 2005.

Since 2000, the project of black queer studies has been outlined in several publications starting with a special issue of *Callaloo* called "Plum Nelly: New Essays in Black Queer Studies" (2000), edited by Dwight McBride and Jennifer DeVere Brody.[151] In April 2000, the conference "Black Queer Studies in the Millenium" took place at the University of North Carolina at Chapel Hill, which resulted in the publication of the volume *Black Queer Studies* in 2005. Among the important theoretical approches currently discussed as contributions to the field are José Esteban Muñoz's *Disidentifications: Queers of Color and the Performance of Politics* (1999), E. Patrick Johnson's *Appropriating Blackness: Performance and the Politics of Authenticity* (2003), and Roderick Ferguson's *Aberrations in Black: Towards a Queer of Color Critique* (2004). Johnson has pointedly formulated his criticism of queer studies in the essay "'Quare' Studies, or (Almost) Everything I Know About Queer Studies I Learned from My Grandmother" (2005).[152] Ferguson gives a definition of his project of a "Queer of Color analysis" which captures the key elements inherent in the recent approaches in the field of black queer studies, and he explicitly emphasizes the importance of the analysis of the intersections of various axes of difference such as race, gender, sexuality, and class for the project of a queer of color analysis:

> Queer of Color analysis [...] interrogates social formations as the inter-sections of race, gender, sexuality, and class, with particular interest in how those formations correspond with and diverge from nationalist ideals and practices. Queer of color analysis is a heterogeneous enterprise made up of women of color feminism, materialist analysis, poststructuralist theory, and queer critique.[153]

In the following, I will focus on how Muñoz and Johnson have used the concept of "disidentification" in their readings of the work of black queer

---

151 Jennifer DeVere Brody and Dwight A. McBride, eds. "Plum Nelly: New Essays in Black Queer Studies," *Callaloo* 23.1 (2000): Special Edition.

152 Other texts that can be read as contributions to the field of black queer theory include: Robert Reid-Pharr, *Black Gay Man*, New York: New York UP, 2001, Philipp Brian Harper, *Private Affairs: Critical Ventures in the Culture of Social Relations*, New York: New York UP, 1999; Samuel R. Delany, *Times Square Red, Times Square Blue*. New York, New York UP, 1999.

153 Roderick A. Ferguson, *Aberrations in Black: Toward a Queer of Color Critique*, Minneapolis: U of Minnesota P, 2004, 149FN1.

performance artists, writers and filmmakers. Their theories grew out of the field of performance studies, but both critics have extended their theoretical approaches to literary texts, such as the writings of lesbian feminists of color, and to the analysis of films, particularly the work of the black gay filmmakers Isaac Julien (Muñoz) and Marlon Riggs (Johnson). To understand disidentification, I will first refer to Louis Althusser's concept of interpellation and subject formation.

3.3 Interpellation

On the basis of Althusser's concept of interpellation, one can argue that subject formations along the lines of gender, race and sexual orientation are a result of the interpellation of individuals as subjects by the dominant ideology and by racist and heteronormative discourses. Since the late 1960s, the present-day meanings of the categories black and gay have emerged through dominant and sub-cultural representations and political strategies by black and gay movements in particular ways. The way one is interpellated as black or as gay depends on these meanings.

The central thesis of Louis Althusser's 1969 essay "Ideology and Ideological State Apparatuses" is that "ideology interpellates individuals as subjects."[154] In the Marxist tradition, the state is explicitly conceived as a repressive apparatus which contains institutions such as the government, the administration, the army, the police, the courts, and the prisons. Althusser adds to this Marxist concept of repressive state apparatuses the concept of ideological state apparatuses, which include institutions such as the educational system, the family, the press, as well as literature and the Arts. There is an obvious difference between repressive state apparatuses and ideological state apparatuses: the former function predominately by the use of force and concern the public

---

154 Louis Althusser, "Ideology and Ideological State Apparatusses," *Lenin and Philosophy, and Other Essays*, London: New Left Books, 1971, 121–173, 160.

domain while the latter function predominately by ideology and concern the private domain.

The role of ideology, understood as "the system of the ideas and representations which dominate the mind of a man or a social group,"[155] is important for the formation of subjects and consequently for the ways in which identity categories are constructed. Althusser states that "all ideology hails or interpellates concrete individuals as concrete subjects. The existence of ideology and the hailing or interpellation of individuals as subjects are one and the same thing."[156] The terms interpellation and hailing are used synonymously. The basic example of interpellation is a scene in which a person walks down the street, is called by a policeman and reacts to the call. Althusser explains this process as follows:

> I shall then suggest that ideology 'acts' or 'functions' in such a way that it 'recruits' subjects among the individuals into subjects (it recruits them all), or 'transforms' the individuals into subjects (it transforms them all) by that very precise operation which I have called interpellation or hailing, and which can be imagined along the lines of the most commonplace everyday police (or other) hailing: 'Hey, you there!'[157]

The subject that is interpellated has an awareness that the person or institution that interpellates "must mean me." This awareness is a precondition for the subject. Althusser maintains that subject formation cannot be a spontaneous process. It is always a response to some hailing, some interpellation, by some aspect of the social.

Judith Butler, Delany, Muñoz, and other queer theorists have applied Althusser's concept of interpellation to the formation of identity categories. Delany argues that the answer to the questions "What makes us gay?" and "What makes us black?" is that black and gay subjects are interpellated in specific ways.

---

155 Althusser, 149.

156 Althusser, 162.

157 Althusser, 162–63.

> Anyone who self-identifies as gay must have been interpellated, at some point, as gay by some individual or social speech or text to which he or she responded, 'He/she/it/they must mean me.' [...] It is the same process of interpellation that 'makes us gay' that also 'makes us black.' Such a process *is* the social construction that everyone so often speaks of and no one seems ever to do anything about.[158]

Delany illustrates how an individual is interpellated as a gay subject with the help of two short examples:

> It doesn't really matter whether someone catches you in the bathroom, looking at the same-sex nude, and then blurts out, 'Hey, you're gay!' and you look up and realize 'you' ('He means me!') have been caught, or if you're reading a description of homosexuality in a text book and 'you' think, 'Hey, they're describing me!'[159]

For those subjects who are interpellated in a pejorative way, it is important to think about ways of resisting this process. Even though Althusser states that all individuals are "*always already* subjects,"[160] one can think of ways in which the power of ideological state apparatuses or the power of heteronormative and racist discourses can be challenged.

Althusser argues that scientific discourse is the only realm outside ideology.[161] His idea for change is that "from within ideology we have to outline a discourse which tries to break with ideology, in order to dare to be the beginning of a scientific (i.e. subjectless) discourse on ideology."[162] Unfortunately, he does not argue convincingly how this could possibly be done if all individuals are "always already" subjects and if scientific discourse is something that is produced by subjects within ideological state apparatuses like the university. Even though Althusser speaks of "bad subjects" once,[163] he does not discuss possibilities of opposition to interpellation.

---

158 Samuel R. Delany, "Some Queer Notions About Race," *Dangerous Liaisons: Blacks and Gays and the Struggle for Equality*, ed. Eric Brandt, New York: New Press, 1999, 259–289.

159 Delany, "Some Queer Notions," 285.

160 Althusser, 161.

161 Althusser, 160.

162 Althusser, 162.

163 Althusser, 169.

3.4 Disidentification

In his study *Disidentifications: Queers of Color and the Performance of Politics*, the Latino performance theorist Muñoz looks at the situation, politics and art of queers of color. He is particularly interested in "the ways in which queers of color identify with ethnos or queerness despite the phobic charges in both fields"[164] and continues the French linguist Michel Pecheux's theory of disidentification to analyze texts (films, performances and novels) by queers of color. This theory of disidentification pays attention to the intersections of the categories race, class, gender, and sexuality. Muñoz states that queers of color are "subjects whose identities are formed in response to the cultural logics of heteronormativity, white supremacy, and misogyny." Recognizing that queers of color inhabit more than one minority position, he argues that as they are interpellated

> by more than one minority identity, they have an especially arduous time of the processes of identification. Subjects who are outside the purview of dominant public spheres encounter obstacles in enacting identifications. Minority identifications are often neglectful or antagonistic to other minoritarian positionalities.[165]

To a significant extent, the identities of black gay men are determined by the categories blackness and gayness, which is an example of an interpellation by two minority identities that are constructed antagonistically, as I have shown when dealing with the construction of gay identity as white and prevailing stereotypes of black heterosexual masculinity. The expression "hailed by more than one minority identity" itself makes clear that Muñoz's theory of disidentification is based on Althusser's concept of ideology and interpellation.[166]

The term "disidentification" was first used by Pecheux. Pecheux distinguishes three modes of dealing with the dominant ideology and calls these modes identification, counteridentification, and disidentification. Whereas so-called Good Subjects identify in the way the dominant ideology interpellates

---

164 Muñoz, *Disidentifications*, 11.

165 Muñoz, *Disidentifications*, 8.

166 There are other important theoretical frameworks Muñoz refers to, among them linguistics, the writings by radical women of color, and psychoanalysis.

them, and "bad subjects" choose counteridentification to rebel against the way they are interpellated. Muñoz sees the strategy of counteridentification as limiting because to counteridentify as a "bad subject," that is, to identify in direct opposition to the dominant ideology, might even validate and confirm the categories of the dominant ideology.[167] In rejecting counteridentification as a mode of resistance, Muñoz takes a Foucauldian approach towards power and resistance. Michel Foucault does not view power solely in the traditional way as a negative force oppressing individuals or groups. Instead, he sees power in a relational way, and in the first volume of his *History of Sexuality* he analyzes the emergence of the category homosexual in the nineteenth century. He demonstrates that, in addition to its policing side, power has a productive side, as well. His way of thinking about power demands new ways of thinking about resistance, too. With regard to power and resistance, Foucault states:

> Where there is power, there is resistance, and yet, or rather consequently, this resistance is never in a position of exteriority to power. [...] These points of resistance are present everywhere in the power network. Hence there is no single locus of great Refusal, no soul of revolt, source of all rebellions, or pure law of the revolutionary. Instead there is a plurality of resistances, each of them a special case: resistances that are possible, necessary, improbable; others that are spontaneous, savage, solitary, concerted, rampant, or violent; still others that are quick to compromise, interested, or sacrificial; by definition, they can only exist in the strategic field of power relations.[168]

Disidentification, then, is the third way of reacting to the way one is interpellated by the dominant ideology. It is a "working on and against, a strategy that tries to transform a cultural logic from within, always laboring to enact permanent structural change while at the same time valuing the importance of local or everyday struggles of resistance."[169] This third mode is the basis for Muñoz's theory. Disidentification is "a strategy that resists a conception of power as being a fixed discourse."[170] "[A] disidentificatory subject

---

167 Muñoz, *Disidentifications*, 11.

168 Michel Foucault, *History of Sexuality: The Will to Knowledge*, London: Penguin, 1990, 95–96.

169 Muñoz, *Disidentifications*, 11–12.

170 Muñoz, *Disidentifications*, 19.

[...] tactically and simultaneously works on, with, and against a cultural form."[171] A Foucauldian approach towards power and towards the resultant complication of any notion of resistance ensures that disidentification is not an apolitical middle ground between assimilationist and antiassimilationist positions. Its political agenda is clearly indebted to antiassimilationist thought.

Judith Butler describes an example of a disidentifactory practice in *Bodies That Matter*. Exploring the possibilities of resistance against ideological subject formations, she reminds us that the term "queer" and an interpellation as queer had pejorative meanings before the term was re-appropriated by a political movement: "The term 'queer' has operated as one linguistic practice whose purpose has been the shaming of the subject it names or, rather, the producing of a subject through that shaming interpellation."[172] Muñoz refers to writings by radical women of color as well as to Pecheux. He argues that the book *This Bridge Called My Back: Writings By Radical Women Of Color*, edited by Chicana feminist critics Gloria Anzaldúa and Cherríe Moraga, is one of the seminal texts of queer theory, even though it is often ignored by white academics within gay, lesbian, and queer studies. Muñoz argues that this text is a valuable example of disidentification as a political strategy because it breaks with previous feminist strategies of identification and counteridentification. He takes the term "identities-in-difference" from third world feminists and uses it as a category for queers of color.

> The identities-in-difference emerge from a failed interpellation within the dominant public sphere. Their emergence is predicated on their ability to disidentify with the mass public and instead, through this disidentification, contribute to the function of a counterpublic sphere.[173]

In the previous chapter I have shown that the black gay anthologies *In the Life* (1986) and *Brother to Brother: New Writings by Black Gay Men* (1991) have a political agenda similar to that of *This Bridge Called My Back*. These publications "contribute to the function of a counterpublic sphere," and consequently, they too can be considered as examples of the strategy of disidentification.

---

171 Muñoz, *Disidentifications*, 12.

172 Judith Butler, *Bodies that Matter: On the Discursive Limits of 'Sex,'* New York: Routledge, 1993, 226.

173 Muñoz, *Disidentifications*, 7.

3.5 Quare/Signifying

In his essay "'Quare' Studies, or (Almost) Everything I Know About Queer Studies I learned from My Grandmother," E. Patrick Johnson puts Muñoz's concept of disidentification in an historical perspective and argues that ever since slavery African Americans have used disidentifcation as a mode of resistance. In order to approach works by queers of color and to point at the shortcomings of queer theory and politics which tend to be exclusionary with regard to race and class, Johnson uses the term "quare" to "draw on the *vernacular* roots implicit in [his] grandmother's use of the word to devise a strategy for theorizing racialized sexuality."[174] He understands quare studies as "a theory of and for gays and lesbians of color."[175] He states that the

> performance strategies of African Americans who labored and struggled under human bondage exemplify this disidentificatory practice. For instance, vernacular traditions that emerged among enslaved Africans – including folktales, spirituals, and the blues – provided the foundation for social and political empowerment. These discursively mediated forms, spoken and filtered through 'black' bodies, enabled survival.[176]

Johnson regards folktales, spirituals, and the blues as "discursive weapons based on an identity as oppressed people."[177] This aspect of Johnson's analysis corresponds to the results of Lawrence L. Levine's study *Black Culture and Black Consciousness*, which emphasizes the potential of resistance in black vernacular expressions such as folktales, songs and verbal games like "playing the dozens." For example, Levine explicates the resistant elements of black songs:

> To state that black song constituted a form of black protest and resistance does not mean that it necessarily led to or even called for any tangible and specific actions, but rather that it served as a mechanism by which Negroes could be relatively candid in a society that rarely accorded them that privilege, could communicate this candor to others whom they would in no other

---

174 Johnson, "'Quare' Studies," 126.

175 Johnson, "'Quare' Studies," 127.

176 Johnson, "'Quare' Studies," 139.

177 Johnson, "'Quare' Studies," 140.

way be able to reach, and, in the face of the sanctions of the white majority, could assert their own individuality, aspirations, and sense of being.[178]

The form of protest Levine describes can also be described as a disidentifactory practice because this mode of resistance works within a hegemonic culture. Levine demonstrates that these strategies of resistance did not end with slavery, and Johnson focuses on how they were taken up and continued by gays, lesbians, bisexuals, and transgendered people of color. For example, he calls attention to Bessie Smith, Ma Rainey, Little Richard, Sylvester, RuPaul, and Blackberri. As will be shown later, Blackberri's songs are a central element on the soundtrack of *Looking for Langston* (see 4.3.3). Johnson also names some rhetorical and performance strategies that are used outside the realm of music:

> Performance practices such as vogueing, snapping, 'throwing shade,' and 'reading' attest to the ways in which black gays, lesbians, bisexuals, and transgendered people demonstrate the ways of devising technologies of self-assertion and summoning the agency to resist.[179]

One of the earliest theoretical texts to connect African American vernacular traditions with black gay culture, especially with the writings of black gay men, is Nero's influential essay "Towards a Black Gay Aesthetic: Signifying in Black Gay Literature" (1991), which was included in Hemphill's *Brother to Brother*. In reading key texts by black gay men, among them Essex Hemphill, Samuel R. Delany, Larry Duplechan, and Craig G. Harris, Nero analyzes how these black gay writers have referred to the black vernacular and to African American literary history. He states that these authors use signifying as a mode of writing. Quoting Henry Louis Gates Jr.'s critical theory based on the African American oral tradition put forward in *The Signifying Monkey*, Nero defines signifying as "'the indirect use of words that changes the meaning of a word or words.'"[180] Nero names certain rhetorical elements that constitute the

---

178 Lawrence W. Levine, *Black Culture and Black Consciousness: Afro-American Folk Thought from Slavery to Freedom*, New York: Oxford UP, 1977, 239–240.

179 Johnson, "'Quare' Studies," 140. See also E. Patrick Johnson, "SNAP! Culture: A Different Kind of 'Reading,'" *Text and Performance Quarterly* 15 (1995): 122–142.

180 Nero, "Toward a Black Gay Aesthetic," 230; Henry Louis Gates Jr., *The Signifying Monkey: A Theory of Afro-American Literary Criticism*, New York: Oxford UP, 1988, 81.

rhetorical strategy of signifying, "capping, loud-talking, the dozens, reading, going off, talking smart, sounding, joining (jonesing), dropping lugs, snapping, woofing, styling out, and calling out of one's name."[181] Most important, he demonstrates that these rhetorical figures can be found in black gay texts.[182]

Signifying is a way of giving information implicitly, because the strategy draws on knowledge shared by those who take part in the communication.[183] Nero argues that signifying is an important strategy for black gay writers for two reasons. First, "the use of signifying by black gay men places their writing squarely within the African American literary tradition," and second, "it permits black gay men to revise the 'Black Experience' in African American literature and, thereby, to create a space for themselves."[184]

As I will argue in my study, this revision of the 'Black Experience' in African American literature has been a project undertaken by the majority of black gay writers. In *The Signifying Monkey* Gates analyzes the ways in which black texts talk to other black texts. He specifically focuses on how Alice Walker's novel *The Color Purple* (1982) can be regarded as a revision of the narrative strategies employed by Zora Neale Hurston in her novel *Their Eyes Were Watching God* (1937). Gates argues that the intertextuality between Walker's and Hurston's texts can be considered as pastiche because "Walker seems to be intent on underscoring the relation of her text to Hurston's, in a joyous proclamation of antecedent and descendant texts."[185] In reading Ishmael Reed's novel *Mumbo Jumbo*, Gates identifies another form of intertextuality between black texts, which, because of Reed's postmodern narrative techniques, he calls parody. According to Gates, both modes of intertextuality are intentional, but he regards pastiche as unmotivated signifying and parody as motivated signifying. Following Nero, I suggest that many texts of black gay writers in the 1980s and 1990s can also be

---

181 Nero, "Toward a Black Gay Aesthetic," 230.

182 See also Geneva Smitherman, *Talkin and Testifyin: The Language of Black America*, Detroit: Wayne State UP, 1986.

183 Nero, "Toward a Black Gay Aesthetic," 230.

184 Nero, "Toward a Black Gay Aesthetic," 231.

185 Gates Jr., *Signifying Monkey*, xxvii.

regarded as embodiments of what Gates calls "the trope of the talking book."[186] The texts speak to earlier black texts by writers such as Nugent, Baldwin, and Hughes, and they employ both forms of signifying, pastiche and parody. As will be shown in chapters three and four, pastiche is prominent in the texts by Corbin, Julien, Dixon, and Kenan, and parody can most prominently be found in Delany's texts. For example, the ways in which Walker's novel refers to Hurston's earlier text is mirrored in Dixon's *Vanishing Rooms*, which I will read as a re-writing of Baldwin's *Giovanni's Room*, and Kenan's *A Visitation of Spirits*, which can be considered a re-writing of Baldwin's *Go Tell It On The Mountain*, whereas the contents and the postmodern experimental style of writing of Delany's "Atlantis: Model 1924" and *The Motion of Light in Water* ironically comment on such elements of the African American tradition as the migration narrative and black autobiography.

In his reading of Baldwin's *Go Tell it on the Mountain*, the literary critic Robert McRuer analyzes the references between Baldwin's text and Kenan's *A Visitation of Spirits*. One conclusion he draws is that Kenan's strategy can be considered unmotivated signifying, an embrace of the earlier text. His conclusion contradicts Gates's assumption about texts by black male and black female writers. Gates assumes that texts by black female writers are characterized by an embrace of earlier black women writers' texts, whereas those by black male writers are sometimes characterized by a denial of black influences or the claiming of white traditions.[187] McRuer states that "contrary to Gates's implication, then, some men 'lovingly bond' with other men as readily as women bond with women,"[188] and he argues that the way Kenan's and Baldwin's texts interrelate "disrupts the gendered dichotomy at work in Gates's theories."[189] If the texts by Corbin, Julien and Dixon, as well as many of the shorter texts in the black gay anthologies, are taken into account, one could

---

186 Gates Jr., *Signifying Monkey*, 127–169.

187 Robert McRuer, *The Queer Renaissance: Contemporary American Literature and the Reinvention of Lesbian and Gay Identities*, New York: New York UP, 1997, 112. McRuer does not refer to *The Signifying Monkey* but to Valerie Smith's reading of a review Gates wrote about Mary Helen Washington's anthology *Invented Lives*.

188 McRuer, 113.

189 McRuer, 113.

argue that texts by black gay men, like those by black women, can be taken as examples of unmotivated signifying. I suggest that the structural disadvantages effected by the intersectionality of race and gender/sexuality in the case of black women writers and race and sexuality in the case of black gay writers is one reason for the similarities in the strategy these texts employ. Delany's irony and his references to alleged white traditions in his texts should not be misunderstood as what McRuer analyzes as "an anxiety of influence that leads [male writers] to critique other (male) writers who have preceded them, repeating and revising those writers' tropes and narrative strategies."[190] I will argue instead that Delany's texts should be read as comments on the strategy of unmotivated signifying many black gay writers used during the 1980s.

The references to earlier writers and periods are not always encoded as re-writings of earlier texts. Sometimes the references are made explicit, and they are formulated as homage to the earlier writers. A prominent example of direct homage to an earlier writer is Walker's 1975 essay "Looking for Zora."[191] The title of the essay was probably an inspiration for the title of Julien's film *Looking for Langston.* In her essay Walker describes her search for the grave of the Harlem Renaissance poet Zora Neale Hurston in Eatonville/Florida. As the exact place where Hurston is buried was in the midst of a neglected cemetery covered over and over with weeds and as it was not visibly marked, Walker decided on the place herself and set up a gravestone with an engraving to remember Hurston.[192] Walker's act of setting up a gravestone is a rather concrete act of claiming a black female literary heritage in order to empower herself and later generations of black female writers. A decade later, black gay writers used the same strategy. Johnson's "quare" intervention in the fields of queer theory and politics was inspired by Walker, too. Walker used the term "womanist prose" rather than feminist prose as a subtitle for her collection of essays in order to emphasize the intersections of race and gender and to separate herself from the white dominance within feminism. Likewise, Johnson uses the term "quare,"

190 McRuer, 112–113.

191 Alice Walker, "Looking for Zora," *In Search of Our Mothers' Gardens: Womanist Prose*, San Diego: Harcourt Brace Jovanovich, 1983, 93–116.

192 Walker, 107.

his grandmother's pronunciation of the word "queer," instead of "queer" to criticize the lack of intersectional analysis in queer contexts.[193]

Beam and Nero also emphasize the connection between black (lesbian) feminism and the politics of black gay men. In the introduction to *In the Life*, Beam writes about the impact black and Chicana (lesbian) feminist writers, among them Audre Lorde, Barbara Smith, Moraga and June Jordan, had on his perception of himself as a black gay man and writer.[194] Referring to Beam's introduction, Nero reinforces the black feminist roots of black gay literature and states that "as black people, we need to continue to imagine unions between black gay men and black feminists as part of a progressive and liberating politics."[195]

In an attempt to go beyond the postmodern politics of difference, the engagement with identities and identity politics, including the approach of strategic essentialism, has recently been criticized in favor of what Ross Posnock calls "cosmopolitan universalism." Arguing that W.E.B. DuBois was the first modern American intellectual, Posnock states in his book *Color and Culture: Black Writers and the Making of the Modern Intellectual* that, in the US, the concept of the intellectual has always already been black. Consequently, he argues that his understanding of universalism is not "a 'color-blind' ideal."[196] Posnock dismisses identity politics because of its tendency to enforce norms of an authentic group identity. His approach is important for my study because in the last chapter of his book, he discusses Delany's writings as an example of this cosmopolitan universalism.[197]

---

193 Johnson, "'Quare' Studies," 151FN1.

194 Beam, "Introduction," 13.

195 Nero, "Black Gay Men and White Gay Men," 125.

196 Ross Posnock, *Color and Culture: Black Writers and the Making of the Modern Intellectual*, Cambridge, Mass: Harvard UP, 1998, 21.

197 Jeffrey Tucker asserts that Delany's texts are rooted in the African American tradition. His approach contradicts Posnock's interpretation of Delany's work as examplary of a cosmopolitan universalism. The debate between the two approaches will be further outlined in my two sub-chapters on Delany's texts "Atlantis: Model 1924" (see 4.4) and *The Motion of Light in Water* (see 5.4).

4   Looking for the Harlem Renaissance

In this chapter I will focus on the way the period called the Harlem Renaissance is referred to in two novels and one film, all three produced between 1989 and 1995: Steven Corbin's novel *No Easy Place to Be* (1989), Isaac Julien's film *Looking for Langston* (1989) and Samuel R. Delany's short novel "Atlantis: Model 1924" (1995). All three texts establish a connection with the 1920s, but they differ in the ways they refer to race, gender, sexuality, and to the Harlem Renaissance and modernism. Corbin's *No Easy Place to Be* engages in a neo-realist style of writing and serves the didactic function of educating the black gay community of the 1980s on their heritage. In addition, the text aims at raising the acceptance and tolerance for black gay men within the larger black community by employing political strategies of the 1980s gay liberation movement. In contrast to Corbin, who depicts the historical period of the Harlem Renaissance without in any way referring to the 1980s, Julien and Delany establish a connection between the 1920s and themselves in the late twentieth century. *Looking for Langston* and "Atlantis: Model 1924" are experimental texts that combine different historical periods. In the first scene of *Looking for Langston*, Julien himself plays the role of the dead Hughes in the coffin. Delany establishes the personal connection by fictionalizing his own Harlem-based family and making his father Samuel Ray Delany Sr. the protagonist of the narrative. Both texts can be regarded as postmodern texts on a number of levels.

Looking for Langston and "Atlantis: Model 1924" are similar in the way they refer to both the Harlem Renaissance and to modernism, which has often been misrepresented as an exclusively white tradition. *Looking for Langston* alludes to African American modernist literature and art: to the art of Aaron Douglass, Bruce Nugent's "Smoke, Lilies and Jade," and to avant-garde photography and filmmaking. Its content connects contemporary discussions about black gay identity with the homosexual dimensions of the Harlem Renaissance. The film language creates a single space that is trans-temporal and trans-cultural. The whole film is filmed in black and white, a stylistic device that unites 1920s archival footage with the newly-directed scenes that refer to the 1980s.

"Atlantis: Model 1924" is an example of experimental writing that positions itself in the modernist tradition. At the center of the narrative is a fictional interracial and queer encounter on New York's Brooklyn Bridge between Harold Hart, a character based on the white modernist poet Hart Crane, and Sam, a character based on Delany's biological father.

Despite these similarities, the texts differ in significant ways. Unlike the critics Muñoz, Gates Jr., Mercer, and others, who take *Looking for Langston* as an example of Julien's anti-essentialist project of deconstructing identities, I will argue that, despite its experimental form, the film partly deals with the 1980s project of appropriating the Harlem Renaissance and Nugent's story "Smoke, Lilies and Jade" for an essentialist black gay political agenda (see 2.3). This attempt can be seen first and foremost by the ways in which Julien changes the contents of Nugent's story and by the way the film comments on Robert Mapplethorpe's photographs of black men. Delany's text, however, ironically treats the expectations of readers who encounter a narrative focusing on the 1920s by a black gay writer of the 1990s. The text raises the expectations of a new version of the re-appropriation of the Harlem Renaissance for black gay ends. However, following the argument Ross Posnock develops in his study *Color and Culture* (1998), I will argue that "Atlantis: Model 1924" positions itself in the modernist tradition and leaves the readers' expectations unfulfilled. In this chapter I will focus first on the 1920s and establish the historical context by referring to recent studies that point out the queer dimensions of the Harlem Renaissance (see 4.1). With this background I will then analyze the three texts by Corbin (see 4.2), Julien (see 4.3), and Delany (see 4.4).

4.1 Race and Representation

The term "Harlem Renaissance" denotes an epoch at the beginning of the twentieth century when African American art and literature flourished in an unprecedented manner and when black people expressed a new self-confidence. One important factor for its beginnings was the Great Migration that started in the first decades of the twentieth century, and one of the reasons for its demise was the Great Depression of the 1930s. Between 1917 and 1930, over one million African Americans migrated from the rural south to the big cities in the north of the USA. Consequently, large black communities evolved in Chicago, Detroit, and Buffalo. The largest black community arose in the Harlem area of New York City. In the 1920s, Harlem became the center of black literary and artistic production. Writers such as Zora Neale Hurston, Langston Hughes, Wallace Thurman, Countée Cullen, Bruce Nugent, and artists like Aaron Douglass and Beauford Delaney are some of the well-known and important figures of the Harlem Renaissance.[198] In his study *Gay New York: Gender, Urban Culture, and the Making of the Gay Male World 1890–1940* George Chauncey describes Harlem in the 1920s as

> a huge black metropolis unlike anything America had seen before, it was home to soaring black cathedrals, thriving businesses, a wide array of social clubs, and Marcus Garvey's militant black nationalist movement, to dozens of elegant nightclubs and hundreds of basement jazz clubs and speakeasies, and to the poets, artists, and novelists whose work produced the Harlem Renaissance.[199]

In 1925 Alain Locke published the anthology *The New Negro*, a book that Arnold Rampersad calls the Harlem Renaissance's "definite text," its "bible." [200] For his anthology Locke collected essays, poems, and stories by prominent African American writers. He included an extensive bibliography with sections on black literature, music and drama. In the foreword of *The New Negro*, Locke expresses his belief in the power of black art and literature for racial uplift. According to Locke, black artists should depict themselves positively in order to raise the public reputation of black people as a whole.[201] Locke's ideas about black art and literature reflected those of W.E.B. DuBois, who urged "Harlem's writers to avoid scandalous topics or low-life depictions,

---

198 For a comprehensive and illustrated study that gives an overview over the Harlem Renaissance and its artists including the topic of homosexuality, see Steven Watson, *The Harlem Renaissance: Hub of African-American Culture, 1920–1930*, New York: Pantheon, 1995.

199 Chauncey, 246.

200 Arnold Rampersad, "Introduction," *The New Negro*, ed. Alain LeRoy Locke, New York: Touchstone, 1997, ix-xxiii, ix.

201 Alain Locke, ed., *The New Negro*, New York: Touchstone, 1997, 3-16.

and instead inculcate a vision of a thoroughly respectable black middle class."[202] Consequently, sexuality and same-sex desires are not an issue in the texts of *The New Negro*. However, in her 2003 study *Gay Voices of the Harlem Renaissance*, when A.B. Christa Schwarz looks at the homosexual proclivities of the Harlem Renaissance writers, she also writes about Locke's homosexuality. In analyzing the correspondence between Locke and other African American men, she comes to the conclusion that there existed what she calls "a gay male, transnational, and, though apparently mainly black, interracial network." She states that

> with Locke as a pivotal figure, the men involved in the gay network formed an invisible, diverse community which was at the heart of the Harlem Renaissance. Some of its members were unrelated to the Renaissance movement, and not all same-sex-interested men involved in the Renaissance participated in the network, but it seems that at least in Locke's perception, numerous well-known and lesser-known writers – 'Jean Toomer – Langston Hughes, Countee Cullen, Lewis Alexander, Richard Bruce – Donald Hayes – Albert Dunham'- counted among his 'spiritual children.'[203]

Compared to the politics and aesthetics promoted by DuBois and by Locke's *The New Negro*, the younger generation of black artists and writers, among them Bruce Nugent, Langston Hughes, Zora Neale Hurston and Wallace Thurman, took a more radical approach towards art. They wrote about homosexuality and prostitution, were critical of an elitist concept of art and literature, and rejected the burden of representation, the notion that they should be representatives of and speak for the entire African American community. Often using a modernist aesthetics, they combined formal experiments with political concerns. For a long time, the modernist aesthetics of many Harlem Renaissance writers was not fully recognized. In his essay "Modernism and the Black Diaspora: Langston Hughes and the Broken Cubes of Picasso," Seth Moglen illustrates how critics have largely attributed the innovative formal experiments to white writers, whereas black writers of the period have been narrowly regarded as

---

202 Joseph Allen Boone, *Libidinal Currents: Sexuality and the Shaping of Modernism*, Chicago: U of Chicago P, 1998, 223.

203 A.B. Christa Schwarz, *Gay Voices of the Harlem Renaissance*, Bloomington: Indiana UP, 2003, 14.

Harlem Renaissance writers, and he argues that, between the 1940s and the 1960s, modernism has been canonized in a "politically narrow and racially exclusionary" way, as a white aesthetic paradigm.[204] This belief has also informed the early African American Studies movement of the 1960s. After surveying studies on modernism and the Harlem Renaissance, Moglen observes that the binarity between white modernism and the black Harlem Renaissance is deeply rooted. Black writers are excluded in important anthologies of modernist writers. According to Moglen, this canonization of modernism as a white phenomenon influenced studies of black Harlem Renaissance scholars, too. See for example Nathan Huggins' *The Harlem Renaissance* (1971) and Houston Baker, Jr.'s *Modernism and the Harlem Renaissance* (1987).[205]

However, Moglen's criticism does not apply to Joseph Allen Boone's study *Libidinal Currents: Sexuality and the Shaping of Modernism*. In his study, Boone has included a chapter on the "Queer Sites of Modernism," which explicitly refers to gay urban spaces of the 1920s and 30s, the Left Bank in Paris and Greenwich Village and Harlem in New York City. These gay urban spaces are the places of origin of what he calls "a neglected alternative modernism"[206] – as opposed to high modernism. The texts Boone considers as constituting this neglected alternative modernism are characterized by experimental styles of writing and by transgressive representations of gender, sexuality, and desire. Boone's argument corresponds with Moglen's emphasis on the political significance of the formal experiments of female, black, and working-class writers in the 1920s.[207] Boone states that some of these texts "foreshadow the rise of what is now being called 'queer' in current gay studies, arts, and politics."[208] The literary anthology *Fire!!* (1926) is a prominent example of the combination of a modernist aesthetic with assumedly disrespectable topics

204 Seth Moglen, "Modernism in the Black Diaspora: Langston Hughes and the Broken Cubes of Picasso," *Callaloo* 25.4 (2002): 1189–1205, 1189

205 Moglen, 1189. For a critical re-evaluation of the scholarship on the Harlem Renaissance, see George Hutchinson, *The Harlem Renaissance in Black and White*, Cambridge, Mass: Belknap-Harvard UP, 1995.

206 Boone, 205.

207 Moglen, 1191.

208 Boone, 205.

like homosexuality and prostitution that contradicted Locke's and DuBois's ideals of black literature.

4.1.1 Dissident Voices

One year after the publication of *The New Negro*, the younger generation of black writers and artists contributed their writings and drawings to *Fire!!*, edited by Wallace Thurman. Even though it was planned as an art quarterly, only one issue of the magazine was produced. With the contribution of the story "Smoke, Lilies and Jade," Bruce Nugent published one of the first fictional accounts of homosexual desire.[209] It is considered the first-known text on that topic by an African American writer. "Smoke, Lilies and Jade" and Thurman's "Cordelia the Crude" are the reason for the magazine's reputation of being more radical, subversive and sexually transgressive than Locke's anthology. Owing to the subject matter of these two texts, homosexuality and promiscuity/polyamory ("Smoke") and prostitution ("Cordelia"), Thomas H. Wirth calls *Fire!!* a "manifesto of revolt against the strictures of the Bourgeoisie."[210]

Likewise, Schwarz states that "sexual dissidence was [...] clearly part of the younger Renaissance writers' transgressive strategies and their rejection of the burden of representation,"[211] and Seth Clark Silberman regards *Fire!!* as the younger writers' answer to Locke's *The New Negro*. In his essay "Lighting the Harlem Renaissance A*Fire!!*: Embodying Richard Bruce Nugent's Boehemian Politic," Silberman states that, by including Thurman's and Nugent's texts, they "aimed to contradict Locke's ideals for Negro fiction."[212] Focusing on Nugent's text, he argues that it is significant for a reason that goes beyond its homosexual

---

209 The editors of *Black Like Us* name three titles and state that these constitute the first works of American gay fiction: Henry Blake Fuller, *Bertram Cope's Year* (1919), Robert McAlmond, *Distinguished Air (Grim Fairy Tales)* (1925), and Bruce Nugent, "Smoke, Lilies, and Jade" (1926) (Carbado, McBride, 10–11).

210 Thomas H. Wirth, "Introduction," *Gay Rebel of the Harlem Renaissance: Selections from the Work of Richard Bruce Nugent*, eds. Bruce Nugent and Thomas H. Wirth, Durham: Duke UP, 2002, 1–61, 48.

211 Schwarz, 42.

212 Seth Clark Silberman, "Lighting the Harlem Renaissance A*Fire!!*: Embodying Richard Bruce Nugent's Bohemian Politic," *The Greatest Taboo: Homosexuality in Black Communities*, ed. Delroy Constantine-Simms. Los Angeles: Alyson, 2001, 254–273, 264.

subject matter. "Smoke" deliberately contradicts Locke's idea of the role of black arts and literature for racial uplift.[213] As the younger writers criticized DuBois and Locke's aesthetic agenda, they deliberately tried to provoke with the topics they covered in *Fire!!*. Hughes addressed the younger generation's agenda in his essay "The Negro Artist and the Racial Mountain:" "We younger Negro artists who create now intend to express our individual dark-skinned selves without fear or shame. If white people are pleased we are glad. If they are not, it doesn't matter... if black people are pleased we are glad. If they are not it doesn't matter."[214]

4.1.2 Queer Readings of the Harlem Renaissance

"Smoke, Lilies and Jade" is one of numerous Harlem Renaissance texts dealing with homosexuality. Since the 1980s, these texts and the homosexual and queer dimensions of the Harlem Renaissance have often been the focus of literary criticism. The critical reception of the queer dimensions of the Harlem Renaissance poets, artists and their works can be divided into three phases. The first phase is characterized by silence and ignorance regarding the topic of homosexuality, the second is characterized by biographical approaches focusing on the homosexuality of the Harlem Renaissance writers, and the third is characterized by queer readings of Harlem Renaissance texts. The analysis of same-sex desires and homosexual subtexts was not an issue in the early works of criticism that were published in the Civil Rights era, when the Harlem Renaissance was re-discovered from a perspective that focused solely on race.[215] In the wake of the gay and lesbian studies movement, however, critics like Eric Garber, Emmanuel S. Nelson and Gregory Woods reclaimed the Harlem Renaissance artists and their works from a gay and lesbian perspective by arguing that the major Harlem Renaissance figures were gay men and lesbians. These critics were not so much concerned with the texts themselves. Instead they took a biographical approach and focused on the lives and relationships

---

213 Silberman, 271.

214 Langston Hughes, "The Negro Artist and the Racial Mountain," *The Nation* June 23 (1926).

215 Dorothea Löbbermann, "Looking for Harlem: (Re)Konstruktionen Harlems als 'queer mecca' 1925–1995," *Amerikastudien/American Studies* 46 (2001): 55–69, 59.

of the Harlem Renaissance writers. After the poststructuralist turn in thinking about identities and identity politics (see 3.1.1), there was a paradigm shift in the approaches that gay and lesbian studies took to the Harlem Renaissance. Critics like George Chauncey, A.B. Christa Schwarz, and Thomas Wirth are more sensitive when arguing for the connections between homosexuality and the Harlem Renaissance. They state that the term "gay" has a specific historically-situated meaning that evolved out of the gay liberation movement of the 1970s. Consequently, the term in its present day meaning cannot easily be used in connection with the 1920s and 30s.

Despite this paradigm shift in acknowledging the queer dimensions of the Harlem Renaissance, the tendency to ignore the intersections of homosexuality and race in the critical analyses of Harlem Renaissance texts still remains. For example, in his 1992 introduction to a new edition of *The New Negro*, Arnold Rampersad demonstrates his ignorance of intersectional and queer-studies approaches to the Harlem Renaissance by stating that "Bruce Nugent was far more concerned with his gay identity than with his sense of race or ethnicity."[216]

One of the first essays examining the Harlem Renaissance from a specifically gay and lesbian studies point of view is Garber's groundbreaking essay "T'aint Nobody's Bizness (Homosexuality in 1920s Harlem)." Owing to three different versions of the essay that were included in different publications, it has become very influential. It was published in Smith's 1983 anthology *Black Men, White Men* (see 2.2). A different version of the piece appeared earlier in the gay magazine *The Advocate*, and a similar but more academic essay was published in 1989 in the influential book *Hidden From History: Reclaiming the Gay and Lesbian Past* under the title "A Spectacle in Color: The Lesbian and Gay Subculture of Jazz Age Harlem."[217] For his work, Garber conducted personal interviews with Nugent, who, in the 1980s, was one of the last witnesses of the Harlem Renaissance.

---

216 Rampersad, xxi.

217 This most recent and elaborate version of the essay is the one I use for my argumentation.

Focusing on the artists and writers of the period, Garber states that most of the artists of the Harlem Renaissance were gay men and lesbians. He argues that "in spite of racial oppression, economic hardship, and homophobic persecution, black lesbians and gay men were able to build a thriving community of their own within existing Afro-American institutions and traditions."[218] He later states that "many of the writers, intellectuals, and artists of what is now referred to as the Harlem Renaissance were homosexual, bisexual, or otherwise sexually unorthodox."[219] Stating that homosexuals did not have to "come out of the closet" during this period, Garber shows an awareness of the historical situatedness of categories of identity.[220] Focusing on Nugent, Garber states that "the most bohemian of them all was Bruce Nugent, who delighted in shocking the prudish with his erotic drawings and his openly homosexual promiscuity."[221] He calls Nugent's experimental short story "Smoke, Lilies and Jade" a "defense of homosexual love"[222] and the "first published essay on homosexuality by an African American."[223] From his choice of words one could get the false impression that Nugent wrote an essay in defense of homosexuality, rather than an experimental piece of modernist fiction.

Charles Michael Smith's essay "Bruce Nugent: Bohemian of the Harlem Renaissance" is also partly based on an interview with Nugent. His essay was published in Beam's *In the Life: A Black Gay Anthology* (1986). In his essay, Smith unambiguously depicts Nugent as gay. Instead of just printing the interview, Smith adds his own interpretations of Nugent's statements. One implicit aim of Smith's interpretation is the legitimization of homosexuality within the black community. For example, when referring to the artists of the Harlem Renaissance, Smith writes that

---

218 Eric Garber, "A Spectacle in Color: The Lesbian and Gay Subculture of Jazz Age Harlem," *Hidden from History: Reclaiming the Gay and Lesbian Past*, eds. Martin B. Duberman, Martha Vicinus, and George Chauncey, New York: New American Library, 1989, 318–331, 321.

219 Garber, 326.

220 Garber, 327.

221 Garber, 327.

222 Garber, 330.

223 Garber, 330.

a number of these artists were gay and lesbian, including Hughes although
Nugent dismisses the notion by saying his feeling about Langston 'is that he
was asexual.' But the emphasis was on one's blackness, not one's gayness.
Nugent was the only one who dealt with homosexuality explicitly.[224]

Even though Nugent explicitly doubts Hughes's homosexuality, Smith
takes Nugent's statement as a proof that Hughes was gay. There are other
aspects in Smith's text that aim at legitimizing homosexuality within the
eyes of the black community, such as Smith's description of Nugent's family
background and the characterization of his parents as respectable "pillars of
society."[225]

Gregory Woods's 1993 essay "Gay Re-Readings of the Harlem Renaissance
Poets" (1993) follows the same paradigm. He states that the homosexuality of
Cullen, Hughes, McKay, and Nugent is a "fact,"[226] and he considers the Harlem
Renaissance as "a cohesive gay community."[227] Taking a biographical approach,
he speaks of "Langston Hughes's clear attraction to young black men," and he
calls Nugent a "gay maverick."[228]

Later scholars take a more cautious approach towards the connections
between homosexuality and the Harlem Renaissance poets. Despite the
unambiguous title of her study *Gay Voices of the Harlem Renaissance* (2003),
Schwarz discusses whether it is appropriate to apply the concept of a gay identity
to earlier historical periods. Referring to Chauncey's *Gay New York* (1994), she
argues that the terminology in which people spoke of sexuality in the 1920s
was not yet determined by the identity categories gay and lesbian, even if some
individuals might have perceived themselves as homosexuals.[229] Likewise, in
the introductory essay to his book *Gay Rebel of the Harlem Renaissance: Selections
from the Work of Richard Bruce Nugent* (2002), Thomas H. Wirth states that "despite

---

224 Charles Michael Smith, "Bruce Nugent: Bohemian of the Harlem Renaissance," *In the Life: A
     Black Gay Anthology,* ed. Joseph Beam, Boston: Alyson, 1986, 209–220, 213–14.

225 Charles Michael Smith, 210.

226 Gregory Woods, "Gay Re-Readings of the Harlem Renaissance Poets," *Critical Essays: Gay and
     Lesbian Writers of Color,* ed. Emmanuel S. Nelson, New York: Haworth, 1993, 127–142, 127.

227 Woods, 128.

228 Woods, 139.

229 Schwarz, 3.

a high concentration of men who were sexually interested in other men, this was not a 'gay community.'"[230] Carbado, Weise, and McBride, the editors of the anthology *Black Like Us* (2002), take an approach similar to that of Schwarz and Wirth in arguing that authors such as Nugent would not have called themselves gay. They emphasize the "caution that must be exerted in equating gay men's nonconformism in the 1920s with their willingness to identify themselves as homosexual or bisexual in the modern context of gay liberation politics."[231] Still, the term gay is used in all three texts, and, somewhat surprisingly given their analyses of the context in which the term "gay" evolved, it is used in all of the titles of the three books.

4.1.3 Richard Bruce Nugent: "Smoke, Lilies and Jade" (1926)

In spite of its central position in the scholarship of the queer Harlem Renaissance, "Smoke, Lilies and Jade" is not the only text of that epoch that includes representations of homoeroticism. In addition to representations of black homosexual characters in texts by white writers, such as Carl Van Vechten's *Nigger Heaven* (1926) and Blair Niles's *Strange Brother* (1932), there are homosexual characters in texts by black writers, too. For example, Claude McKay's novel *Home to Harlem* (1928) depicts the homosexual character Billy Biasse;[232] the character's nickname "the wolf" alludes to the 1920s sub-cultural term "wolf," which was used for homosexually interested men who displayed what Chauncey calls a "marked masculinity."[233] There are two poems by Langston Hughes that are often referred to by black gay men of the 1980s and 90s, "Poem [2]" (1932),[234] which is included in *Looking for Langston*, and "Café 3 A.M." (1951).[235] The six-line poem "Poem [2]" starts and ends with the sentence "I loved my friend" and in its subheading it says that it is "for F.S." These initials

230 Wirth, 21.

231 Carbado, McBride, 12.

232 Claude McKay, *Home to Harlem*, Boston: Northeastern UP, 1987, 92; 30–31.

233 Chauncey, 86–97.

234 Langston Hughes, "Poem [2]," *The Collected Poems of Langston Hughes*, eds. Langston Hughes, Arnold Rampersad, and David E. Roessel, New York: Knopf, 1995, 52.

235 Langston Hughes, "Café: 3 a.m," *The Collected Poems of Langston Hughes*, eds. Langston Hughes, Arnold Rampersad, and David E. Roessel, New York: Knopf, 1995, 406.

have led to some speculation, and in *Black Men/White Men* F.S. has been identified as the merchant seaman Ferdinand Smith. As "Café 3 A.M." is from 1951, it is not a Harlem Renaissance text. The narrator describes a scene in a café where the police are looking for homosexuals, "fairies" and "lesbians."[236] The poem rejects the popular belief that homosexuals are "degenerates" and defends homosexuality by referring to God and the evolution: "But God, Nature, or somebody made them that way."[237]

In both of Thurman's novels, *The Blacker the Berry* (1929) and *Infants of the Spring* (1932), there are male and female homosexual characters. One, for example, is Paul Arbian in *Infants of the Spring*, who is based on Thurman's friend Richard Bruce Nugent. The allusion to Nugent is made clear by Arbian's last name, which sounds like Nugent's initials (RBN = Arbian). Taking a rather problematic biographical approach to Thurman's novel in his study *The Harlem Renaissance: Hub of African American Culture 1920–1930* (1995), Steven Watson even quotes a passage from *Infants of the Spring* that refers to Arbian in order to back up his biographical chapter on Nugent.[238] Arbian is depicted as a dandy.[239] As an artist, he paints pictures with homoerotic motifs, and he has homosexual acquaintances. What is more, he is very open about his sexuality, which is not limited to homosexual or heterosexual encounters. Being asked whether he preferred homosexuality or heterosexuality, Arbian answers: "'I really don't know. After all there are no sexes, only sex majorities, and the primary function of the sex act is enjoyment. Therefore I enjoyed one experience as much as the other.'"[240]

Arbian makes this statement after telling his friends at Niggeratti Manor about a (homo-) erotic dream he had. Arbian's account of the dream clearly alludes to Nugent's short story "Smoke, Lilies and Jade." Arbian tells his friends that he dreamed he was in a field of beautiful flowers, among

---

236 During the 1920s and 30s, Hughes would probably not have used the term "lesbian."

237 Hughes, "Café 3 a.m."

238 Watson, 90.

239 See also Elisa F. Glick, "Harlem's Queer Dandy: African-American Modernism and the Artifice of Blackness," *MFS Modern Fiction Studies* 49.3 (2003): 414–442.

240 Wallace Thurman, *Infants of the Spring*, Boston: Northeastern UP, 1992, 47.

them "white lilies, red lilies, pale narcissi, slender orchids, polychromatic pansies, jaundiced daffodils, soporific lotus blossoms."[241] This list of flowers signifies homosexuality. Chauncey states that the use of names of flowers for homosexual men, such as "pansy," was so common in the 1920s and 1930s that "they were sometimes simply called 'horticultural lads.'"[242] What is more, the lilies directly refer to the lilies in the title of Nugent's story and, as Charles C. Eldredge has shown, among modernists, calla lilies were easily identifiable as a symbol of homosexuality and bisexuality.[243] Arbian's narration of the dream continues and becomes more explicit:

> I lay down. Then I became aware of a presence. An ivory body exuding some exotic perfume. Beauty dimmed my eyes. The physical nearness of that invisible presence called to me, lured me closer. And as I crept nearer, the perfume pervaded my nostrils, inflamed my senses, anesthetized my brain. My hand reached out and touched a silken forelock. Involuntarily, my eyes closed and I was conscious of being sucked into it until there was a complete merging. For one brief moment I experienced complete ecstasy.[244]

By the use of the term "ivory," the body is marked as white, whereas the gender is not specified. Like the male character in Nugent's "Smoke, Lilies and Jade," the presence is called Beauty. At the end of the quotation, Arbian makes the sexual nature of the encounter in the dream between him and Beauty explicit, a reference to the sexually explicit narrative of "Smoke, Lilies and Jade." In the short account of Arbian's dream, Thurman has captured the key elements that made "Smoke, Lilies and Jade" scandalous: the homoeroticism indicated by the setting in a field of flowers, the interracial sexuality between the black Arbian and the white body, the indeterminacy of the body's gender, and the sexual overtones in Arbian's account of his dream.

---

241 Thurman, 45.

242 Chauncey, 15.

243 For an account of the symbolism of the calla lily, see Charles C. Eldrege, Eldrege, "Calla Moderna: 'Such a Strange Flower,'" Georgia O'Keeffe and the Calla Lily in American Art, 1860–1940, eds. Barbara Buhler Lynes and Georgia O'Keeffe, New Haven: Yale UP, 2002, 4–37.

244 Thurman, 45.

As there are direct references to "Smoke, Lilies and Jade" in *No Easy Place to Be*, and as one scene in *Looking for Langston* can be considered a direct adaptation of Nugent's short story, I will now refer to those elements in the story that were subsequently taken up by Corbin and Julien.

Even though "Smoke, Lilies, and Jade" is frequently called the first text about homosexuality written by an African American, this characterization implies the danger of a narrow interpretation focusing on homosexuality alone. In addition to Alex's homosexual desires for Beauty, the text presents the intersections of various differences, among them race, sexuality, gender and can also be called a text about a black protagonist with interracial, bisexual, and polyamorous (sexual) desires. One could therefore argue that the text embodies what nowadays would be called the representation of queer desire.

Before reading the first sentence of "Smoke, Lilies, and Jade," the reader encounters a text whose experimental form is directly visible on the page. To a large part, it consists of sentence fragments and ellipses that are represented by dots. Boone argues that these ellipses correspond to the reality of the story's protagonist. He states that Nugent's ellipses "break the horizontal flow of language with worldless gaps that, repeating from line to line, visually create vertical 'paths,' literal openings, on the page that evoke the protagonist's aimless footsteps as he cruises the city."[245] Such breaks in the horizontal flow of language and such vertical paths can also be found in the use of two parallel columns on the pages of Delany's "Atlantis: Model 1924," which I will refer to in the last section of this chapter (see 4.4).

"Smoke, Lilies and Jade" is written in a stream of consciousness style. The text is framed by the description of its protagonist Alex, who is alone in his room lying on his bed. He is "smoking a cigarette thru an ivory holder...inlaid with red jade and green... ."[246] At the beginning of the narrative, Alex thinks of his past, the death of his father, and arguments with his mother, who cannot understand his bohemian lifestyle. In addition to Alex's room, there are other

245 Boone, 220.

246 Richard Bruce Nugent, "Smoke, Lilies and Jade," *Fire!!*, ed. Wallace Thurman, Metuchen, N.J: Fire!! Press, 1982, 33–391, 34.

settings, among them a street at night, a cafeteria, a field of lilies, a party, a speakeasy, and a fair by the sea, which is probably Coney Island. Smoke is a recurrent motif uniting these different settings.

After leaving the room at night, Alex meets a man in a street. The setting is similar to a cruising situation. The man addresses Alex in Spanish and asks for a match, and then the two men go to Alex's room to have sex. Alex refers to the man as Beauty, and later also calls him Adrian. The sexual encounter between the two men depicted in "Smoke, Lilies and Jade" is one of the transgressive elements of the narrative. As Adrian's body is described as white, e.g. "two strong white legs [...] firm white thighs,"[247] the interracial nature of the encounter adds a second element of transgression to the homosexuality.[248] However, neither homosexuality nor interracial love is represented as an area of conflict. Something else is troubling Alex's mind, and that is his love for two people. In addition to Beauty, he is in love with a black woman named Melva, and it is his affection for both of them that is the reason for his inner conflicts:

> he would like Beauty to know Melva...they were both so perfect...such compliments...yes he would like Beauty to know Melva because he loved them both...there...he had thought it...actually dared to think it...but Beauty must never know...Beauty couldn't understand...indeed Alex couldn't understand...and it pained him...almost physically...and tired his mind... Beauty...Beauty was in the air...the smoke...Beauty...Melva... Beauty...Melva... Alex slept...and dreamed[249]

What follows is a description of the dream Alex has, one that is the basis for a scene in *Looking for Langston*. This dream is the result of Alex's initial belief that he has to decide between Beauty and Melva. He dreams that he is in "a

---

247 Nugent, 37.

248 As the first words Beauty speaks are in Spanish, it is debatable whether he is represented as white or Latino/Hispanic. As Beauty's body is explicitly referred to with the word "white" repeatedly throughout the narrative, I take the encounter between Alex and Beauty to be an interracial encounter between a black and a white man. In my reading of Alex as black I follow Boone, who argues that "Alex's awareness of his blackness is simply presented as part of his life, rather than as a fact that needs to spelled out for uncomprehending readers" (Boone, 228), and I contradict Schwarz, who considers Alex to be "racially unidentified" (Schwarz, 126).

249 Nugent, 36–37.

field of blue smoke and black poppes [sic] and red calla lilies."[250] Searching on his hands and knees, he first meets Beauty and later Melva. Beauty's and Melva's physical appearances are vividly described, starting with their feet and legs and ending with their eyes. In the descriptions of their naked bodies, the difference in gender and race is clearly marked. Both of them say only one identical sentence: "I'll wait Alex."[251] In his dream, Alex reacts confusedly each time he hears this sentence. He kisses Melva and continues his search. He cannot make a decision between the two.

Alex's transition from confusion and a state of innocence towards self-actualization follows the structure of the quest-narrative. After awaking from the dream in which he only dreamed of kissing Melva, Alex thinks "he *would* like to kiss Beauty's lips."[252] However, he smokes a cigarette instead, thinking about the dream he just had. In the narrative, a kiss on the lips between two men is represented as being more taboo and shameful than the sex act, and the kiss between Alex and Beauty marks the transition from innocence to knowledge and emancipation. At first, Beauty kisses Alex's lips while Alex pretends to be asleep, and then Beauty and Alex kiss each other with their eyes open:

> Beauty's lips touched his...pressed hard...cool...opened slightly...Alex opened his eyes...into Beauty's...parted his lips...Dulce...Beauty's breath was hot and short...Alex ran his hand through Beauty's hair...Beauty's lips pressed hard against his teeth...Alex trembled...could feel Beauty's body...close against his....hot...tense...white...and soft...soft...soft.........[253]

Boone rightly argues that this kiss signifies that "an ultimate barrier of self-actualization has been crossed."[254] After this kiss, Alex introduces his lovers to each other at a place called Forno's: "Alex looked toward the door...there was Melva...Alex beckoned...Melva this is Adrian...Beauty held her hand...they talked...smoked."[255] In the last passage of the text, Alex's inner conflict is once

250 Nugent, 37.
251 Nugent, 37.
252 Nugent, 37.
253 Nugent, 38.
254 Boone, 231.
255 Nugent, 38.

again visualized before it is finally resolved. The last passage of the text that is set at Coney Island is characterized by the naming of opposites that stand for Alex's conflicting feelings for Melva and Beauty: the upward and downward movements of the rollercoaster and the ferris wheel, the change from day to dawn symbolized by sunset and subsequent moonrise, the contrast of the sound of the sea and the sound of the train, and finally Alex's memories of Melva's and Beauty's kisses.[256] After the sensual experience of these opposites, Alex no longer feels the need to decide between his two lovers, and the conflict is resolved by Alex's realizing: "one *can* love two at the same time."[257]

The end of the narrative shows the way in which the form of "Smoke, Lilies and Jade" corresponds to its contents. The vivid depiction of space and movement represents the inner thoughts and conflicts of the protagonist. In his analysis, Boone has observed the intersection of metropolitan modernity, literary modernism, and marginalized identity. Putting emphasis on the significance of gay urban spaces for the development of alternative modernist forms, Boone focuses on the homosexual dimensions of "Smoke, Lilies, and Jade." He argues that the story dramatizes "the internal process by which a black person comes to acknowledge, give name to, and act upon his homosexual desires."[258] This characterization is reminiscent of the 1970s Coming Out paradigm of the gay liberation movement, and Boone himself considers the possibility of reading "Smoke, Lilies and Jade" as "a variant of the coming-out paradigm of much gay fiction."[259] However, Boone also states that "this coming-out narrative is produced through a series of identifications that cross and recross multiple categories – in particular, those of sexuality (hetero/homo/bisexuality), biological sex (male/female), race (black/white/Latin), and aesthetics (Wildean decadence/high modernism/Harlem Renaissance)."[260] On the grounds of the formal experiments of Nugent's story and the transgressive themes crossing categories of race, gender, sexuality and social positioning, one could well

---

256 Nugent, 39.

257 Nugent, 39.

258 Boone, 223.

259 Boone, 223.

260 Boone, 223–224.

regard the story as a queer narrative.[261] As will be shown at the end of this chapter, the fragility and fluidity of categories of difference is a prominent topic in Delany's "Atlantis: Model 1924". Referring to modernism, the form of Delany's text supports his project of deconstructing the authenticity of race and (male) homosexuality.

4.2 Steven Corbin: *No Easy Place to Be* (1989)

Steven Corbin's *No Easy Place to Be* is set in Harlem during the Harlem Renaissance. In its depiction of the period, the novel takes an approach, similar to Garber and Woods, of the first wave of those gay and lesbian studies scholars whose aim was the excavation of the Harlem Renaissance's homosexual dimensions. Corbin's novel pursues two somewhat contradictory aims: on the one hand, it refers to the period of the Harlem Renaissance by depicting some of its notable figures, and, on the other, it consolidates the 1980s identity categories of black gay man and black lesbian.

Unlike most black gay anthologies and novels of the 1980s that were either self-published or published by small independent presses, *No Easy Place to Be* was published by Simon and Schuster, a major publishing house. This fact alone, however, did not secure the novel's success. There was only one printing of the hardcover edition; it was not re-printed or distributed as a paperback, and it remained largely unnoticed by literary critics. As Corbin lived and worked in Los Angeles at the time the novel was published, he was not personally affiliated with the group of black gay men living in the cities on the East Coast who contributed their writings to the anthologies *In the Life* or *Brother to Brother* (chapter 1.1). Corbin published two more novels that were more successful than his debut. His second novel *Fragments That Remain* was published by Gay Men's Press in London in 1993, and his third novel *A Hundred Days from Now* was published by Alyson in 1994. While writing *No Easy*

---

261 See also Boone, 232.

Place to Be, Corbin worked as a teacher of creative writing at UCLA. In 1994, Corbin died of AIDS-related complications.

Corbin's perspective on the Harlem Renaissance is determined by the gay and lesbian studies movement of the 1970s and 1980s and the black gay movement of the 1980s. With the depiction of homosexuality during the Harlem Renaissance, his novel fictionalizes an often ignored and underrepresented part of black history. In contrast to many texts that were written during the 1920s, *No Easy Place to Be* is not a document of experimental literature. It is a neo-realist novel with meticulously researched historical references. I will show that Corbin reluctantly reflects on the process of constructing a black gay and lesbian past through intertextual references and metafictional elements. However, the decision to authenticate the narrative through neo-realist devices, such as references to historical figures of the Harlem Renaissance serves the purpose of revising dominant historiography by claiming and consolidating the contested identity categories black gay man and black lesbian.

Of course, Corbin can only construct and present one version of "reality." After the linguistic turn, the idea of representing "reality" through literature has become obsolete because structuralist and poststructuralist thinkers have shown the essential role language has in the construction of reality. Opposing the view that realist modes of representation simply depict a reality independent from and prior to the text, Roland Barthes has introduced the term "reality effect." Barthes argues that the reality effect, the impression that the depicted world is close to what the reader knows as the real world, is achieved because of the fact that the fictional text is highly constructed and contains references to the knowledge of the reader's cultural realm.[262] Following Barthes, Winfried Fluck argues that "realism is no more (and no less) than a system of rhetorical strategies in order to claim special authority for one's own interpretation of reality. It does not simply reflect or mirror reality, but offers a version of it, based on certain assumptions about the nature of the real and the best way

---

262 Roland Barthes, "The Reality Effect," *The Novel: An Anthology of Criticim and Theory 1900–2000*, ed. Dorothy J. Hale. Malden MA and Oxford UK: Blackwell, 2006, 229–234. See also Winfried Fluck, *Inszenierte Wirklichkeit: Der Amerikanische Realismus 1865–1900*, München: Fink, 1992, 25–33.

of gaining knowledge about it."²⁶³ In this sense, Corbin presents a black gay and lesbian version of the Harlem Renaissance, and the reality effect depends on a number of devices, such as the inclusion of historical persons, detailed descriptions of settings and cultural and political organizations of the period.

In contrast to texts by Julien, Delany, Kenan, and Dixon, Corbin's text depicts black gay identity without contradictions. Corbin's novel is exceptional in omitting stylistic devices reflecting on the process of referring to the homosexual dimensions of black cultural history. For that reason, it serves as a foil for my reading of the other texts.

The story of the three sisters Miriam, Velma, and Louise Brooks is told by an omniscient narrator who reveals the inner thoughts of all of the novel's characters. Consequently, the reader does not have to engage actively in the construction of the narrative. Adding to this effect is the fact that the detailed descriptions of the settings in the novel read like the stage directions in a play or screenplay. The chapters alternately focus on the experiences of the three sisters. The reality effect depends on the historical references and the detailed description of persons and places, which also explain the era of Harlem in the 1920s to readers who are not familiar with the time. The novel depicts, for example, the factors that positively influenced the Harlem Renaissance: the new self-esteem of African Americans after the participation of black soldiers in World War I, and the effects the Great Migration had on life in Harlem. It introduces important intellectuals of the time, such as W.E.B DuBois and Alain Locke and their publications. Corbin refers back to the 1920s to educate his readers about the position of black homosexual men and women in the Harlem Renaissance. I will argue that the concepts he uses to depict homosexuality are influenced by the 1980s black gay political discourse. Consequently, his particular picture of homosexuality is implicitly connected with the circumstances of black gay men and lesbians in the 1980s.

Relying on George Lukács' definition of the historical novel, Hutcheon argues that the historical novel, in contrast to historiographic metafiction,

---

263 Winfried Fluck, "Surface Knowledge and 'Deep' Knowledge: The New Realism In American Fiction," *Neo-Realism in Contemporary American Fiction*, ed. Kristiaan Versluys, Amsterdam and Atlanta: Rodopi, 1992, 65–85, 67.

deals with an historical period as a microcosm and the novel's protagonist as a type.[264] This characterization also applies to *No Easy Place to Be*. The Harlem Renaissance is represented as a microcosm, and each of the novel's characters embodies a typical strand of the period. For example, each of the three sisters stands for a different facet of social and political life in Harlem. Miriam, a political activist and follower of Marcus Garvey, works as a nurse. Velma is a black writer associated with the writers and artists of the period. The very light-skinned Louise works as a showgirl at the Cotton Club and decides to pass as white. At first glance, it is surprising that Corbin returns to more standardized narrative forms during a period when much of black literature is influenced by the innovative experiments of historiographic metafiction.

Historiographic metafiction makes transparent the processes through which constructed cultural norms appear as naturally given and thus real. The texts themselves point to the processes of their production, and devices such as unreliable narrators, gaps in the chronological order or multiple alternative endings make the reader aware of the constructed character of the text. One of the effects of this approach is the insight that a given cultural order is constructed and arbitrary. Such an approach is radical because it questions the epistemological foundations of any societal system, but some might argue that it can also have negative consequences for the political agenda of minority groups. If everything is arbitrary and culturally constructed, the basis on which one can work towards political change is highly unstable. For this very reason, some writers have returned to realistic modes of representation.

Since the 1980s and 1990s, writers of ethnic and sexual minorities have used neo-realist devices in order to challenge the dominant white heteropatriarchal view on history. The decision for a neo-realist style is a reaction to the postmodern experiments in fiction that emerged since the 1960s.[265] Mark Shechner states that "the list of new realists includes Chinese-American writers, Native-American writers, and Black or Afro-American writers, and while there

---

264 Linda Hutcheon, *A Poetics of Postmodernism*, New York: Routledge, 1988, 113.

265 Alfred Hornung, "Postmoderne bis zur Gegenwart," *Amerikanische Literaturgeschichte*, ed. Hubert Zapf, Stuttgart and Weimar: Metzler, 1994, 304–375, 365–366.

is a long and rich history of Black writing in America, Black writers are still seeking to be heard outside their own communities."[266] Schechner argues that a neo-realist style is the "most efficient" mode of writing for minority writers in order to be heard and recognized and states that within these ethnic groups, texts by female writers are the most provocative.[267] I contend that Corbin's pro-feminist and gay perspective in *No Easy Place to Be* supports Shechner's argument, because Corbin seeks recognition for the hidden history of black gay men and black lesbians. Corbin presents an alternative narrative of the Harlem Renaissance which includes homosexuality. One should thus regard Corbin's project and other neo-realist writings since the 1980s not as a naïve project that ignores structuralist and post-structuralist insights, but as a reaction to what some might perceive as the limitations of historiographic metafiction. In this respect, neo-realist writings can follow a progressive agenda even though they are not experimental literature.

The texts that belong to the genre of historiographic metafiction, such as the novels of Ishmael Reed and, as I will argue, Delany's "Atlantis: Model: 1924" (see 4.4), and Kenan's *A Visitation of Spirits* (see 5.2), depict identity as a socially constructed category and treat the process of identity formation as necessarily incomplete. In these texts, identity is a concept under constant negotiation which draws on disparate and hybrid cultural sources. Such a postmodern negotiation of identity would interfere with the didactic aims of *No Easy Place to Be*. On a formal level, some critics might regard a return to more standardized forms of writing as traditional and conservative, but one should also take into account that writers such as Corbin who address the central topics of the political movements of the late twentieth century do not act out of a conservative impulse and one can thus reject the reproach of neo-realism being a conservative project.

Instead of supporting a conservative agenda, *No Easy Place to Be* supports the political struggle of the black gay and black (lesbian) feminist movements of the second half of the twentieth century, and the depiction of Velma, in

---

266 Mark Shechner, "American Realisms, American Realities," *Neo-Realism in Contemporary American Fiction*, ed. Kristiaan Versluys, Amsterdam and Atlanta: Rodopi, 1992, 27–50, 32.

267 Shechner, 32.

particular, illustrates the position of black female writers in a racist and patriarchal society. Velma is depicted as an emancipated woman who reflects on her situation as a black female writer and criticizes her fellow male writers for their lack of awareness of the significance of gender. In a conversation with her lover Scott, she states, "You and I both experience racial oppression in our lives and in literature, right? For you, that's where it stops. For me, it extends to my life as a woman, as well."[268] The explicit accounts of the ways in which Velma and her sisters are exposed to patriarchal structures and male violence evokes the position of black women, lesbians and gay men during the 1980s. The parallel structure of Velma's circumstances and those of many black female and gay writers during the 1980s aims at legitimizing the black feminist and black gay political agenda of the 1980s.

4.2.1 Coming Out in the Harlem Renaissance

The didacticism of the novel extends to the way Corbin depicts female and male homosexuality, for he aims at raising the readers' tolerance and acceptance of black gays and lesbians, and to the way it empowers black lesbian and gay readers. As male and female homosexuality is most prominently shown in the characters Rudy and Miriam, I will focus my attention on the stages of their emancipation. In showing Rudy's and Miriam's quest and emancipation as black homosexuals in terms of a progression from innocence to maturity, Corbin applies the motif and structure of the salvation narrative that has been central to African American literature since the slave narratives.[269] The exemplary representation of their quest, which finally leads to closure, serves as a model for black gay men and black lesbians in the 1980s.

I suggest that the way Rudy's and Miriam's homosexuality is represented mirrors the political context of the 1980s. Corbin's way of depicting homosexuality implies a trans-historical and essentialist conception of identity categories which can also be found in the early studies of the homosexual

---

268 Steven Corbin, *No Easy Place to Be*, New York: Simon and Schuster, 1989, 135.

269 Maria Diedrich, *Ausbruch aus der Knechtschaft: Das Amerikanische Slave Narrative Zwischen Unabhängigkeitserklärung und Bürgerkrieg*, Stuttgart: Steiner, 1986, 37–40.

dimensions of the Harlem Renaissance. Several examples support the argument that homosexuality is conceptualized in an essentialist way in order to relate the 1920s to the 1980s rather than to disclose the ambiguities and contradictions connected with constructions of identities. For example, when Rudy talks to Velma about his homosexuality for the first time, he refers to the essentialist notion of a homosexual nature defining his whole self, "'Velma, it's not a passing condition or a choice – it's the way I am.'"[270] Later in the novel, Rudy remembers the one time when he had sex with Velma and thinks to himself:

> it became clear, like a drug kicking into effect, that he'd rather be with a man. *What am I doing here?* reverberated through him. Entering her, he decided that Velma Brooks was the last word and period in a chapter he was closing on himself. For the first time in his life, he felt in touch with himself.[271]

This quotation illustrates how the process of Rudy's maturation follows the pattern of the salvation narrative. The single event of heterosexual intercourse divides Rudy's life in two essentially different phases. First, he is detached from himself, and afterwards, he feels redeemed and prepared to seek out sexual partners of the same gender to fully emancipate himself as a homosexual man. The same idea of "feeling in touch with oneself" because of one's freedom to choose a sexual partner of the same gender is also highlighted in the way Miriam is depicted. For her, the experience of having sex with another woman is described in terms of being released from a life-long sentence. Afterwards she feels newly born. After having sex with her friend Agnes for the first time, her inner thoughts are explained to the reader:

> she couldn't explain how she felt, but wouldn't trade it for anything in the world. It occurred to her that she's been released from something. A darkness, a morass, an ignorance pertaining to the total working parts of her anatomy. Like inhaling the sweet breeze of a second wind, she thought, until now, she hadn't lived, not *really* lived.[272]

---

270 Corbin, 85.

271 Corbin, 149.

272 Corbin, 326.

In juxtaposing the "darkness" and "morass" of her existence with "the sweet breeze of a second wind" in having sex with Agnes, Miriam thinks that so far she had not really lived. Here, too, she evokes a salvation narrative and suggests that homosexual persons feel newly born once they have sex with a person of the same gender. The first homosexual act is represented as so powerful and even sacred that it can change one's level of consciousness and function as a way to salvation.

In directly addressing topics specific to the process of coming out, for example, conflicts within the family, with one's social surroundings and the belief that homosexuality is only a phase in the development towards heterosexuality, *No Easy Place to Be* demonstrates its rootedness in late twentieth-century discussions about coming out as a political strategy for gay men and lesbians. In the 1960s, this strategy partly came into being as a consequence of the persecution gay men and lesbians experienced during the McCarthy era (see 5.1.1). Publicly declaring one's homosexuality was a strategy of avoiding blackmail.[273] Coming out has become an important and effective strategy for gay men and lesbians to consolidate their identities and gain recognition on a personal level and as a political collective. Coming-out narratives frequently divide the lives of gay men and lesbians into two phases, an unhappy youth, and a fulfilling adulthood after a successful coming out. Recently, the strategy of coming out has been critically questioned because of its inherent tendency to homogenize the different biographies of gay men and lesbians in accordance with the model of the coming-out narrative.[274]

The problems Miriam faces in a talk with the leaders of UNIA (Universal Negro Improvement Association), the political organization she works for, mirror the repression many homosexual men and women were in during the McCarthy era, but they also allude to the way black leaders dealt with black homosexual activists. Miriam is confronted with the UNIA leaders' suspicion of her being a homosexual woman a long time before she herself considers

---

273 On the situation of homosexual men during the McCarthy era see Corber, *Homosexuality*.

274 See Volker Woltersdorff, *Coming Out: Die Inszenierung Schwuler Identitäten Zwischen Auflehnung und Anpassung*, Frankfurt a.M.: Campus, 2005; Samuel R. Delany, "Coming/Out," *Shorter Views: Queer Thoughts and the Politics of the Paraliterary*, Hanover, NH: Wesleyan UP, 1999, 67–97.

this possibility. After she emancipates herself, she thinks about the way she would now react on the basis of her newly won self-esteem:

> She didn't fancy living a double life, as Louise probably had to do before her disappearance. But now, she thought a person's sexual orientation was a petty ground upon which to be charged with misconduct, so long as it didn't infringe upon or embarrass the organization. Yes, they were expected to procreate and flourish, but there were enough folks making babies that any contribution she couldn't make wouldn't be missed.[275]

Miriam's idea that homosexuals are forced to live a double life is closely connected to the strategy of coming out. Likewise, the term "sexual orientation" is informed by sociological theories about homosexuality stemming from the second half of the twentieth century. Miriam's thoughts can be read as a comment on the position black homosexual women and men have had in black political organizations throughout the twentieth century. For example, in 1928, W.E.B. DuBois dismissed the NAACP activist Augustus Granville Dill, who was the business manager of *The Crisis*, because he was arrested for a homosexual contact in a public restroom.[276] Similarly, in 1963 Bayard Rustin was denied the role of director of the march on Washington on the grounds of his homosexuality,[277] and Eldridge Cleaver verbally attacked James Baldwin because of his homosexuality (see 5.1.3). Miriam's thoughts also contradict the argument that homosexuality is a danger for the black family. This position was formulated in Nathan and Julia Hare's 1984 study *The Endangered Black Family: Coping with the Unisexualization and Coming Extinction of the Black Race*, and it was controversially debated in the late 1980s.[278]

Rudy's and Miriam's homosexuality affects their relations to their families. As Rudy's parents do not know anything about their son's homosexuality, Scott concludes that Rudy came to New York because of the

---

275 Corbin, 327.

276 Chauncey, 198.

277 Jeanmarie, 5–6.

278 Nathan Hare and Julia Hare, *The Endangered Black Family: Coping with the Unisexualization and Coming Extinction of the Black Race*, San Francisco: Black Think Tank, 1984.

freedom from oppression the metropolis grants.[279] Miriam, instead, decides to tell her sister Velma about her love for Agnes. After the first shock, Velma tries to understand her sister:

> Velma was shocked, a trifle repulsed. She struggled against being judgmental. She wondered how long Miriam had been this way, and suddenly understood why she had never dated men after George. She'd gotten used to homosexuals, but she never thought for a moment that one could be blood-related.[280]

In recognizing that her own sister is homosexual, Velma highlights the gay and lesbian movement's popular slogan "we are everywhere." In showing both Miriam's fear of telling her sister about her love for Agnes and Velma's reactions and conflicting feelings about Miriam's homosexuality, the novel explains two different facets of a coming-out process. The reader is didactically led to understand the consequences of the fact that, within hegemonic discourse, everyone is first assumed to be heterosexual. Miriam's coming out further suggests that everyone, including family members one has known since childhood, can be homosexual.

During their homosexual emancipation, Rudy and Miriam are confronted with common and stereotypical beliefs about homosexuality. Thinking that he "would have made the transition into heterosexuality, like a caterpillar metamorphosing into a butterfly"[281] once he reached adulthood, Rudy himself holds on to and then rejects the psychoanalytic idea widely held until the 1980s that homosexuality is an adolescent phase that will be overcome after puberty. In his talk with Scott about his homosexuality, Rudy revises the stereotype that homosexual men want to be like women[282] – "I've never had the desire to put on anybody's dress"[283] – and once again argues in favor of homosexuality by stating that it is "as natural as heterosexual attraction."[284] Likewise, Velma

---

279 Corbin, 152.

280 Corbin, 411.

281 Corbin, 149.

282 Sinfield, 9–31.

283 Corbin, 153.

284 Corbin, 153.

states that Rudy is "too masculine ... too good-looking to be that way."[285] In addition to these examples that revise common beliefs and stereotypes about homosexuality, Corbin refers to the 1970s and 1980s discourse of "gay pride." For example, Rudy is described as someone who "went after men who, like himself, knew what they were and celebrated it."[286] Referring to this passage, Löbbermann rightly argues that the idea of celebrating one's sexual identity is a result of the politics of the Gay Liberation Movement.[287] Corbin combines his use of concepts and political strategies from the 1980s with the terminology of same-sex desire of the 1920s. He never uses the terms "gay" and "lesbian" to describe male and female homosexuality. Instead, he uses contemporary terms of the 1920s such as "freakish" or "bulldiker."

4.2.2 Signifying on "Smoke, Lilies and Jade"

The characters in the novel, Rudy, Velma, and Scott can be interpreted in at least two ways: as a reference to three historical writers of the Harlem Renaissance, or to the fictional characters of Nugent's story "Smoke, Lilies and Jade." I will first consider the historical references, and in a second step, I will consider the references to "Smoke, Lilies and Jade." The constellation of Rudy, Velma, and Scott and their arrangements with their godmother Mrs. Vanderpool evoke the constellation of Langston Hughes, Zora Neale Hurston, Alain Locke, and Charlotte van der Quick Mason. The novel depicts the ambivalent role of white patrons who financed African American artists and writers because they wanted to support "primitive" and "exotic" art. Mrs. Vanderpool is based on the white patron Charlotte van der Veer Quick Mason,[288] the self-announced "godmother" who financially supports Velma and Rudy. She says, "Let me say that my ideal of Negro literature centers around the primitive. Gay people, full of music and dance. And that primitive flavor is unique to your race. I see the work reflecting the exoticism of the jungle, if you will. Give me something gay. Keep

---

285 Corbin, 85.

286 Corbin, 275.

287 Löbbermann, "Looking for Harlem," 59.

288 For information on Mason, see Watson, 144–147.

the protest."[289] There are many other parallels between the historical personas and the novel's characters. For example, like Scott, who introduces Rudy and Melva to Mrs. Vanderpool in the novel, Locke introduced Hughes and Hurston to Mason's patronage. Like Mrs. Vanderpool in the novel, Mason insisted on being called "godmother," and Hurston, like Velma, received a car from her patron. The novel also takes up the conflicts surrounding Hurston's and Hughes's staging of a folk opera that led to the end of their arrangement with Mason.

Whereas there are many fictional representations of Harlem Renaissance writers and artists in the novel, Nugent, a central figure of the queer Harlem Renaissance, is never mentioned. Nugent's striking absence is one reason for the argument that Rudy serves the function of a replacement of the historical Nugent. In addition, there are other similarities between Nugent and Rudy. Rudy is represented as a bohemian. His style of clothing is very casual, and on their first meeting Velma realizes

> his shabby clothes – a wrinkled, fading shirt inside an army green pullover sweater, uncreased pleated pants with sagging cuffs, baggy at the knees, and a pair of beat-up wing-tip shoes that looked as if they'd belonged to his father, perhaps his grandfather, made him appear informal, unpretentious, bohemian.[290]

Rudy is quite self-assured in his clothing. Later on he even gives the advice: "Do what I do, wear what's comfortable."[291] Moreover, like Alex in "Smoke, Lilies and Jade," Rudy only lives for the moment and wonders, "Couldn't folks just go with the flow of life's momentum without gratuitous expectations?"[292]

In addition to these parallels between historical persons and the characters in the novel, Hughes, Hurston, and Locke are also included as fictionalized historical characters. Such an inclusion and "relegation of historical personages

---

289 Corbin, 116. Later on in the novel, the fictionalized Zora Neale Hurston gives Rudy and Melva the advice to treat the white patrons strategically when she states: "Do what I do. Play little happy-go-lucky darky writer and bat your eyelashes a lot. When I call I say, 'This is your lil ol' primitive child.' They just love stuff like that" (Corbin, 131).

290 Corbin, 44.

291 Corbin, 86.

292 Corbin, 86.

to secondary roles"[293] are one major characteristic of the historical novel. "In many historical novels, the real figures of the past are deployed to validate or authenticate the fictional world by their presence, as if to hide the joins between fiction and history in a formal and ontological sleight of hand."[294] According to Barthes, the inclusion of historical persons in fictional texts is one device granting the "reality effect" of a novel.[295]

I will now focus on how Rudy, Melva, and Scott allude to the fictional characters of Nugent's story "Smoke, Lilies and Jade." The intertextual references to the story show that Corbin combines a postmodernist device with a neo-realist depiction of the Harlem Renaissance. The most direct reference to "Smoke, Lilies and Jade" can be deduced from the name "Velma." Velma is an anagram of the name "Melva," the female character in Nugent's story. I suggest that the constellation of Melva, Alex, and Beauty in "Smoke, Lilies and Jade" serves as a basis for the relationship of the three friends Velma, Rudy, and Scott. Rudy's character is loosely based on Alex, the protagonist of "Smoke, Lilies and Jade," and there are also references to its author Nugent. Scott is loosely reminiscent of Beauty. The relationship between Velma, Rudy, and Scott develops just after Rudy and Velma meet Scott for the first time. Scott invites them for a midnight picnic on Brooklyn Bridge. Interestingly, the scene is set at the same place as the queer encounter between Sam and Harold Hart in Delany's "Atlantis: Model 1924" (see 4.4.3). The time and place of their meeting is informative. As "the nighttime walkways of the city's downtown bridges have traditionally been heavy homosexual cruising areas, practically since their opening,"[296] a context open to sexual possibilities is directly evoked in this scene.

After drinking wine and smoking marijuana, Rudy, Scott, and Velma emphasize their mutual friendship with an embrace. At first, Velma feels excluded from Rudy's and Scott's hug:

---

293 Hutcheon, 114.

294 Hutcheon, 114.

295 Barthes, 232.

296 Samuel R. Delany, "Atlantis Rose. Some Notes on Hart Crane," *Longer Views: Extended Essays*, Hanover, NH: UP of New England, 1996, 174–250, 213.

> She [Velma] walked toward [Scott], her arms outstretched for an embrace.
> Scott walked toward her, passing her, and threw his arms around Rudy,
> who half-heartedly returned the hug. Velma stood motionless, not knowing
> what to do.

But when she joins the two men in their embrace a few moments later, the three of them become a "triangle of inebriated passion."[297] The passage on the bridge is a foreshadowing of their relationship. During the course of the novel, each of them will have sex with the other two. However, the constellation in *No Easy Place to Be* is more complicated than that in "Smoke, Lilies and Jade." The relationship between Velma, Rudy, and Scott is determined by jealousy as well as by their sexual identities. Whereas Velma loves both men and enjoys having sex with them, Rudy, after their first sexual encounter, does not want to pursue a sexual relationship with Velma. He is sexually attracted to Scott, who in turn wants a monogamous relationship with Velma. Nevertheless, he once had an enjoyable homosexual experience when he lived in Paris, and once he even tries to make Velma jealous by having sex with Rudy.

Velma points out to Rudy the complications connected with her being in love with two men. At the same time, her remark illustrates that her being in love with two men – "one can love two at the same time"[298] – is a good theme for literature, a twofold reference to Nugent's short story as well as Corbin's novel.

> 'Everything's so damn crazy. I'm in love with Scott. You're in love with Scott;
> Scott loves me; I'm in love with you. Gosh! There must be a novel in there
> or something, wouldn't you say? At least.'[299]

This quotation is a metafictional element that makes transparent the reference to Nugent as well as Corbin's own construction of the triangle of Rudy, Velma and Scott. However, even if this metafictional element points to the project of fictionalizing the Harlem Renaissance transparent, it does not altogether question constructions of identity. In highlighting the complications connected with Velma's being in love with two men and with Rudy's homosexuality,

---

297 Corbin, 100.

298 Nugent, 39.

299 Corbin, 309.

No Easy Place to Be points at the dreamlike and utopian character of the transgressive elements that Nugent presents in "Smoke." Altering the bisexual and interracial dimensions of "Smoke, Lilies and Jade" into a narrative that presents only black characters with static homosexual and heterosexual identities, Corbin strengthens black gay identity and supports an afrocentric black gay agenda. This erasure of racial and sexual ambiguity underlines the 1980s project of constructing a distinct black gay identity as a strategy to counter homophobia within black communities and racism within the white dominated gay community.

At one point, the novel indirectly refers to "Smoke, Lilies and Jade." Rudy is awakened by Velma because of a conflict that ends in a fight between the two friends. Like Alex in "Smoke, Lilies and Jade," Rudy was lying in his bed dreaming, and he thinks afterwards, "had he known, or barely sniffed the nature of her 'emergency,' he wouldn't have budged from his Murphy bed. As it was, she'd awakened him from a wet dream he was having about Scott."[300] Because of the parallels between Melva and Alex and Velma and Rudy, the wet dream Rudy refers to is arguably an allusion to the dream described in "Smoke, Lilies and Jade."

Rather than homosexuality or bisexuality, Nugent presents the fact of Alex's being in love with two persons at the same time as an area of conflict,[301] and this is exactly the focus *No Easy Place to Be* takes in referring to "Smoke, Lilies and Jade." In contrast to Nugent, who tells his story from Alex's perspective, Corbin puts the female protagonist Velma at the center of the narrative. Whereas "Smoke, Lilies and Jade" concentrates on Alex's love of Beauty rather than his love of Melva, she – as Velma – rather than Rudy is the one who has to come to terms with her love for two persons.

In "Smoke, Lilies and Jade," Beauty is depicted as a white man, adding the transgressive element of interracial love to the topics of homosexuality and polyamory. Corbin omits this dimension from the relationship of Rudy, Velma and Scott, all of whom are black. Nevertheless, by emphasizing Scott's physical beauty, he alludes to the character Beauty in Nugent's story. When

---

300 Corbin, 362.

301 Schwarz, 135.

Velma meets Scott for the first time, she thinks: "If Adonis was Negro, (...) he would look like this."[302] In his study *When Harlem Was In Vogue*, David Levering Lewis characterizes Beauty as a "Hispanic Adonis."[303] As it is more than likely that Corbin knew Lewis's 1981 study at the time he wrote his novel, one could cautiously argue that he uses the name "Adonis" to refer to Beauty. Adonis, the emblem of male beauty in Greek mythology, is frequently referred to in the gay sub-culture and has become a gay icon. By comparing Scott, a black man, to the white Adonis, Corbin directs the reader's attention to the beauty of black men. This strategy for empowering black men is comparable to the 1960s slogan "black is beautiful." In the context of this black gay narrative, it also encourages black gay readers to recognize the beauty of other black men as well as their own beauty.

No Easy Place to Be also refers to "Smoke, Lilies and Jade" by taking up the short story's symbol of the lily. The lilies from the title of Nugent's story play a central role in Corbin's description of Louise's act of passing. The homosexuality in "Smoke, Lilies and Jade" is closely connected to Alex's dream, which is set in a field of "poppies and red calla lilies."[304] In *No Easy Place to Be*, the lily is less a symbol of homosexuality or bisexuality, than of femininity. Calla lilies are an important element in the way Corbin describes the relationship between Louise and Vittorio, her Italian husband, who gives her calla lilies every time they meet and later even calls her by the pet name "Calla Lily." On their first date,

> he handed her a crisp, freshly cut calla lily wrapped in white tissue paper. Louise handled the long green stem and sniffed the bell-shaped flower with a deep breath, though there was nothing to smell.[305]

Throughout the novel, the calla lily is the symbol of Louise's passing. Calla lilies are white flowers with a South African origin. Like a calla lily, Louise has black roots and a white appearance. By emphasizing the odorlessness of the calla lily, he also indicates a lack of substance and authenticity. The freshness of the lilies

---

302 Corbin, 90.

303 David L. Lewis, *When Harlem was In Vogue*, New York: Knopf, 1981, 197.

304 Nugent, 37.

305 Corbin, 196.

indicates the state of their relationship. Whereas on their first meeting the lily is "freshly cut," it is wilting[306] after Vittorio finds out that his wife is black.

Owing to the dreamlike atmosphere, the calla lilies in "Smoke, Lilies and Jade" are red rather than white. The image of the red calla lilies is taken up again in *No Easy Place to Be*. After Vittorio's failed suicide attempt, there are "blood-splattered calla lilies"[307] in the room, real red calla lilies as opposed to the surreal red lilies in "Smoke, Lilies and Jade." This tragic end to Louise's attempt at passing can be read as a reinforcement of the popular motif of the tragic mulatto and is reminiscent of texts such as Nella Larsen's 1929 novel *Passing*. Louise's decision to pass as white ends in disaster. With regard to both of Delany's texts, I will show that he employs the passing motif to different ends. Sam's passing in "Atlantis: Model 1924" and Delany's passing narrated in his autobiographical memoir *The Motion of Light in Water* point at the fragility and fluidity of the category of race and contradict the trope of the tragic mulatto.

The ways in which Corbin takes up and leaves out elements from Nugent's story is an expression of skepticism concerning interracial love and sexuality. By depicting Rudy, Velma, and Scott as black, he omits the interracial dimension of "Smoke, Lilies and Jade." Corbin alters the transgressive and fluid elements of Nugent's story, bisexuality, polyamory and interracial sexuality, to an unambiguous narrative depicting characters who arrive at static homosexual and heterosexual identities, and whose sexual desire is solely directed at other black people. By altering the positive symbol of the calla lily from "Smoke, Lilies and Jade" that stands for Alex's love for the white man Beauty into the blood-red calla lilies representing the violence and racism connected to Louise's passing and her failed marriage with Vittorio, Corbin suggests that interracial relationships are doomed to fail.

Unlike Delany's "Atlantis: Model 1924," a text that supports the idea of an anti-essentialist approach towards identities (see 4.4.2), *No Easy Place to Be* aims at the consolidation of black gay and lesbian identities and it can also be read as an introduction to the Harlem Renaissance. It is thus aimed at a black

---

306 Corbin, 437.
307 Corbin, 440.

readership both heterosexual and homosexual and also at white queer readers who might not know much about black cultural history. As I have shown, the novel depicts conflicts of (black) homosexuals, such as the position of homosexuals in black political organizations, the relationship between homosexuals and their families, and conflicts connected with the process of coming out. It also refers to the inner thoughts of Rudy, a black homosexual man, and Miriam, a black homosexual woman. The novel represents their sexual emancipation as redemption. Both want to be part of the larger black community rather than a part of the white-dominated homosexual sub-culture. Both are in love with an African American person, and both dedicate their lives and work to contribute to black arts (Rudy) and black politics (Miriam). Consequently, the novel supports the politics established in the early anthologies of black gay and lesbian writings. In promoting same-gender love within the African American community, in showing Rudy and Velma's affiliations with black traditions, and in indirectly referring to Nugent's "Smoke, Lilies and Jade," *No Easy Place to Be* aims at consolidating black gay and lesbian identities. It does so by constructing the Harlem Renaissance as a myth of origin specific to 1980s and 90s black gay and lesbian culture.

4.3 Isaac Julien: *Looking for Langston* (1989)

Isaac Julien's film *Looking for Langston* was released in 1989 during the prime of black gay cultural activism. As one might expect, it takes up many of the political debates that are characteristic of these years, such as negations of black gay identity, the criticism of white gay racism and the dominant construction of gayness as a white identity, the debate about interracial sexuality, and questions concerning a specific black gay history that reaches back to the Harlem Renaissance.[308] For the production of *Looking for Langston*, its director Julien brought together notable cultural activists and artists and cultural theorists from two different countries, the UK (for example Sunil Gupta, Jimmy Somerville, Stuart

308 Isaac Julien, dir., *Looking for Langston*, London: BFI, 2006, DVD.

Hall, and members of the Sankofa film collective) and the USA (among them Essex Hemphill, Wayson R. Jones, Blackberri, and Toni Morrison). This transnational collaboration of black and white, gay and straight intellectuals led to a fusion of different discussions and approaches towards identities and identity politics, and one might even call the film an example of Paul Gilroy's paradigm of the Black Atlantic.[309] Many discussions in the 1990s around representations of black masculinity and representational intersectionality (see 3.1.2), constructions of gay whiteness (see 3.1.3), the threat of HIV/AIDS (see 3.1.4) as well as the excavation of the queer dimensions of the Harlem Renaissance (see 4.1) were once again fueled by Julien's film. José Esteban Muñoz even takes *Looking for Langston* as one starting point in developing his theory of disidentification (see 3.4), and in his article "Somewhere Out There: The New Black Queer Theory" Rinaldo Walcott regards Julien's film as one important text that influenced the emerging field of black queer studies (see 3.2).[310] As the film contains poetry, images, criticism, music, and performances by 1980s black gay cultural activists, Muñoz regards it as the "slippery center"[311] of late 1980s black gay cultural activism.

Julien's representational strategy is rooted in British Cultural Studies, a school of thought inextricably linked to Stuart Hall. Hall pleads for a new form of black politics and for new ways of representing black subjects. In stating that "the question of the black subject cannot be represented without reference to the dimensions of class, gender, sexuality and ethnicity,"[312] he supports an intersectional approach towards identities and identity politics. Hall sees his ideas of a new politics of representation exemplified in the films of black British film collectives like Black Audio Collective and Sankofa.[313] In these films, the black subject is positioned among the axes of race, gender, sexuality, and

---

309 Paul Gilroy, *The Black Atlantic: Modernity and Double Consciousness*, Cambridge, Mass: Harvard UP, 1993.

310 Walcott.

311 José Esteban Muñoz, "Photographs of Mourning: Melancholia and Ambivalence in Van der Zee, Mapplethorpe, and *Looking for Langston*," *Disidentifications: Queers of Color and the Performance of Politics*, Minneapolis: U of Minnesota P, 1999, 57–74, 57.

312 Hall, 28. See also Mercer, "Dark and Lovely," 221.

313 Another example he gives is Hanif Kureishi's and Stephen Frear's 1985 film *My Beautiful Launderette* (Hall, 30).

class, and the filmmakers deliberately reject the "burden of representation," the need to produce positive images of marginalized groups to represent the whole group. Julien, by way of his work as a member of the Sankofa film collective, has made films such as *Territories* and *Passion of Remembrance*. In them he has helped to establish the new aesthetic and political paradigm Hall refers to in his theoretical approach.[314] Julien is intellectually and personally rooted in black British cultural studies, and his films can be read as a contribution to a discourse on identity and trans-culturalism rather than as a didactic film for black gay men and the larger black community. In this respect, it differs from *No Easy Place to Be*. The film's involvement in academic discussions is one reason for its success. Whereas Corbin's novel, which came out in the same year as *Looking for Langston*, was all but ignored within the academy, *Looking for Langston* to this day is repeatedly taken as a point of reference by scholars concerned with African American studies, black British cultural studies, and queer theory.

The main reason for the popularity of the film is that different audiences have taken an interest in the film. For example, black gay men, the larger black community, the larger gay and lesbian community, academics working in various disciplines, and art curators have all contributed to its success. Before the film was made, there were hardly any positive filmic representations of black gay masculinity whatsoever. Black gay men in the US, as well as in the UK, were eager to see themselves represented on the screen. With its artistic production of beautiful black male bodies and despite its critique of white gay racism, the film also appealed to the larger gay community. Moreover, the negative reactions of the Hughes estate regarding the inclusion of several poems by Langston Hughes probably added to the film's popularity. Academics working in film studies, African American studies, gay and lesbian and queer studies, and film studies still refer to the film as an example of the different facets of discussion surrounding the topic of identity.

---

314 Hall himself participated in the production of *Looking for Langston* as a voice-over narrator. He is listed as "British voice" at the end of the film to indicate that the new politics of representation also questions contemporary understandings of Britishness, and thereby reveal Britishness as a particular ethnicity rather than a universality.

Because of its references to the African American gay movement of the 1980s, its affiliations with black British cultural studies and its intervention into debates about the representation of black masculinity, Julien's film contributed to a specific political discourse. However, the political effectiveness of his aesthetics has been questioned because of the experimental and avant-garde style of the film, its academic leanings and its non-linear narrative. At the 1988 conference Black Film/British Cinema, Judith Williamson asked whether such an aesthetic speaks to an audience that is rooted within the social movements.[315] José Arroyo turns her argument around and argues that Julien's films have been distributed in the US exactly because of their experimental style.[316] He further states that a contemporary audience used to the images of music videos have the competence of reading Julien's film. Arroyo is doubtful whether "a more 'accessible' form would automatically translate into larger audiences and thus greater political effectiveness."[317] *Looking for Langston* has been debated within cultural studies by black and white critics alike. Furthermore, it was quite successful at international gay and lesbian film festivals. The recent release of the film on DVD and the fact that *Looking for Langston* is frequently shown in film programs accompanying international art shows[318] demonstrate that there is still an interest in the film, nearly twenty years after it was made.[319]

4.3.1 Cinematography and Black Queer History

A brief comparison to Rodney Evans's 2004 film *Brother to Brother* and its flashback to the 1920s helps to make clear the particular way in which *Looking*

---

315 See Judith Williamson, "Two Kinds of Otherness," *Black Film, British Cinema*, ed. ICA, London: Institute of Contemporary Arts, 1988, 33–37.

316 José Arroyo, "The Films of Isaac Julien: Look Back and Talk Black," *Cinemas of the Black Diaspora: Diversity, Dependence, and Oppositionality*, ed. Michael T. Martin. Detroit: Wayne State UP, 1995, 318–339, 335FN3.

317 Arroyo, 335FN3.

318 See for example the film programs of Documenta 11 (2002) and of the exhibition "New York – States of Mind" at *Haus der Kulturen der Welt* in Berlin (2007).

319 Over the last decade, Julien has produced innovative work for the museum employing an even more experimental film language using devices such as split screen projections. His recent work, for example the installations *Paradise Omeros* and *True North*, focus on questions of ethnic and (trans)national identity and still consider sexuality as a line of difference.

for Langston connects three different historical moments. In *Brother to Brother*, the elderly Bruce Nugent character guides the young fictional protagonist Perry on a tour of the Harlem Renaissance. They go back in time and visit 1920s Harlem. As invisible observers, they go to a rent party at Niggeratti Manor, the house where Nugent, Thurman, and others resided during the 1920s, and which is depicted in Thurman's 1932 novel *Infants of the Spring*. Nugent points out Thurman, Hughes, and Hurston. In a later scene we see them reading some negative reviews after the publication of their literary magazine *Fire!!*. Unlike the scenes that are set in the 1980s, these scenes are filmed in black and white. The contrast between past and present is made clear through the use of black-and-white film and color film. Nugent, who lived in both periods, has the role of a messenger who mediates between the 1920s and the 1980s to help the young black gay Perry.

The cinematic device of using black and white or color film to denote past and present is not employed in *Looking for Langston*. On the contrary, Julien's exclusive use of black and white images fuses different historical periods into a unified narrative. In connecting three different historical periods, *Looking for Langston* constructs a genealogy of black homosexual/gay art. The three points of reference are the Harlem Renaissance of the 1920s, the late 1960s, and the 1980s, the decade in which the film was made; this connection is already established in the credits of the film even before the first image is shown. The first title reads "A Meditation on Langston Hughes (1902–1967) and the Harlem Renaissance." In the opening credits it says that the film features poetry by Bruce Nugent and Essex Hemphill, and a third title says that the film was made "In Memory of James Baldwin (1924–1987)."

The very first sequence shows historical black and white footage of 1920s Harlem. We see a subway train on a bridge heading towards Harlem. The image of a subway train on a bridge is taken up again in a later scene. This time the scene is set in 1980s London. Consequently, the image of the train on the bridge not only links the 1920s to the 1980s, but it also connects Harlem with London, the place where Julien works and lives.[320]

320 The opening sequence of *Looking for Langston* is once again taken up in the first sequence of Evans's *Brother to Brother*, showing Perry, who is inside a wagon of a subway train, crossing the East River.

The example of the two images of a train on a bridge, one an archival image from 1920s Harlem, the other a newly-directed scene filmed in London, indicates the technique of collage. Througout the film, there is a combination of archival film footage, photographs and radio features from the beginning of the twentieth century with directed scenes, all of them filmed in black and white, in order to establish a connection between different periods of black cultural production. The archival footage shows black artists at work: there are sequences that show Hughes reciting his work, and we see Bessie Smith as well as parts of Oscar Micheaux's films *10 Minutes to Live*, *Go Down Death* and *The Killer*. The style of the collage also applies to the soundtrack. With a few exceptions, it is non-diegetic and it consists of voiceover narration and music combining texts by black British and African American artists and intellectuals. For example, we hear the music of the black gay singer Blackberri, the poetry of Essex Hemphill, and a recording of Toni Morrison's funeral address for James Baldwin.

After establishing Harlem as one of the film's locations, the film shows historical footage of a funeral, supposedly Hughes's funeral in 1967. The historical funeral of Hughes is the introduction to the first directed scene. This scene subtly reveals the connection between the three historical periods, and it establishes the space in which most of the directed scenes take place. Mourners are standing around an open coffin to mourn Hughes's death. There are flowers and candles. The viewer who is looking for Hughes in the coffin discovers the filmmaker Julien, who is lying in the coffin playing the dead Hughes. In the spoken commentary to the recent DVD-edition of the film, Julien gives two explanations for his decision to play the dead Hughes himself. First, it is an ironic comment on Roland Barthes's theory of the death of the author. Second, it can be read as a comment on the AIDS crisis, a comment that directly connects this scene to the 1980s. The sound track of this scene consists of Toni Morrison's 1987 funeral address for James Baldwin at St John the Devine Church on Harlem's 125th Street, establishing a link between the funeral of Hughes in 1967 and that of Baldwin in 1987.[321] What is more, the scene is composed like

321 Mark Nash, "Langston in Retrospect," "Looking for Langston:" *A Film by Isaac Julien* [DVD Booklet], ed. British Film Institute, London: BFI, 2006, 4–6, 5.

a photograph out of James Van der Zee's *Harlem Book of the Dead*, an aestehtic device that once more evokes the Harlem of the 1920s.[322] In his essay "The Absent One: The Avant-Garde and the Black Imaginary in *Looking for Langston*," Manthia Diawara observes that the combination of the 1967 funeral "with the 1920s costumes and the black-and-white film stock creates a mood that is simultaneously that of the Harlem Renaissance, of 1967 (when Hughes died), and of the present, denoted by the presence of contemporary black British actors around the casket."[323] The combination of these different periods of time in one scene indicates the approach of the film as a whole. Rather than asking whether Hughes was a homosexual, it refers to the Harlem Renaissance and to the 1960s to negotiate contemporary constructions of race, gender and sexuality. As Henry Louis Gates puts it, "We look for Langston, but we discover Isaac."[324] Muñoz argues that the way the film juxtaposes and connects two generations of black homosexual/gay men and their art, for example the poems by Hughes and Hemphill, is an example of "call and response," a trope of the African American oral tradition:

> Julien makes use of call-and-response to historicize black gay male history and contextualize recent queer African American cultural production. This technique is rooted in black vernacular tradition while being a new and innovative approach to filmic production.[325]

The funeral ceremony takes place at the top floor of a building which is the main setting of the film. The spatial center of the film, a speakeasy, is located in the same building one floor below the place where the funeral ceremony takes place in the first scene. It is striking that the two venues are not separated by walls or doors. Without a single cut, the camera slowly and vertically moves from the top floor (funeral) to the floor below (speakeasy). The

322 For the way the aesthetics of Van der Zee is employed in the film, see Muñoz, "Photographs of Mourning."

323 Manthia Diawara, "The Absent One: The Avant-Garde and the Black Imaginary in *Looking for Langston*," *Representing Black Men*, eds. Marcellus Blount and George P. Cunningham, New York and London: Routledge, 1996, 205–224, 206.

324 Henry Louis Gates Jr., "Looking for Modernism," *Black American Cinema*, ed. Manthia Diawara, New York: Routledge, 1993, 200–207, 202.

325 Muñoz, "Photographs of Mourning," 62.

camera movement visualizes the transgression of time and place, and it stops with a shot of the guests in the speakeasy, which is reminiscent of a black and white photograph. The people in the room do not move, and the scene looks like a freeze frame. However, there are billows of smoke moving across the screen. A giant mirror ball hangs from the ceiling, and its reflections add to the effects of the lighting, which makes the place appear slightly unreal. Until the very last scene, the viewer does not get much information about the building itself, its exact location, and the way it looks from the outside. It becomes clear, however, that the speakeasy is not located on the ground floor of the building because there is a stairway leading downstairs to the first floor.

After establishing the connection between the different periods, as well as this space as a center of the film, we now see the title of the film. In later scenes, the frozen image of the guests in the speakeasy comes to life. Jazz music is heard, and the many black men, a few white men, and a female couple, all of them in tuxedos, drink and dance with each other. At the end of the film, hostile intruders, characterized in the credits as "thugs and police," enter the speakeasy in order to attack the dancing men. The music changes from jazz to 1980s house music,[326] and the costumes of the intruders can be easily identified as 1980s clothing. The attackers approach the building, which we now see from the outside. In the commentary, Julien identifies the building as the back of London's gay club "Heaven." Three elements, house music, the clothing, and the gay club clearly denote the 1980s. However, in the last scene, when the intruders enter the Club, the people in the club have disappeared, and one of the angels I will shortly refer to is laughing.

Even though the film is constructed as a collage without a linear storyline, there are three main characters around which the film evolves, Alex, Beauty, and Karl. Alex and Beauty are also the names of the characters of Nugent's "Smoke, Lilies and Jade," and there is one dream sequence in the film set in

---

326 Concerning the involvement of black gay men in the development of House Music, see Anthony Thomas, "The House the Kids Built: The Gay Black Imprint on American Dance Music," *The Greatest Taboo: Homosexuality in Black Communities*, ed. Delroy Constantine-Simms, Los Angeles: Alyson, 2001, 327–336.

a field of lilies, an image which directly signifies on Nugent's story. However, Alex can also be interpreted as the character who embodies Langston Hughes. In a scene after the title "Looking for Langston" appears, we see him connected to historical footage of Langston Hughes reading his poem "The Ballad of the Fortune Teller," accompanied by a jazz quartet. While the sound track continues, there is a cut, and we see a close-up of a record player. The camera slowly moves to the left, and we see Alex. Alex is linked to the historical Hughes by means of the sound and the image of the technical apparatus that has conserved Hughes's poem.

Karl is one of the few white men in the speakeasy. His name reminds us of Carl Van Vechten, a white photographer and author of the controversial novel *Nigger Heaven* (1926). Van Vechten was sexually interested in black men, and he has been criticized for exploiting black culture. Karl is depicted as a white homosexual man, and, as I will argue below, he embodies the racist white gay gaze on the black body.

Similar to the way many black gay writers of the 1980s refer to the past, Julien turns to Nugent, Baldwin, and Hughes in order to gain respect for black gayness in the 1980s, as well as to empower black gay men. Throughout the film, we see black men dressed as angels displaying huge posters with the faces of Hughes, Nugent and Baldwin. There are also angels on the top balcony observing and illuminating the scene below with high intensity bulbs.[327] The angels can be read as icons denoting a new and fragile black gay culture that takes the three writers as guides. Diawara states that the posters can also be read as "shields against prejudice and intolerance."[328] The Angel symbolizes homosexuality, and it is prominent in many works connected with 1980s and 1990s gay culture.[329] The black angels, who hold up large pictures of Hughes, Nugent and Baldwin, adapt the symbolism of the larger white dominated gay community and connect it with topics specific to black gay men.

---

327 Not all of the angels are black. One of the angels on the balcony is embodied by the British white gay activist and singer Jimmy Somerville.

328 Diawara, 222.

329 See for example in the titles of Derek Jarman's film *The Angelic Conversation* (1985) and Tony Kushner's play *Angels in America* (1992).

As Julien himself says in the DVD-commentary, this angel motif is also reminiscent of the aphorism about the Angel of History which Walter Benjamin develops from Paul Klee's painting *Angelus Novus*.[330] Like Delany, Julien explicitly refers to white intellectual and aesthetic traditions as a way of negotiating black gayness. Benjamin's Angel is a symbol that critically signifies progress. It has spread its wings and is blown backwards towards the future. It has directed its eyes towards the past, which it perceives as one single catastrophic event. Like the face of Benjamin's Angel, Julien's camera is directed at the past, and it visualizes a history of black male homosexuality that is always in danger of being erased by racism, homophobia, the AIDS crisis, and the dominant historiography.[331]

Despite this visualization of the fragility of black male homosexuality, the audience confronted with this view of the present and the past is not left helpless and passive. The assignment of actively retrieving the black gay past can be compared to the concept and symbol of Sankofa. "Sankofa" is the name of the filmmaking collective Julien co-founded in 1984. The word belongs to the Akan language of Ghana. It can be translated as "We must go back and reclaim our past so we can move forward; so we understand why and how we came to be who we are today."[332] Sankofa is symbolized by a bird. Like the Angel of History, the bird looks at the past while moving forward: "Visually and symbolically 'Sankofa' is expressed as a mythic bird that flies forward while looking backward with an egg (symbolizing the future) in its mouth."[333] Benjamin's Angel of History has no other choice than to look at the catastrophic past while (s)he is blown towards the future. The Sankofa bird, however, symbolizes an active agency in the reclaiming of the past:

---

330 Walter Benjamin, *Illuminations*, London: Fontana, 1973.

331 John Akomfrah and the Black Audio Collective also refer to Benjamin's Angel of History. Their documentary *The Last Angel of History* (1996) explores the connections between African American culture and Science Fiction.

332 This translation of the term "sankofa" is given on the homepage of Haile Gerima's 1995 film *Sankofa*, (Haile Gerima, *Sankofa*. <http://sankofastore.com/catalog/homepage.php>, accessed May 1, 2007).

333 Learning Center WEB DuBois, *The Meaning of the Symbolism of the Sankofa Bird*, <http://duboislc.net/SankofaMeaning.html>, accessed May 5, 2007.

'Sankofa' teaches us that we must go back to our roots in order to move forward. That is, we should reach back and gather the best of what our past has to teach us, so that we can achieve our full potential as we move forward. Whatever we have lost, forgotten, forgone or been stripped of, can be reclaimed, revived, preserved and perpetuated.[334]

In its conceptualization of a specific black gay history, Looking for Langston connects the meanings of both symbols. Like the Angel of History, it shows an awareness of the threats and dangers black homosexual men are confronted with, and, like the Sankofa bird, it pleads for active agency in the retrieval of a black gay history.

hooks understands the connection of the film to the past as a strategy of self-empowerment and recognition: "the poetic voice of the film passionately states, 'I long for my past.' A longing that is reiterated when we are told 'it's not wrong for the boy to be looking for his gay black fathers.' Such testimony speaks about the connection between the recognition and self-actualization."[335] hooks reads the way Hughes, Nugent and Baldwin are depicted to be the younger black gay artist's (Julien's) representation of his black gay fathers. Likewise, Diawara states that "Julien's revisiting of the place of the Renaissance, his dances with the ancestor figures, are sounding steps of the black imaginary that transfer the power and the knowledge of the ancestors to the young generation."[336]

However, the film does more than merely construct black gay fathers. Critics like Gates and Mercer have argued that the very strategy of appropriating the Harlem Renaissance writers as well as Baldwin for a contemporary discourse on black gay identity is reflected in Looking for Langston. In this respect, the film differs significantly from a purely historical novel like No Easy Place to Be. Looking for Langston does not explicitly state that the Harlem Renaissance poets were homosexual; it is not concerned with the assertion of a trans-historical black gayness. Diawara rightly argues that the film presents homosexuality as a new political dimension within black culture specific to a 1980s context.

334 Learning Center WEB DuBois.

335 bell hooks, "Seductive Sexualities: Representing in Poetry and on Screen," Yearning: Race, Gender, and Cultural Politics, Boston: South End, 1990, 193–201, 199.

336 Diawara, 221.

In *Looking for Langston*, (...), the discourse of blackness, symbolized by Langston Hughes and other figures of the Harlem Renaissance as well as by James Baldwin, constitutes the Absent One. The younger generation's attempt to identify with them in the film, to fill in the void left by their absence, to stand in their place, is a way of shifting the issues away from those debated during the Harlem Renaissance, to using these figures to confront new themes of the discourse of blackness, i.e. homosexuality.[337]

Similarly, Gates argues that the film contributes to discussions in the 1980s about identity politics and considers its evocation of the historical Harlem Renaissance to be "a self-reflexive gesture." He states that

there is a relation, even a typology, established between black British cinema of the 1980s and the cultural movement of the 1920s that we call the Harlem Renaissance. By its choice of subject, the film brings out, in a very self-conscious way, the analogy between this contemporary ambit of black creativity and an historical precursor.[338]

One could argue that the main difference between *No Easy Place to Be* and *Looking for Langston* is the way in which *Looking for Langston* makes clear the project of constructing a trans-historical and trans-cultural discourse around issues of race, gender, and sexuality. Julien achieves the transparency by fusing the different periods of time, the different poetic voices and aesthetic paradigms all in one space, in which he embodies the dead Langston Hughes. The self-reflexive effect is achieved through the possibilities of cinematic language.

In his aesthetics, Julien uses an approach that is based on Paul Gilroy's paradigm of the Black Atlantic. The influence of the black British cultural studies school of thought becomes apparent in comparison with Corbin's text. Whereas Corbin constructs a linear progression from the Harlem Renaissance to the 1980s and includes debates about the importance of African roots for identity and identity politics, Julien puts forward a non-linear narrative and fuses different locations. Other than referring back to cultural *roots* in the sense of a clearly defined location, he stresses the *routes* that particular persons as well

---

337 Diawara, 217.

338 Gates Jr., "The Black Man's Burden," 232.

as discourses surrounding race, gender, class, and sexuality take as a model for dynamic concepts of identity and identity politics. Gilroy states that

> marked by its European origins, modern black political culture has always been more interested in the relationship of identity to roots and rootedness than in seeing identity as a process of movement and mediation that is more appropriately approached via the homonym routes.[339]

Looking for Langston represents blackness in accordance with the routes-paradigm as a category that is not confined within national borders. Similar to Gilroy, Julien conceptualizes black British gay identity in relation to African American culture and politics. He refers to Hughes and the Harlem Renaissance and constructs a direct link between African American history and the black diaspora in Britain. Julien thus affirms the centrality of African American discourses in conceptions of the black diaspora.

The centrality of African American discourses, culture, and politics in conceptualizations of the black diaspora has recently been challenged by scholars such as Michelle Wright and Tina Campt. In their studies on the black diaspora outside the US and the UK both critically discuss the term "Black Atlantic" and use the term "diaspora" in order to shift the emphasis away from exchanges in the Western Hemisphere.[340]

Wright challenges Gilroy for another reason. In *Becoming Black* she criticizes Gilroy for centering his theory on race alone and for being uncritical of heteropatriarchal structures. In contrast to Gilroy, she understands blackness as

> a social category produced in relation to both gender and sex categories. (...) Only when we see Black subjectivities produced through, rather than in exclusion to, these categories do we arrive at theories of the Black subject that successfully negotiate the ideal and material formations that must predicate Black subject formations.[341]

---

339 Gilroy, 19.

340 Wright, *Becoming Black*, Campt, *Other Germans*.

341 Wright, *Becoming Black*, 7.

Both Kobena Mercer and Stuart Hall have also repeatedly emphasized the need to understand the category blackness through the inclusion of gender and sexuality.[342]

Even though *Looking for Langston* is no theoretical text, one can argue that black subjectivities are understood through the intersections of race, gender, and sexuality. In this regard, Julien's aesthetic approach corresponds to that of those black British cultural theorists who are more aware of gender and sexuality than Gilroy is according to Wright and Campt.

Despite the film's "self-reflexive gesture" and despite its connection to black British cultural studies, it should nevertheless be read as a text that confirms the homosexuality of Hughes and other Harlem Renaissance poets rather than as a text that aims at deconstructing identity categories. One example is the way the Langston Hughes estate reacted to the film. In order to prevent a connection between the poet's name and homosexuality, certain passages that feature Hughes reading his poetry were censored. Some poems had to be removed from the American edition of the film, the screening of the film was blocked twice, and the sound had to be turned down while showing the film at the New York film festival.[343] The politics of the Hughes estate is grounded in a reading of the film as confirming the identity category black gay man by referring to the homosexuality of Hughes and other Harlem Renaissance poets. Even though the film does not explicitly state that Hughes and others were homosexuals, I will argue below that the film refers to the Harlem Renaissance in order to support black gayness from a perspective informed by afrocentric black gay discussions of the 1980s (see 4.3.3).

4.3.2 The Burden of Representation

The way black masculinity is depicted in *Looking for Langston* is one realm that reveals Julien's intervention into one-dimensional representational politics. Julien considers *Looking for Langston* to be a contribution to the redefinition

---

342 See Mercer "Dark and Lovely;" Hall, "New Etnicities."

343 Molly Shinat, "Black History and Desire," "Looking for Langston:" *A Film by Isaac Julien* [DVD Booklet], ed. British Film Institute, London: BFI, 2006, 14–19, 19. Charles I. Nero, "Fixing Ceremonies: An Introduction," *Ceremonies: Prose and Poetry*, Essex Hemphill, San Francisco: Cleis, 1992, xi-xxiii, xii.

of black masculinity. In a conversation with hooks, when talking about his project to produce alternative images of black masculinity that contest racist stereotypes, he argues that his aim is to "portray the kind of construction of black masculinity which is something that's very fragile and vulnerable."[344] *Looking for Langston* does indeed establish a different aesthetics than the hard images of black men represented in the iconography of Black Nationalism (see 3.1.2). In contrast to this attempt to represent a hard black masculinity, Julien's project is to depict black men as "fragile and vulnerable," a project which is acknowledged by Gates:

> Surely one of the salient features of the work is its attitude towards the corporeal, the way in which the Black body is sexualized. Gloria Watkins has noted that Nina Kellgren's camera presents the Black male body as vulnerable, soft, even passive, in marked contrast to its usual representation in American film. It's a way of disrupting a visual order, a hardened convention of representation.[345]

Likewise, hooks states that "contrary to the popular stereotype, in *Looking for Langston* black men appear vulnerable, shed the protective shield of hardened masculinity."[346] However, while thinking along the same lines as Gates and hooks, Diawara has argued that Julien's way of depicting black masculinity runs the risk of stereotyping black gay masculinity. He states that the way black men are pictured in the film tends to establish a new standard of beauty for black gay men rather than disrupting beauty standards altogether. Diawara argues that "it is possible to criticize *Looking for Langston* itself for stereotyping black gayness through its glamorization of their clothes and linking of their culture to nightclubs, song, and dance."[347] However, he also acknowledges that Julien is very much aware of this danger. According to Diawara, Julien uses this aesthetic in spite of the danger that it might be uncritically read as a confirmation of racist stereotypes.

---

344 Isaac Julien, *Diary of a Young Soul Rebel*, London: BFI, 1991, 132.

345 Gates Jr., "Looking for Modernism," 203.

346 hooks, "Seductive Sexualities," 198.

347 Diawara, 222.

Julien takes the risk of replicating the racial stereotype of the thick-lipped negro precisely to reposition the black subject as the desiring subject, not the alienated object of the look – to represent the black man who wants (to look at) another black man.[348]

It is difficult to establish whether the strategy of producing alternative images of black men in the way it is done in *Looking for Langston* is politically effective. The fact that the film was successful at gay and lesbian and at queer film festivals might indicate that the overtly white audience at these festivals uncritically consumed the representations of beautiful black men, ignoring those aspects of the film that are critical of the white gay objectifying gaze (see 4.3.4).

The protagonist of James Earl Hardy's 1994 novel *B-Boy Blues* refers to the film poster of *Looking for Langston*, which is a good example of the way black men are depicted in the film:

And there was – a full-length framed poster for the film *Looking for Langston*. I didn't care for the movie, but the poster is hot – two nude, gorgeous brothers sleeping in a semi-69 position.[349]

This statement indicates that Diawara's concern about the failed disruption of beauty standards is not unfounded. The poster of *Looking for Langston* shows a film still that is fashioned after a 1952 homoerotic photograph by the white homosexual photographer George Platt Lynes. The poster shows a black and white image of two black men intimately lying on a bed, one resting his head in the lap of the other. Platt Lyne's portraits and fashion photographs are well-known for their "expressionist lighting, suggestive posturing, and the use of surreal props."[350] All three of these characteristics, the expressionist lighting, the suggestive posturing, and the surrealism, describe the aesthetics of the cinematography of *Looking for Langston*. In the case of the film poster, the disruption of beauty standards has another dimension. In arranging the photo of the film poster, which is also a film still, Julien has adapted and altered

348 Mercer, "Dark and Lovely," 225.

349 James Earl Hardy, *B-Boy Blues*, Boston: Alyson, 1994, 142.

350 British Film Institute, "Biographies," "*Looking for Langston:*" *A Film by Isaac Julien* [DVD Booklet], ed. British Film Institute. London: BFI, 2006, 37–41, 40.

Platt Lyne's original image that shows an interracial couple by depicting two black men. Platt Lynes's 1952 photograph is called "John Leaphart and Robert 'Buddy' McCarthy."[351] The black man rests his head in the lap of the white man with his eyes closed. The head of the white man is not visible. The arms of the men in the two photos are in exactly the same positions. This alteration is a re-appropriation of Platt Lyne's photo from a black gay perspective. There is a similar alteration in the appropriation of Nugent's "Smoke, Lilies and Jade."

Despite the approaches of critics who have argued that Julien's film reflects processes of identity formation and that it takes an anti-essentialist approach to the categories blackness and gayness, I will now explore to what extent the film supports the 1980s project of confirming a black gay identity rooted in black cultural traditions. In doing so, I will focus on two aspects, the way Julien transforms Nugent's interracial bisexual narrative "Smoke, Lilies and Jade" to a black male homosexual narrative and the way the photographs of Robert Mapplethorpe are negotiated in the film.

4.3.3 Adapting "Smoke, Lilies and Jade"

In Nugent's "Smoke, Lilies and Jade," Alex dreams of meeting a man called Beauty in a field of lilies. This dream is enacted as a scene in *Looking for Langston*. This dream sequence starts right after Alex observes the black man Beauty and the white man Karl sitting at a table. Alex is standing in the speakeasy with his back turned towards the bar. For a short moment, Alex and Beauty hold eye contact, a contact that is immediately cut short by Karl, who violently bangs a bottle of champagne on the table in order to regain Beauty's attention. We hear the two men laughing underneath the soundtrack that consists of the track "Call me a freakish man." Another black man (perhaps one of Karl's former lovers) enters the speakeasy, glances at Karl, who arrogantly rejects him. Alex turns around, takes a sip of champagne and gazes at the smoke of his cigarette. The subsequent dream sequence as a whole is framed by cigarette smoke, which alludes to the title of Nugent's story. In addition to the cigarette smoke at the beginning of Alex's daydream,

---

351 David Leddick, *George Platt Lynes 1907–1955*, Köln: Taschen, 2000, 152.

the scene ends when he imagines lighting a cigarette in the bedroom where he and Beauty are lying on a bed. Throughout the scene, the soundtrack consists of the voice-over narration of a passage from "Smoke, Lilies and Jade," which the images on the screen illustrate. Alex imagines himself walking in a field of grass. There are white flags and a few puddles in which his image is reflected. He meets Beauty, who is standing naked in a field of lilies. Alex touches his body. Like Beauty in Nugent's story, he speaks only one sentence (it is one of the few occasions in which diegetic sound is used): "I'll wait." The second half of the scene takes place in a bedroom. First, we shortly see Karl and Beauty undressing, but Alex imagines himself to take the place of Karl. Beauty and Alex are lying on the bed. The setup of the scene is the same as the image of the film poster described above: Beauty rests his head in Alex's lap.

Diawara and hooks do not connect their interpretations of the scene in the field of lilies to Nugent's "Smoke, Lilies and Jade." Gates states that the story "receives perhaps the most elaborate and effecting tableau vivant in the film."[352] Later in his essay he argues that "the importance of open-textured films such as *Looking for Langston* is in presenting an aesthetics that can embrace ambiguity."[353] In Julien's adaptation of Nugent's story, however, the racial and sexual ambiguity of "Smoke, Lilies and Jade" is changed to a rather unambiguous narrative. Instead of representing Alex's interracial and bisexual relationship to Beauty, a white man, and Melva, a black woman, the film depicts Beauty as a black man and omits Melva altogether. What is more, the excerpts from "Smoke, Lilies and Jade" that are read in the voice-over narration are deliberately altered. In addition to some minor omissions that make the excerpt more easily comprehensible and the fact that every time the name Alex is used in Nugent's text, the voice-over narrator in the scene uses the personal pronoun he, there are two important alterations that change the sense of the text as a whole.

The first major alteration concerns Alex's inner conflict because of his love for two people. The second part of Alex's dream in Nugent's story, in

---

352 Gates Jr., "The Black Man's Burden," 232.

353 Gates Jr., "The Black Man's Burden," 238.

which he encounters the naked Melva, whom he kisses on the lips, is omitted in *Looking for Langston*. His resulting confusion and his inner conflict because of his love for both Beauty and Melva are altered into a conflict in which he has to come to terms with his homosexuality. The second major alteration concerns the omission of the racial markers that can be found in Nugent's story. Whereas in "Smoke, Lilies and Jade," Beauty's naked body is repeatedly described as white, the scene shows a black man standing in the field of Lilies. In the story, Beauty's whiteness is once again emphasized: "Alex trembled... could feel Beauty's body...close against his...hot...tense...white...and soft...soft... soft."[354] The voice-over narrator in the scene simply omits the word "white" and adjusts the narrative to the image of the two black men on the screen. This adaptation shows that, whereas Julien's avant-gardist form and film language may be open and ambiguous, the effect of the appropriation of "Smoke, Lilies and Jade" for the black gay project is unambiguous. It is rooted in the plea for "black men loving black men" (see 2.4), an ideal, the film seems to suggest, that was realized in the Harlem Renaissance.

The soundtrack of the next scene consists of Blackberri's song "Blues for Langston," in which the singer directly addresses Hughes in the first line: "Langston I'm singing this Blues for you."[355] The lyrics of the song embody the project of the film as a whole, as well as of much of black gay culture in the 1980s: a younger generation of black gay men looks at their black homosexual forefathers to reclaim and construct their own history. For this purpose, the title of Hughes's memoirs of the 1930s *I Wonder as I Wander* (1956) is taken up in the first line of the third stanza and altered to directly connect Hughes with the singer who states "I wonder as you wondered."[356] The singer speaks as part of a collective "we" that can be read as black gay men in the 1980s. Like the poets of the Harlem Renaissance, they use language, literature and art to

---

354 Nugent, 38.

355 Edition Salzgeber, ed. *Begleitheft zu Isaac Juliens* "Looking for Langston," Berlin: Salzgeber, 1989, 2. Salzgeber is the German distributor of *Looking for Langston*. As the company did not want to interfere with the film's images by adding German subtitles, they edited this accompanying text that contains the complete texts of the film's soundtrack in order to make sure that the German speaking audience understood the contents.

356 Edition Salzgeber, 5.

"find power in our words."[357] The singer states that he does not want Hughes's name to be forgotten or to be remembered in the wrong way. For this reason black gay men of the 1980s are asking if there is "a life that you've hidden/one you felt was forbidden," and try to reveal "what's true" about a possible hidden side of Hughes's life.[358] Alluding to Hughes's poem "Montage of a Dream Deferred" (1951), the singer asks in the first line of the second stanza, "Whatever happened to the dream deferred?" As a soundtrack to the scene that comes directly after Alex's dream, the line refers to the homoerotic dream about Beauty rather than the dream of racial equality in Hughes's poem.[359]

Both the appropriation of Nugent's story "Smoke, Lilies and Jade" and the subsequent song "Blues for Langston" by Blackberri (whose name evokes Thurman's novel *The Blacker the Berry*) construct a black gay heritage that directly and unambiguously connects Hughes, Nugent and the 1920s with black gay men in the 1980s.

4.3.4 Gay Whiteness

In one scene, the archival footage of the film shows 1920s black artists producing their work, and the voice-over narration states:

> It was a time when the negro was in vogue. White patrons of the Harlem Renaissance wanted their black artists and writers to know and feel the intuitions of the primitive. They didn't want modernism, they wanted black art to keep art and artists in their place. By the end of the twenties, negroes were no longer in vogue, patrons found other uses for their money. Sophisticated New Yorkers turned to Noel Coward and colored artists began to go hungry. History, the smiler with the knife under the cloak.[360]

Like *No Easy Place to Be*, this scene depicts the dependency of many Harlem Renaissance artists on the money of their white patrons. Their dependency on white people and the lack of autonomy on the side of black people are also the

---

357 Edition Salzgeber, 5.

358 Edition Salzgeber, 5.

359 For a special feature on Blackberri including an interview and songs, listen to the November 2001 edition of JD Doyle's monthly radio program Queermusicheritage (JD Doyle, *Queer Music Heritage*, <www.queermusicheritage.us/nov2001.html>, accessed February 27, 2008).

360 Edition Salzgeber, 9.

topic of the following scene, in which the dominance of whiteness within the gay subculture is criticized. In this scene, the white man Karl, played by John Wilson, becomes the focus of attention.

The white man's name Karl is an allusion to the white writer and photographer Carl Van Vechten, author of *Nigger Heaven* (1926). He was what Hurston called a "Negrotarian," a white person who supported the New Negro Movement. Watson characterizes Van Vechten as "a tall, ungainly, homosexual dandy"[361] and states that his "support for the New Negro Movement mixed literary appreciation, low-life voyeurism, race consciousness, sexual attraction, and a sensitive nose for fashion."[362]

Drawing on Van Vechten, Mapplethorpe, and Platt Lynes, *Looking for Langston* establishes the exploitative ways in which black culture is represented in works by three white homosexual men. This is one framework for reading the way the film depicts gay whiteness. In the scene I will now refer to, gay whiteness is linked to the way racist stereotypes of black men are taken up in the white gay sub-culture. It explicitly alludes to discussions about the way the white gay photographer Robert Mapplethorpe depicts black men. Mapplethorpe is known for photographic representations of gay sadomasochistic sexual practices and images of black men that date from the mid-1980s. He died in 1989 from AIDS complications. In their essay "True Confessions," Julien and Mercer criticize these photographs for confirming racist stereotypes of black masculinity rooted in colonial fantasy. Hemphill's attitude, put forward in the essay "Does your Mama know about me," is very much in accordance with Julien and Mercer's essay. He states that "it is virtually impossible while viewing Mapplethorpe's photos of Black Males to avoid confronting issues of exploitation and objectification," and argues that Mapplethorpe's work "artistically perpetuates racial stereotypes constructed around sexuality and desire."[363] He particularly criticizes the fact that Mapplethorpe depicts black bodies and parts of black bodies without their heads.

---

361 Watson, 98.

362 Watson, 98.

363 Essex Hemphill, "Does Your Mama Know About Me," *Ceremonies: Prose and Poetry*, San Francisco: Cleis, 1992, 41–47, 43.

Mapplethorpe's eye pays special attention to the penis at the expense of showing us the subject's face, and thus, a whole person. The penis becomes the identity of the black male, which is the classic racist stereotype recreated and presented as Art in the context of a gay vision.[364]

Mercer modifies the argument he and Julien put forward in "True Confessions" in a later essay because of "the homophobic right-wing attacks on Mapplethorpe."[365] One could read the Mapplethorpe-scene from *Looking for Langston* as an illustration of the arguments from Hemphill's and Julien and Mercer's essays. The facts that Julien is the director and that the poem is written and performed by Hemphill support such a reading.

Mapplethorpe's photographs from his *Black Book* are included in the film in a special way. They are projected on white canvases in a dark room. All of these photos show the naked bodies of black men who are sometimes depicted without their heads. The scene visualizes blackness and whiteness as opposites. Whereas the naked black men are represented as passive objects, the white man Karl, dressed in white underwear, actively walks through the room touching the canvases. The soundtrack of this scene consists of Essex Hemphill reading his poem "If His Name Were Mandingo," which addresses some racist stereotypes white gay men have when they encounter black (gay) men.

> You don't notice many things about him. He doesn't always wear a red ski cap, eat fried chicken, fuck like a jungle. He doesn't always live with his mother, or off the street. Or off some bitch as you assume.[366]

In using the personal pronoun "you", the voice of the black gay poet and activist Hemphill directly addresses the white gay man on the screen. As the poem itself is not directed to one particular white man, I suggest that it is also directed at those white viewers who identify as gay. Karl is negatively depicted as a dinge queen (see 2.4). His sexual desire for black men is depicted

---

364 Hemphill, "Does Your Mama," 42–43.

365 Muñoz, "Photographs of Mourning," 70. For an essay consisting of two parts that reveal Mercer's turn in thinking about Mapplethorpe's work, see Kobena Mercer, "Reading Racial Fetishism: The Photographs of Robert Mapplethorpe," *Welcome to the Jungle: New Positions in Black Cultural Studies*, New York: Routledge, 1994, 171–220.

366 Essex Hemphill, "If His Name Were Mandingo," *Ceremonies: Prose and Poetry*, San Francisco: Cleis, 1992, 156.

as objectifying and abusive, because he is solely interested in stereotypical images of black male bodies. In addition, Hemphill's poem suggests that Karl holds racist beliefs about black men.

With regard to white-dominated cultural productions, black critics have repeatedly criticized the representational practice of including only one black person, who then bears the burden of representing black people in general. Such a situation is reversed in *Looking for Langston*; there is only one elaborated white gay character who stands for all white gay men. Muñoz maintains that the way gay whiteness is represented in *Looking for Langston* might have a liberating effect on black gay viewers. Julien's film shows that Mapplethorpe's *Black Book* contains racist images whereas at the same time it opens up a new possibility for black gay men to see these images. In addition to depicting the images of *Black Book*, the scene shows how these images are viewed and touched by a white gay man. One could argue with Muñoz that, by including the white gay gaze, Julien takes the images from *Black Book* out of the hands of white gay men and enables black gay men to "partially recycle and hold on to these representations."[367] While pointing at the exploitative character of Mapplethorpe's photographic practice, Muñoz reads the way the images of Mapplethorpe are represented in the film as an example of the strategy of disidentification (see 3.4) and argues that through the depiction of the racist white gay gaze, black (gay) viewers are enabled to disidentify with the images on the screen.[368] Thus, Julien's filmic commentary on Mapplethorpe's photographs has at least two effects. It is critical of white gay identity positions, whereas at the same time, it is empowering for black gay viewers.

Julien's alteration of Platt Lynes's photograph, his implicit critique of Van Vechten, his more direct critique of Mapplethorpe and the alteration of Nugent's interracial and bisexual narrative to a black gay narrative are best understood if his affiliations with more afrocentric black gay activists like Hemphill are considered. However, whereas the re-appropriation of the works of the white artists Platt Lynes, Van Vechten, and Mapplethorpe can be read as acts

---

367 Muñoz, "Photographs of Mourning," 72.

368 Muñoz, "Photographs of Mourning," 72.

of resistance to the ways in which these white homosexual artists have depicted the black male body, the appropriation of Nugent's narrative has to be seen in context of the 1980s strategy of constructing a black gay cultural heritage.[369]

4.4 Samuel R. Delany: "Atlantis: Model 1924" (1995)

I have argued that, in depicting the homosexual dimensions of the Harlem Renaissance and in constructing Nugent as a black gay forefather, Corbin refers to the sexually dissident writers of the Harlem Renaissance in order to gain recognition and acceptance within the larger black community. He pursues this didactic aim by choosing the genre of the historical novel (see 4.2). On a formal level, Julien's approach is more experimental. He uses the style of the avant-garde cinema, but, in his adaptation of "Smoke, Lilies and Jade," he transforms the transgressive dimensions of Nugent's story to an unambiguous black gay narrative (see 4.3.3). Delany's strategy is different from both Corbin's and Julien's. With his short novel "Atlantis: Model 1924," he aims neither at the black community's recognition of black gayness nor at the self-empowerment of black gay men. In fact, "Atlantis: Model 1924" is not even a black gay narrative.

The short novel is the first of three texts collected in the volume *Atlantis: Three Tales*, which was published by Wesleyan UP in 1995. The fact that a number of Delany's more recent writings are published by university presses indicates a growing academic interest in his writings. In addition to the three fictional texts contained in *Atlantis*, a new edition of his autobiographical memoir *The Motion of Light in Water* was published by Minnesota UP. Most of Delany's more recent non-fictional writings are collected in three volumes published by Wesleyan UP, and the two essays that comprise *Times Square Red, Times Square Blue* about the gentrification of Times Square were published by New York UP.

---

369 In his later films, for example *Young Soul Rebels* (1991) and *The Attendant* (1993), Julien chooses a representational strategy that depicts interracial (gay) sexuality as transgressive with the potential to subvert normative constructions of desire and sexuality.

These editions by university presses, the inclusion of parts of "Atlantis: Model 1924" in *The Norton Anthology of African American Literature*, as well as Delany's position as a professor of Comparative Literature, contribute to the fact that there is a growing number of studies concentrating on his later writings. These texts are largely concerned with academic debates surrounding issues of literary criticism, race, sexuality, and class in a more direct way than his earlier Science Fiction texts. Regarding these professional affiliations with the academy, one might argue that his recent fictional texts are written as commentaries on debates within academic disciplines such as queer studies or African American studies rather than as books directed at the empowerment of a political collective. This also explains the exceptional approach his fictional texts take towards issues surrounding black gay masculinity.

In contrast to *No Easy Place to Be* and *Looking for Langston*, the categories race and sexuality in "Atlantis: Model 1924" are represented as fluid rather than fixed. Instead of constructing a myth of origin of black gayness by referring back to the 1920s, the novel questions the reality of origins altogether. This goal is achieved on the level of content as well as on a formal level, by the experimental structure of the text.

Whereas Corbin and Julien change the sexual ambiguity represented in "Smoke, Lilies and Jade" in favor of clear-cut sexual identities, Delany's text is similar to Nugent's. His experimental style alludes to modernist forms. New York is represented as an urban space with manifold possibilities. Ross Posnock demonstrates that the idea of an anti-essentialist approach towards identities is also taken up on a formal level in the narrative. He characterizes the aesthetics of the novel as a collage and states that in collage "all is borrowed and reworked, originality is never primary, but only derived."[370] Owing to the experimental aesthetics of collage and the constant negotiation of questions of identity, Delany's text can be characterized as historiographic metafiction.[371] Rather than creating Harlem as a microcosm and the characters as types, Delany draws

---

370 Posnock, 293.

371 Hutcheon. Löbbermann reads "Atlantis: Model 1924" as historiographic metafiction, too (Dorothea Löbbermann, *Memories of Harlem: Literarische (Re)Konstruktionen eines Mythos der Zwanziger Jahre*, Frankfurt am Main: Campus, 2002, 22).

on disparate cultural sources and connects the narrative to himself and his position as the author. The connection between "Atlantis" and Delany becomes clear when he refers to a later stage in Sam's biography as well as to his own persona:

> After eighteen years, when, in his second marriage, he would have his first son, also named Sam, he finally forgot the last fragments of what had happened on the bridge in between – the young man with his ravings, the rower in the boat below.[372]

Sam's first son, also named Sam, is Delany himself. Like Julien, who plays the dead Langston Hughes in the coffin, the inclusion of the persona of the author in this fictional text can be read as an ironic comment on Barthes's dictum of the death of the author. Contrary to the death of the author, the above quotation refers to the birth of the author, whose aesthetics is influenced by the divergent origins represented in "Atlantis: Model 1924."

On the level of contents, the text refers to two aesthetic traditions, Modernism embodied by the poet Harold Hart, a fictional character based on Hart Crane, and the Harlem Renaissance represented by the family of Sam, the protagonist of the novel. In 1923, the seventeen-year-old black protagonist Sam moves from Raleigh, North Carolina to New York City in order to stay with his older siblings. As part of the great migration, all have left North Carolina for New York. The connection between the author Samuel R. Delany and the 1920s is directly established by the characters based on the writer's biological family.[373] This generation of the Delany family can be regarded as representative of what W.E.B. DuBois labeled the talented tenth because they received a higher education and pursued successful careers.

I will now analyze the ways in which Delany's narrative differs from

---

372 Samuel R. Delany, "Atlantis: Model 1924," *Atlantis: Three Tales*, Middletown, CT: Wesleyan UP, 1995, 1–121, 121.

373 Sam is based on Samuel Ray Delany Sr., the author's father, who came to New York in 1923. Sam's older siblings Lucius, Hubert, Elsie, and Corey are also based on relatives of Delany. Hubert is based on Hubert T. Delany, the writer's uncle who later became an NAACP activist, and the characters of Elsie and Corey are based on Sarah (Sadie) and Elisabeth (Bessie) Delany, whose memoir is published under the title *Having Our Say: The Delany Sisters' First 100 Years* (Sarah Louise Delany, Annie Elizabeth Delany, and Amy Hill Hearth, *Having Our Say: The Delany Sistsers' First 100 Years*, New York: Kodansha International, 1993).

the 1980s project of constructing a myth of origin of black gayness rooted in the literature and art of the Harlem Renaissance. Following Löbbermann and Posnock, I will show in what respects this strategy is subverted and treated ironically in "Atlantis: Model 1924," and I will focus on the alternatives the narrative offers for questions of origins and identities, specifically the (post-)modernist idea of multiple origins that the narrative reflects on a formal level as well as on the level of content.

4.4.1 Meta-Signifying

At the end of Sam's first evening in New York, Sam walks with his brother Hubert and Hubert's girlfriend Clarice to Harlem's Mount Morris and finally sees the Manhattan skyscrapers in the distance.[374] I suggest that the conversation which evolves among them can be read as an ironic signification on African traditions and as a comment on Henry Louis Gates's theory of Signifying itself (see 3.5). During their conversation, Clarice tells Sam that he should walk on top of the Brooklyn Bridge if he wants to see the skyscrapers. She sneezes three times, and the noise she makes is spelled: "*Eshu!*" The first time, the reader does not understand the meaning of the word. As it is printed with an initial capital letter, one might rather think of a name than the word for a sound: "'Now what Sam – *Eshu!*' Clarice pulled her coat around her – 'Sam should do, if he wants to see skyscrapers, is take a walk across the Brooklyn Bridge.'"[375] It is only when Clarice sneezes for the second time that the reader learns that "*Eshu!*" stands for the sound of the sneeze. The word "Eshu" evokes an additional dimension of meaning. Lawrence W. Levine has shown that "Eshu" is the name of a divine Yoruban trickster figure.[376] Gates has based his theory of Signifying on different variations of this figure to which he refers with the name "Esu-Elegbara," or "Esu." According to Gates, "these variations on Esu-Elegbara speak eloquently of an unbroken arc of metaphysical presupposition and a pattern of figuration shared through time

---

374 Delany, "Atlantis," 26–28.

375 Delany, "Atlantis," 27.

376 Levine, 103.

and space among certain black cultures in West Africa, South America, the Carribean, and the United States."[377] Gates lists the qualities of the figures of Esu that different scholars have found, and this list reads like a list of words that, in addition to characterizing Sam's walk on top of the Brooklyn Bridge to which I will refer below, relates to the narrative as a whole. Gates states that "a partial list of these qualities might include individuality, satire, parody, irony, magic, indeterminacy, open-endedness, ambiguity, sexuality, chance, uncertainty, disruption and reconciliation, betrayal and loyalty, closure and disclosure, enceasement and rupture."[378] During their conversation, Clarice sneezes each time she mentions the Brooklyn Bridge. Her sneeze implicitly connects the bridge with the dimensions of meaning of Gates's list. As the whole passage closes with Clarice's statement "'Over the bridge – *Eshu!* That's what I'd want to do,'"[379] the word "Eshu" and its connection to the bridge is once more emphasized. In Delany's narrative the word "Eshu" has no meaning whatsoever. It is an onomatopoetic word denoting the sound of Clarice's sneeze. The repeated use of a word that is central for what is arguably the most influential theory of African American literary criticism, but devoid of any meaning, can be read as an ironic comment on Gates's theory of Signifying.

On the one hand, this passage evokes the black literary tradition and thereby connects "Atlantis" to this tradition, on the other hand, it ironically questions the validity of a specific African tradition because here, the word "Eshu" does not refer to the Yoruban trickster figure, it solely refers to the sound of the sneeze. However, the word evokes Gates's theory and this unfixed meaning of the word opens the text for a deconstructive reading. Consequently, this passage connects the critical practice of deconstruction with African American literary criticism. This passage also reflects Delany's own position as an African American writer with strong poststructuralist leanings. This way of referring to black literary theory is itself humorous and ironic, and it can be analyzed in terms of parody. As Gates's theory itself has become an important

---

377 Gates Jr., *Signifying Monkey*, 6.

378 Gates Jr., *Signifying Monkey*, 6.

379 Delany, "Atlantis," 28.

part of the black tradition, one could read Delany's strategy as a signification on Gates's theory itself and characterize it as an ironic strategy of meta-signifying. It is a humorous reaction to the project of formulating a distinct African American literary theory which acknowledges Gates's project and at the same time questions the validity and use of a distinct African American literary theory.

4.4.2 Inventing Origins

There is a similarity between Delany's earlier Science Fiction writings and "Atlantis: Model 1924," even though the genre of Science Fiction refers to the future and "Atlantis: Model 1924" refers to the past. In both cases, a utopian aspect is related to the search for cultural roots. "Space" is a recurrent metaphor within afrofuturist literature, art, and music, most notably in the music and performances of the avant-garde jazz musician Sun Ra.[380] The afrofuturist claim to be an alien and to originate in space signifies on the African American motif of searching for one's roots. However, rather than going back to Africa, afrofuturists like Sun Ra combine the roots-motif with a utopian aspect. Similar to the metaphor of Space and Science Fiction, Atlantis is a metaphor combining the search for roots with a utopian aspect.

In his essay "Verloren unter Sternen: Das Mothership und andere Altenativen zur Erde und ihren Territorialien," cultural studies theorist Diedrich Diedrichsen looks at the myth of the water babies that can be found in slave narratives. According to this myth, pregnant slaves who were thrown overboard during the middle passage bear their children under water. Their babies are said to be the founders of a new under-water-culture. Diedrichsen states that the new Atlantis of the water babies is an alternative place combining African roots with the struggle for black liberation.[381] This connection of the middle passage with the image of Atlantis also evokes Gilroy's concept of the Black Atlantic as a postmodern paradigm of black diaspora culture.

---

380 One of Sun Ra's numerous recordings is called "Atlantis" (Sun Ra and his Astro-Infinity Arkestra, *Atlantis*, New York: Saturn (ESR 507 Intergalactic Series II) LP, 1969).

381 Diedrich Diedrichsen, "Verloren Unter Sternen: Das Mothership und Andere Alternativen zur Erde und Ihren Territorialien," *Loving the Alien: Science Fiction, Diaspora, Multikultur*, ed, Diedrich Diedrichsen, Berlin: ID Verlag, 1998, 105–133, 109.

Similar to Julien whose aesthetic approach is based on the dynamic model of the Black Atlantic paradigm, Delany rejects the search for cultural roots as a basis for identity and identity politics. Instead, the Atlantic Ocean evokes the routes that black subjects took and uses them as a basis for a dynamic concept of blackness. Additionally, in referring to space and the under-water culture of Atlantis, Delany's approach is not limited to the transgression of national borders, but, by going beyond the confinements of the earth, it does not even have to position itself solely in relation to concepts of nation and nationality.

The middle passage is not only evoked in the motif of Atlantis. Next to Crane's *The Bridge*, Robert Hayden's epic poem "Middle Passage" (1946) is the second important intertext Delany chooses for his narrative. Four quotations from "Middle Passage" serve as epigraphs to the chapters of "Atlantis: Model 1924." Löbbermann explicates the connections between these epigraphs and the contents of the narrative. Sam's arrival in Harlem is introduced with the epigraph "Voyage through death/ to life upon these shores."[382] The drowning man underneath the bridge is connected with those African slaves who drowned during the middle passage: "lost three this morning leapt with crazy laughter/ to the waiting sharks, sang as they went under."[383] The dreamlike image of Manhattan Sam sees from the Brooklyn Bridge is mirrored in Hayden's "fata morgana's lucent melting shore,"[384] and the thought of the Brooklyn Bridge as a loom exemplifying the process of history, a motif Delany takes up from Crane's *The Bridge* is also introduced in the epigraph from Hayden's poem, "Shuttles in the rocking loom of history, the dark ships move, the dark ships move."[385] [386]

Löbbermann analyzes the ways in which the image of Atlantis is evoked in the recurrent images referring to water and the description of subterranean places.[387] By using these images and emphasizing subterranean places such

---

382 Delany, "Atlantis," 3.

383 Delany, "Atlantis," 57.

384 Delany, "Atlantis," 75.

385 Delany, "Atlantis," 101.

386 Löbbermann, *Memories of Harlem*, 57–58.

387 Löbbermann, *Memories of Harlem*, 48–53.

as Cathay, a shop selling magic tricks located in a subway station,[388] Delany transfers the myth of Atlantis to 1920s New York. The references to Atlantis do not merely evoke the utopian dimension of Space and Atlantis in African American culture. As the myth of Atlantis goes back to ancient Greek culture deriving from Plato's dialogues "Timaios" and "Critias" (about 360 BCE), it exemplifies the ancient ideal of human civilization rooted in European high culture. Delany makes the connection to Plato explicit by using an excerpt from "Critias" as an epigraph to the second part of "Atlantis: Model 1924."[389] These different dimensions of the meaning of Atlantis exemplify Delany's overall strategy of referring to cultural sources that include African American culture as well as European and European-American cultural traditions.

The relationship of the novel to a modernist aesthetics is already established by its title as well as by the painting on the cover of the book. The title refers to the white modernist poet Hart Crane, author of the long poem *The Bridge* about the Brooklyn Bridge, the last part of which is called "Atlantis."[390] Jeffrey Allen Tucker points out that the title of the novel "may be a variation of the article by Earnest Boyd published in the *American Mercury* that mentions Crane, entitled 'Aesthete: Model 1924.'"[391] The book cover, too, refers to modernist aesthetic traditions as well as to the Brooklyn Bridge. It depicts an artwork by Joseph Stella called "The Voice of the city of New York interpreted, 1920–22: The White Way, I." Stella's work is an abstract representation of the Brooklyn Bridge. It is one panel of a work consisting of five panels depicting skyscrapers and bridges. The work as a whole is reminiscent of a religious altarpiece. There is indeed a historical relation between Crane's and Stella's works: The first 1930 edition of Crane's *The Bridge* was illustrated with works by Stella.[392]

---

388 The reference to Cathay evokes Christopher Columbus's search for the riches of China that had been described by Marco Polo as well as Crane's poem *The Bridge*.

389 Delany, "Atlantis," 19.

390 In addition to "Atlantis: Model 1924," Delany wrote an essay on Hart Crane in which he explicates the references to Crane's *The Bridge* (Delany "Atlantis Rose").

391 Jeffrey A. Tucker, *A Sense of Wonder: Samuel R. Delany, Race, Identity, and Difference*, Middletown, CT: Wesleyan UP, 2004, 227.

392 Klaus Reichert, "Zu Hart Cranes The Bridge," *Die Brücke/The Bridge*, ed. Hart Crane and Ute Eisinger, Salzburg: Jung und Jung, 2004, 161–167, 167.

The typeset of the pages supports the thesis that the form of the novel alludes to modernism: many of the pages are set in two parallel columns that are separated by a gap. The two separate columns disrupt the linearity of the narrative. They are separated by a gap in the middle of the page, and the ways the contents of these columns interrelate has to be constructed by the reader. Posnock states that this stylistic device is a means "to render materially the experience of simultaneity."[393] In creating simultaneity between disparate elements, the typesetting of Delany's novel is similar to the space of simultaneity that Julien creates in his experimental film narrative, which combines three historical epochs in a single space (see 4.3.1).

I will refer to one example that is illustrative of the way the different columns relate to one another. When Sam climbs the stairs to the top of the bridge, there is a group of white boys, one of whom is "copper-haired,"[394] walking down the stairs. This group of boys is a memory trigger for Sam, who remembers his black friends from home, the dark-skinned Lewy and the red-haired John. These memories are described in the columns on the right side of the page. Sam remembers when Lewy – with the help of Sam's father – constructed a clock-dial

> drawn on a piece of parchment, inked in reds and blacks and greens and suggesting some medieval illuminated compass, now marked with a time scale of three fourteen-minute intervals, each divided in two, then further divided in three, with the major divisions indicated by signs from the zodiac and the smaller ones notated in Hebrew letters, representing a special, ancient, mystic time scale, out of Africa from before the dawn of the West – which Lewy had just made up.[395]

Lewy's invented clock is connected to Sam's repeated recognition of different clocks in New York. Lewy's clock suggests and illustrates that cultural origins are always constructions. Lewy is quite aware of the implications connected with his project of inventing a mystic time scale. Sam's father tells him that white boys do not do things like that. The reader can assume that, as the white

---

393 Posnock, 262. On the topic of spatiality in Delany's writings, see Jürgen Joachimsthaler "'the spaces between the columns'. Die Text-Räume und Raum-Texte des Samuel R. Delany," *Zeitschrift für Anglistik und Amerikanistik* 55 (2007): 395–416.

394 Delany, "Atlantis," 62.

395 Delany, "Atlantis," 63–64.

boys belong to the dominant culture, they do not feel the need to refer to a separate tradition. However, with his time scale Lewy does not aim at historical accuracy or at cultural purity. On the contrary, he defends his use of Hebrew letters against John's criticism that he should have used Arab or Egyptian letters. Lewy's obvious invention of origins has a direct effect on Sam. It lessens his desire to be as dark-skinned as his father and Lewy rather than light-skinned and sometimes mistaken for white.[396]

The column on the left side of the page is a letter one of the editors of the anthology *The Poetry of the Negro* wrote to a co-editor, supposedly during the 1960s. Posnock deduces from the title of the anthology that the left column consists of "excerpts (either actual or fictive) of Langston Hughes and Arna Bontemps regarding their 1949 anthology."[397] However, as the writer of the letter mentions incidents from the late 1950s and early 1960s, such as Braithwaite's death in 1962, Posnock's suggestion does not seem correct. Tucker also states that the column features the exchange of letters between Bontemps and Hughes, and he suggests that the letters were written "during their editing of a second edition of *The Poetry of the Negro*."[398] However, as the writer discusses which authors they should include in the anthology, it is doubtful that they are simply editing a second edition. In the column it becomes clear that the writer of the letter is influenced by the black studies discourse of the 1960s.

Like the column on the right, this column makes it clear that race and origin are inventions. The editors are planning to include Toomer's work in the anthology even though he did not want to be read solely as a black writer. There are two writers whom the editors believe are not African American writers, but they are planning to include the writings of these authors in the anthology anyway:

> By the way, I also sponsored Frank Lima for his Opportunity. We should let him pass for colored if he wishes. I thought he was Puerto Rican at the time. Nobody would object to a Mexican identifying as a Negro. Not even a black muslim or a black panther. And I will not object to a couple or so poems by

396 Delany, "Atlantis," 64.

397 Posnock, 291.

398 Tucker, 222.

Mason Jordan Mason so long as we make it plain in the biographical note that at least we are not sure. He certainly writes in Negro, as Karl Shapiro says of Tolson. And he's good.[399]

The inclusion of this letter can be read as an ironic comment on approaches that divide literature according to the identities of their writers. The column on the right says that white boys do not invent clocks with mystic and ancient time scales. The same is true for literary anthologies. White editors do not publish anthologies under the label of the whiteness of their contributors (even if there are many anthologies that solely feature white writers). The black studies movement of the 1960s was important because it focused on texts that were in danger of being forgotten in the collective cultural memory, and a number of texts were reprinted because of the interest fuelled by the appearance of African American studies departments. But the critique formulated in this column and in the novel as a whole is clear. One should be aware of the consequences of the division of literature on the grounds of categories that are constructed and arbitrary. The fact that the writer of the letter suggests letting certain writers "pass for colored" signifies on the motif of the tragic mulatto, which Corbin reinforces in his narrative. By extending this critique to the 1980s category "black gay writer," one can question the effectiveness of grounding one's politics and aesthetics on categories that are constructed and arbitrary. In the light of this critique, it is ironic that "Atlantis: Model 1924" is the first text of Delany's oeuvre to be included in the *Norton Anthology of African American Literature*.

The openness and the constructed character of the categories of race and sexuality are also reflected on the level of content. The consequences of different concepts of race are directly addressed in a remembered conversation between the protagonist Sam and his friends John and Lewy that took place in Raleigh, where Sam grew up. Even though the three boys are black, their differences are emphasized: Lewy is dark-skinned, Sam very light-skinned, and John has red hair. In the course of the conversation, Lewy, who sometimes likes to playfully take on other identities like "Batouta the Moor,"[400] directly

---

399 Delany, "Atlantis," 64.
400 Delany, "Atlantis," 26.

addresses the question of origins and states that he has multiple origins rather than only one. I will look at Lewy's plea for multiple origins in some detail, because it is informative of the aesthetics of the text as a whole as well as of the way Delany approaches questions of origins and identities.

Working on his first job, one of Sam's co-workers is also called Louis "who spelled his name completely differently from Lewy down home."[401] In realizing that the two phonetically identical names are spelled differently – in realizing the different etymological origins – Sam anticipates his later memory of Lewy's plea that he is free to choose his origins. Lying on his bed, Sam recalls an episode from his time in Raleigh, a walk he took with his friends. He remembers Lewy saying:

> 'Now me – I'm going to originate everywhere...from now on. I've made up my mind to it.' [...]'From now on, I come from all times before me – and all my origins will feed me. Some in Africa I get through my daddy. And my momma. And my stepdaddy. Some in Europe I get through the library: Greece and Rome, China and India – I suck my origins through my feet from the paths beneath them that tie me to the land, from my hands opened high in celebration of the air, from my eyes lifted among the stars –' [...] '– and I'll go on originating, all through my life, too,' Lewy said. 'Every time I read a new book, every time I hear something new about history, every time I make a new friend, see a new color in the oil slicked over a puddle in the mud, a new origin joins me to make me what I am to be – what I'm always becoming. The whole of my life is origin – nowhere and everywhere. You just watch me now!'[402]

In this quotation, the afrofuturist idea of utopian roots is emphasized once again by Lewy's use of the grammatical construction "I am going to originate." His use of the future tense in connection with cultural origins connects utopia with the search for cultural roots. The origins Lewy names are manifold, and he does not put them in any hierarchical order. At first, he names his African origins, which he gets through his parents. However, these origins are not conceptualized biologically, because Lewy emphasizes that the role of his stepfather for his African origins is as important as that of his biological parents.

401 Delany, "Atlantis," 28.
402 Delany, "Atlantis," 114–115.

The role of literature and history as origins for his sense of self is equally important, and these cultural origins are not limited to African American culture, for he particularly names Greece and Rome, China and India: Lewy claims both white European and Eastern traditions as his own. He counts the earth he lives on as well as space among his origins. In short, Lewy refuses to reduce his origins to the realm of biology or to African American culture and history. Lewy's recurring positive references to Jewish culture and history – "And I'll be the Ancient Rabbi who understands the Cabala's secrets and can speak them backwards" – support his plea for multiple origins, and they stand in opposition to John's and Sam's anti-Semitic sentiments. Throughout the novel, Sam, Lewy, and John read and swap adventure magazines that feature Eastern, Egyptian[403] and Arabian stories.[404]

Lewy's statement that he originates everywhere is reminiscent of Paul Arbian, the Bruce Nugent-character of Thurman's *Infants of the Spring* (see 4.1.3). Like Lewy, Arbian also insists on his manifold origins. Ordered by Dr. Parks, a character based on Alain Locke, to go back to a "pagan heritage for inspiration and the old masters for form,"[405] Arbian replies: "What about the rest?" [...] "My German, English, and Indian ancestors [...]. How can I go back to African ancestors when their blood is so diluted and their country and times

---

403 In the beginning of the short novel, there is already an allusion to Egypt: While Sam travels from Raleigh to New York, he repeatedly recognizes the train's "tut-tut-tut-tut-tut," which reminds him of a song (Delany, "Atlantis," 4). It is only later that the reader learns that this song is "'In Old King Tutankhamen's Day' with its infectious refrain 'Old King Tut-tut-tuttut-tut-tut-tut...'" (Delany, "Atlantis," 26). This cultural reference to Egypt is taken from its context and onomatopoetically refers to something completely different, the sound of the train.

404 One of these stories is entitled "Imprisoned with the Pharaohs" (Delany, "Atlantis," 120). At the end of the narrative, Sam stops reading these stories because his English teacher in night school tells him that he should only read "the finest and greatest of what had been written in English literature" (Delany, "Atlantis," 120). The opposition of great English literature and adventure magazines can be read as an ironic comment on Delany's own profession as a science-fiction writer. On Delany's thoughts concerning the relation between literature and what he calls the paraliterary genres, see Samuel R. Delany, "The Paradoxa Interview: Inside and Outside the Canon," *Shorter Views: Queer Thoughts and the Politics of the Paraliterary*, Hanover, NH: Wesleyan UP, 1999, 186–217. See also Stephanie A. Smith, "A Most Ambiguous Citizen: Samuel R. 'Chip' Delany," *American Literary History* 19 (2007): 557–570.

405 Thurman, 237.

so far away? I have no conscious affinity for them at all."[406] Regarding Arbian's statement, Elisa F. Glick argues that "Paul does not seek to divorce himself from his racial identity, but rather to recognize its complexity, which includes German, English, and Indian, as well as African ancestors, and to locate his own cultural production in the broader context of American cultural nationalism."[407] In this respect, Lewy's position is similar to that of Arbian. Both of them employ a strategy of disidentification with the dominant discourse, a discourse that works to place their identities within the realm of African American culture.

The combination of different and disparate origins parodies the mono-cultural approach of those Black Nationalists who regard the embrace of their African roots as the only way to salvation (see 5.1.3). It evokes debates within the African American community that were already prominent during the Harlem Renaissance, particularly Marcus Garvey's political project of organizing the return to Africa for African Americans in order to enable them reconnect with their cultural roots. The parodistic approach is reminiscent of Ishmael Reed's Neo-HooDooist aesthetics.[408] Reed also combines elements from different cultural realms that include but are not limited to African traditions.

Rather than distancing themselves from African American traditions, Arbian (in "Smoke") and Lewy (in "Atlantis") embrace these traditions and then extend their influences to other cultural realms that are often believed to be separate from African American culture. Their strategy of claiming their white European origins is a way of resistance against the dominant ideology which interpellates black people by connecting their identities to specific black traditions. Against the background of Lewy's statement, the meaning of the manifold references of Delany's narrative becomes clear. In including his father and his extended family in the narrative, Delany refers to his own biological origins. However, these origins are no more important than the numerous other influences that include but are not limited to African American cultural traditions, among them Hart Crane, Joseph Hayden, Jean Toomer, Oscar Wilde, and Paul Robeson.

---

406 Thurman, 237.

407 Glick, 424.

408 Pierre-Damian Mvuyekure, "American Neo-HooDooism," *The Cambridge Companion to the African American Novel*, ed. Maryemma Graham, Cambridge, UK: Cambridge UP, 2004. 203–220.

Lewy, Sam and John themselves discuss the political dimensions of Lewy's statement:

> 'How you gonna stay a nigger,' John asked, 'if you come from so many places?' 'Look,' Lewy said. 'Knowing all I really come from, that won't stop anybody calling me a black bastard,' which startled Sam. (...) 'That don't stop anybody from calling you a nigger, calling Sam a black boy, calling me colored, calling you a redheaded African, calling Sam a Negro, calling me black. And I guess we're what we're called, no matter where we're from. That's what calling means – that's all. It isn't no more important than that.' [409]

Lewy explicitly points out the societal process by which individuals are interpellated as subjects (see 3.3). Subject formations and the social construction of identities are revealed to be ideological processes grounded in the use of language. Lewy explains that the process of interpellation and subject formation has nothing to do with one's biological family or some imagined essence of one's identity by stating that "we're what we called, no matter where we're from." Lewy, Sam, and John share the experience of being interpellated in a pejorative and racist way. The knowledge of the way interpellation functions does not lead Lewy to embrace his African roots as a strategic basis of resistance. On the contrary, he refers to other origins, such as white European traditions, and thus employs a strategy of appropriation to resist being interpellated in a shameful way. This strategy of appropriation can also be characterized as a disidentificatory practice of resistance (see 3.4). Working from within the hegemonic discourse, Lewy's appropriation of origins that are believed to be the origins of white America is a way to transform the meaning of what American origins are. Lewy's knowledge of the very real material consequences of the identity category "race" does not stop him from claiming his multiple origins. On the contrary, this bastardization of origins is a strategy of resistance against racism. Rather than agreeing with Lewy that being called by racist insults is unimportant, Sam replies that "it's pretty important, what they call you, when it means where you got to live, got to go to school, even what you got to work at.' [410]

---

409 Delany, "Atlantis," 115–116.
410 Delany, "Atlantis," 116.

Both Posnock and Tucker analyze Lewy's plea for his multiple origins, and they come to different conclusions. Tucker takes Lewy's claim as an example of strategic identity politics and as an example of an emphasis on African American cultural traditions that he tries to locate in all of Delany's writings. He argues that Lewy's statement shows that he is "rooted in his blackness in a manner that does not amount to a fixing as much as it is a base to return to after drawing sustenance from other cultural locales."[411] The idea of "a base to return to" suggests that his blackness is more important than the other origins Lewy mentions, and it also supports the concept of a strategic essentialism which suggests that, despite the constructed character of all identities, it might be useful to strategically refer to one's black identity as if it had an essence in order to have a firm standpoint from where to speak. Posnock, however, states that Lewy's statement is directed against "the rhetoric and ideology of authenticity."[412] He argues that "by dispersing origin everywhere, Lewy desacralizes it, or, more precisely, bastardizes it. Thus, he deprives the logic of identity of metaphysical grounding and mitigates its capacity to forment violence."[413] Rather than arguing in favor of strategic essentialism, Posnock conceptualizes identity in terms of hybridity.

Tucker, however, does not want to give up the idea of strategic identities altogether and suggests a differentiation between the cultural and social dimensions of identity categories. He supports the project of transcending the idea of specific African American origins on a cultural level whereas he emphasizes the importance blackness has on a social level. This separation of a cultural and a social realm when it comes to discussions around identities is somewhat arbitrary because it seems to me that both realms are inextricably linked. Racism also occurs on a cultural level, and the claiming of different cultural traditions can in fact be an act of resistance on a social level.

In "Atlantis," there is an illustrative example of the way the cultural and the social spheres affect each other. Meeting Hart on top of the Brooklyn Bridge,

---

411 Tucker, 222.

412 Posnock, 293.

413 Posnock, 293.

Sam tells him about a school-performance of Oscar Wilde's *The Importance of Being Earnest* at the traditionally black college where he lived as boy. Sam does not consider a black cast performing a play by Oscar Wilde peculiar. Hart's immediate reaction, however, echoes the white supremacist belief that the black cast is not entitled to lay claim on the play because it is part of a white cultural heritage, and it evokes Sam's indignation. Hart lacks the vocabulary to explain his thoughts: "'I'm sorry – but the idea of *The Importance of Being Earnest* in blackface – well, not blackface. But as a minstrel –' The man's laughter fractured his own sentence. '...Really!'"[414] Thinking about the school performance again, Hart changes his mind and argues that the all-black cast of the Wilde play might effect some change in racist societal structures, and he speculates about the effect such a performance would have on a white audience: "I wouldn't be surprised if it's the sort of thing that all white people should be made to see – Shakespeare and Wilde and Ibsen, with Negro actors of all colors, taking whichever parts. It would probably do us some good."[415] Hence, the black cast of this production of Wilde's play has a direct effect on Hart's perception of the privileges connected with whiteness. Hart even generalizes his insight and applies it to all white people. This is an example of the way in which the social and the cultural level are linked.

Tucker's conclusion from the conversation between the three boys is that they "understand that Lewy will always be interpellated – and will identify himself – as 'black.'"[416] In contrast to Tucker, for whom the result of the boys' conversation is the fact of blackness, I contend that Lewy's claiming of multiple origins is drawn as a strategy of resistance against the interpellation as black. Rather than primarily referring to his African roots, he challenges the dominant discourse by disidentifying with both black and white cultural traditions.

Tucker rightly emphasizes the social dimensions of blackness and the references to African American culture in "Atlantis." However, rather than

---

414 Delany, "Atlantis," 79.

415 Delany, "Atlantis," 79.

416 Tucker, 224.

limiting the references to black cultural traditions, Delany positions his narrative in the broad field of American culture in order to transform the notion of American literature as a whole. In doing so, he takes up a strategy employed by African American modernists. As Hutchinson states,

> African American modernists were right to make claims on the national identity. It is up to us to reconceive what 'American modernism' is, and also to begin thinking of American literature less as a tradition (or set of separate traditions) following noble lines of descent than as the continually reforming product of historical fields of action, power, and experience.[417]

On the level of the narrative, Lewy's statement intervenes in a normative concept of American identity, and the novel as a whole can be seen as challenging reductive and traditionalist notions of American literary traditions. The strategy employed by Delany's narrative is similar to the all black cast of *The Importance of Being Earnest*, which changes Hart's notion of what he first considers a white cultural history, and to Lewy, who lays claim on all different sorts of cultural traditions. Delany connects his narrative to black cultural traditions, such as the migration narrative, Robert Hayden and Jean Toomer, as well as to Crane and white modernist traditions, in order to transform the segregationist discourse on modernism and the Harlem Renaissance. As Posnock states, Delany "makes an imaginative and precise intervention into modernist and African American literary history, a move evident from the start as Delany invokes traditional African American narrative tropes – 'up from slavery' and the journey north – only to give them new turns."[418]

4.4.3 Deconstructing Black Gay Myths of Origin

Delany's "undermining [of] the authority of identity/difference"[419] can also be observed with respect to the 1980s project of grounding the emerging identity category "black gay man" in the literature and culture of the Harlem Renaissance. In her essay "Looking for Harlem: (Re)Konstruktionen Harlems

----

417 Hutchinson, 447.

418 Posnock, 287.

419 Posnock, 293.

als 'queer Mecca', 1925–1995," Löbbermann asks in how far Delany engages in, comments on and subverts the 1980s project of constructing the Harlem Renaissance as a myth of origin for black queer culture. Löbbermann states that "Atlantis" achieves two goals. First, it engages in the project of constructing cultural origins by referring to the 1920s, and, second, it simultaneously deconstructs this project through Sam's naïveté and his own and his family's heterosexuality.[420] She maintains that this deconstruction was necessary in the early 1990s because the notion of a queer Harlem Renaissance was already in danger of becoming a cliché.

In her analysis, she focuses on the second part of the novel in which Sam meets the white poet Hart on top of Brooklyn Bridge.[421] Despite the fact that the conversation between Sam and Hart does not lead to Hart's desired result of taking Sam with him to his apartment in Brooklyn, Löbbermann speaks of a "gay encounter" between Hart and Sam.[422] She argues that the two men are constructed as two homoerotic father-figures who enable Delany's identity as a black gay writer. Likewise, Tucker states that the way the Brooklyn Bridge is depicted as a setting in "Atlantis" "links Delany's biological and literary fathers."[423] Löbbermann regards the encounter between the two men as an encounter between two aesthetic paradigms that have often been regarded separately, the Harlem Renaissance represented by Sam and modernism represented by Hart.

Tucker, however, interprets the encounter from a perspective that emphasizes the racial and sexual identities of the two men and states that "Atlantis is [...] characterized less by a politics of universalism than by its attempts to connect, and connect itself to, specific African American and gay

---

420 Löbbermann, "Looking for Harlem," 56.

421 The encounter on the bridge is depicted as Hart's unsuccessful try to pick up Sam. The scene alludes to the "Cutty Sark" – chapter of *The Bridge*. In "Atlantis Rose" Delany states that "with its account of the unsuccessful pick-up, 'Cutty Sark' is the true center of unspoken homosexual longing, the yearning for communication, in *The Bridge*." (Delany, "Atlantis Rose," 221).

422 Löbbermann, "Looking for Harlem," 64.

423 Tucker, 229.

cultural histories."[424] If one follows Löbbermann and Tucker, one could argue for the intersectionality of the categories homosexuality and blackness even though there are no black and gay/homosexual characters in the narrative.

I will now look at the encounter between the young black supposedly heterosexual Sam and the white homosexual poet Hart in more detail and then investigate in how far one might call it a heterotopian encounter. The encounter on the bridge with Hart's monologue and his failed homosexual pick-up can be read as a signification on what Delany calls "the homosexual genres." In the second part of his essay "Atlantis Rose... Some Notes on Hart Crane," Delany analyzes three poetic forms of the homosexual genre and states that these forms

> have been readable as gay or homosexual by gay or homosexual men and women in their particular times. (...) Most recently however – say, since the 19th century – the aspect that might be cited as most characteristic of this genre or genres is that they are structured so that straight, gay, male, or female readers and critics can read the homosexuality *out* of them, for whatever reason, whenever it becomes necessary or convenient.[425]

Delany distinguishes three poetic forms constituting the homosexual genre. He characterizes the second form as a "narrative that takes place in a world where homosexuality is never mentioned and is presumed not to exist – but where the incidents that occur have no other satisfying explanation," and he states that *The Bridge*'s sub-chapter "Cutty Sark," Crane's poetic depiction of an unsuccessful homosexual pick-up, is an example of such a text.[426] In Sam's encounter with Hart on the bridge, Delany alludes to "Cutty Sark." In fact, homosexuality is the only satisfying explanation for the incidents on the bridge, and the homosexual context of this scene is invoked on several symbolical levels: the sailor with the fan, the sea, the setting of the scene in a homosexual cruising area, and the references to Oscar Wilde. For example, at the beginning of their conversation, Hart states his name as Sebastian Melmouth, the

---

424 Tucker, 229.

425 Delany, "Atlantis Rose," 200.

426 Delany, "Atlantis Rose," 202.

pseudonym Wilde took while living in France.[427] He also states that he lives at One-ten Columbia Heights, Apartment c 33, but he later explains that that the apartment number is incorrect and that it was, in fact, Wilde's cell number in Reading. In his frequent references to Wilde, Hart uses a modernist stylistic device to encode male homosexuality, a strategy that is also used in "Smoke, Lilies and Jade," which explicitly refers to Wilde four times.[428] Sam, however, lacks the ability to decode these references.

Even though Hart becomes more and more explicit in trying to seduce Sam, he does not explicitly utter his sexual intentions. His pass at Sam is so veiled that he, because of his sexual naïveté, misunderstands what his encounter with Hart is about. Still, the elements that constitute this scene contribute to its reading as queer, and Löbbermann is right in characterizing the encounter between Sam and Hart as a "gay encounter."[429]

In Atlantis, male homosexuality is represented by a white writer who is based on the poet Crane. Delany alludes to Crane's experimental text *The Bridge* and its homosexual dimensions on a formal level, as well as on the level of contents. At first glance, the frequent references to Wilde also evoke a white homosexual lineage. As I have shown in the early black gay anthologies, as well as in Corbin's and Julien's texts, such exclusive references to white homosexual traditions are not typical of black gay texts of the 1980s and 90s. On the contrary, one of the aims of black gay texts of the period is the construction of a specific black gay history and culture. Unlike Karl in *Looking for Langston*, the white homosexual Hart is not represented as racist. Revising his initial negative judgment of the all-black cast of *The Importance of Being Earnest*, he is self-critical. His revised attitude towards the school-performance is one example that indicates the way in which Delany reveals the societal and all-pervasive elements of racism rather than the racism of individuals.

In his encounter with Sam, Hart uses the name "Wilde" as a chiffre for homosexuality. After Wilde's trial for homosexuality in 1895, such a reference

---

427 Delany, "Atlantis," 78.

428 Boone, 465FN59.

429 Löbbermann, "Looking for Harlem," 64.

would have been decodable by those seeking out homosexual encounters. The homosexual context of Sam's crossing the Brooklyn Bridge also evokes Walt Whitman's poem "Crossing Brooklyn Ferry," describing a man taking a ferry from Manhattan to Brooklyn.[430] Crane directly refers to Whitman's homosexuality in the "Cape Hatteras"-chapter of *The Bridge*, where he describes Whitman as an American homosexual poet. Delany continues Crane's reference to Whitman by directly referring to Crane's homosexuality in his own narrative. He thereby consciously continues a tradition of white homosexual American poets and sets himself in the position of a legitimate heir to this tradition. This lineage is also one of different aesthetic paradigms. The difference between Whitman and Crane mirrors the difference between romanticism and modernism, and the difference between Crane and Delany mirrors that between modernism and postmodernism. The way the lineage of the three poets is constructed establishes a link between these aesthetic paradigms. Thereby "Atlantis: Model 1924" is connected to American literary history. Delany's references to a homosexual heritage represented by the white men Wilde and Crane have to be regarded in connection with his reference to white aesthetic traditions and with Lewy's claiming his multiple origins. By referring to Wilde and Crane, Delany himself lays claim to traditions that some people would not regard as appropriate origins for a black writer. This strategy can be interpreted as a disidentifactory strategy of resistance. Rather than opposing the dominant discourse of a lineage of white gay masculinity that is reflected in literature by establishing a distinct black gay canon, his narrative transforms the notion of a white gay tradition from within. Consequently, the references to white homosexual traditions can also be read as strategy of treating this cliché ironically.

The structure of the novel implicitly links two events: first, Sam's first experiences of New York, particularly his arrival at Grand Central Station and his subsequent first ride on the subway at the beginning of the novel, and second,

---

430 Walt Whitman, "Crossing Brooklyn Ferry," *Leaves of Grass*, New York: Signet, 1954, 144–149.
    Even though the poem describes a ferry crossing, it is sometimes referred to by the title
    "Crossing Brooklyn Bridge." The construction of Brooklyn Bridge started in 1869. The bridge
    was opened for the public in 1883 when Whitman was 63. He died in 1892.

his walk on top of the Brooklyn Bridge at the end. On entering the walkway of the bridge, he finds a deserted booth with a weathered sign announcing a toll of one cent, the same amount of money he had to pay for his first subway ride. However, in contrast to the subway scene, when Sam sees "people cascading down the steps, breaking to left and right of him, like water at a rock,"[431] there are no other pedestrians on their way to the top of the bridge; there are just two black girls and a few white boys on their way downstairs.[432] The subway ride and the walk on top of the bridge directly refer to the last two chapters of Hart Crane's poem The Bridge: In "The Tunnel," Crane describes a subway ride from Manhattan to Brooklyn[433] and in "Atlantis," he gives a triumphant description of the Brooklyn Bridge.

Sam's walk on top of the bridge is depicted as a disorienting experience that contradicts the conception he has so far gained of life in New York. The experience of walking high above the East River affects Sam's sense of time and space. The detailed descriptions of clocks and Sam's perception of the exact time can be found throughout the novel: at his arrival at Grand Central Station,[434] and while he waits in a queue at the post office. In contrast to Sam's awareness of clocks and the exact time, his sense of time is disrupted while he is on top of the bridge.[435] Wondering "how many epochs could those waters clock, passing under the bridge?,"[436] Sam regards the whole bridge and the water running underneath as a clock whose time scale has a much greater

---

431 Delany, "Atlantis," 13.

432 Delany, "Atlantis," 62–65. In juxtaposing the black girls' "shiny shoes" and "white socks" (Delany, "Atlantis," 62) with the white boys' "ragged socks" and "worn shoes" (Delany, "Atlantis," 65), Delany makes the difference in class between these two groups explicit. Referring to the boys' shoes and socks, Sam thinks that they are the kind of boys who do not invent ancient clocks like Lewy. However, Sam's reason for this thought seems to be their class-based exclusion from a higher education rather than their secure position in the social structure that would make it unnecessary for them to invent their own origins.

433 The description of Sam's first realization that one has to insert coin in a slot beside the turnstile for admission is reminiscent of the same account in The Bridge. Hart Crane and Ute Eisinger, Die Brücke/The Bridge, Salzburg: Jung und Jung, 2004, 116. For the ways in which Delany refers to Crane's poem, see Delany's essay "Atlantis Rose...Some Notes on Hart Crane."

434 Delany, "Atlantis," 11.

435 The frequent mentioning of clocks mirrors Sam's memory of Lewy's invention of a clock with "a special, mystic time scale" while they were still living in Raleigh (Delany, "Atlantis," 64).

436 Delany, "Atlantis," 66.

dimension than the clocks he has observed so far. In a surrealistic way, Sam even extends this image to a man in a boat on the East River whom he sees urinating into the water: "Man as water clock...?"[437] After leaving the bridge, Sam tries "to figure out how long he'd been talking with the man on the bridge. 'Maybe twenty, twenty-five minutes.' Probably it was over thirty. Could it have been an hour?"[438] On his way back to Harlem, however, Sam is taken by surprise when he sees a clock: he realizes that he is already 40 minutes late for his appointment with his siblings at Elsie and Corey's apartment.[439] He will arrive at their apartment almost 90 minutes late. In addition to his loss of sense of time, he also loses his sense of space. As there are gaps between the planks of the wooden walkway, the walkway seems to disappear if one walks across the bridge at a certain speed. Consequently, Sam has "the disorienting experience of being suspended more than a hundred feet in mid-air above glass-green water."[440] His sensation of being suspended in the sky once again alludes to the beginning of the narrative. Upon his arrival at Grand Central Station he is eager to see the New York sky, but he only gets to see the artificial sky that is painted on the ceiling of the station,[441] and, as he immediately takes the subway to travel to Hubert's place, he does not see the sky before his arrival in Harlem. The contrast between the artificial sky and the subway ride, on the one hand, and Sam's sensation of being suspended in the sky, on the other, juxtaposes the limitations of everyday life with a space uninhibited by such boundaries.

Sam's conversation with a policeman on the Manhattan side of the bridge is significant because it demonstrates Sam's unease after his experiences on the bridge. He is confused by the suspension of time and place he has just experienced and wants recognition from an officer. The conversation with the policeman is reminiscent of Louis Althusser's concept of interpellation

---

437 Delany, "Atlantis," 68.

438 Delany, "Atlantis," 99.

439 Delany, "Atlantis," 100.

440 Delany, "Atlantis," 66.

441 Delany, "Atlantis," 11; Tucker states that the watery color of the painted sky "suggests the submerged city of Atlantis" (Tucker, 210).

and subject formation (see 3.3). Althusser's basic example of interpellation is a scene in which an individual is interpellated by the police with the words "Hey you, there!"[442] Realizing that his information on the drowning man is much too vague, Sam leaves. Still, he "glanced back, hoping the officer would be marking it down on his pad – at least the time or the place or something – in case, later, it came up."[443] Here, Sam's desire that the officer will write down the time or the place of the incident is juxtaposed with his experience of the disruption of time and space on top of the bridge. The absence of these parameters, which throughout the novel are depicted as structuring Sam's life, leads him to seek reassurance from a representative of the state. Sam's desire to be validated by a state official in order to re-establish the order of subject positions is juxtaposed to the space of the bridge, where all categories are fluid.

During Sam and Hart's encounter on the Brooklyn Bridge, both the dimensions of space and time and the rules of language, as well as societal norms, are disrupted. Consequently, one could argue that the bridge is represented as a heterotopia. Michel Foucault has defined the term "heterotopia" in a 1967 lecture which was later published under the title "Different Spaces." Foucault states that, in contrast to utopias which have no real places,

> there are also, and probably in every culture, in every civilization, real places, actual places that are designed into the very institution of society, which are sorts of actually realized utopias in which the real emplacements, all the other real emplacements that can be found within the culture are, at the same time, represented, contested, and reversed, sorts of places that are outside all places, although they are actually localizable. Because they are different from all the emplacements that they reflect or refer to, I shall call these places 'heterotopias,' as opposed to utopias.[444]

As the subtitle of Delany's 1976 novel *Trouble on Triton* (whose protagonist is also named Sam) is "An Ambiguous Heterotopia," a reference to the subtitle "An Ambiguous Utopia" of Ursula K. Le Guin's 1974 novel *The Disposessed*, one

---

442 Althusser, 163.

443 Delany, "Atlantis," 100.

444 Michel Foucault, "Different Spaces," *Aesthetics, Method, and Epistemology*, eds. Michel Foucault and James D. Faubion, New York: New Press, 1998, 175–185, 178.

can safely say that Delany is familiar with Foucault's concept and used it in his fiction.[445] Löbbermann states that the Bridge is constructed as a "queer space" where societal norms, as well as the norms of language, are invalid.[446] In this respect, the bridge can be regarded as having "the ability to juxtapose in a single real place several emplacements that are incompatible in themselves:"[447] the encounter of the black, supposedly heterosexual, and sexually naïve Sam who just arrived from North Carolina and resides in Harlem, with the white homosexual modernist poet Crane, who lives in Brooklyn.

The queer dimensions of the encounter on the bridge are directly invoked on several levels. As in *No Easy Place to Be*, the setting of the bridge implies its function as a cruising area for homosexual men.[448] Sam's walk from Manhattan to Brooklyn evokes the journey from Manhattan to Brooklyn described in Whitman's "Crossing Brooklyn Ferry" and thereby alludes to a homosexual literary tradition. A sexually transgressive dimension is also evoked by the first person Sam encounters on the bridge, a sailor with a Japanese fan smiling at him.[449] At the beginning of the twentieth century, the sailor was "the central figure of the [gay] subculture."[450]

Right at the beginning of the conversation between Sam and Hart, Hart talks about a man in a boat on the East River, whom he and Sam observed earlier while the man was urinating into the water. Hart says: "'Lord, he was hung! Like a stallion! Pissed like a racehorse, too!' He looked over, grinning behind his glasses. 'To see it from up here at all, someone's got to throw a stream as thick as a fire hose. It was something, ey.'"[451] As both the man's urinating into the river and Hart's description of the act lie outside what Sam

---

445 See also Marvin Chlada, *Heterotopie und Erfahrung*, Aschaffenburg: Alibri, 2005.

446 Löbbermann, "Looking for Harlem," 68.

447 Foucault, "Different Spaces," 181.

448 Delany, "Atlantis Rose," 213.

449 Delany, "Atlantis," 65.

450 Chauncey, 78. Another example of the figure of the Sailor denoting male homosexuality can be found near the end of Baldwin's *Giovanni's Room* when David escapes from his fiancée Hella. He goes to Nice and meets a sailor with whom he gets drunk and has sex. James Baldwin, *Giovanni's Room*, New York: Delta, 1956, 102.

451 Delany, "Atlantis," 76.

has learned to consider socially acceptable behavior, his reaction is surprise and amusement. The man in the boat might even be interpreted as a direct allusion to Foucault's "Different Spaces," because at the end of his text, Foucault considers the ship to be "the greatest reservoir of imagination" and "the heterotopia par excellence."[452]

During their conversation, Hart and Sam talk about such different people as Oscar Wilde, John Augusts Roebling and his son Washington Roebling who were the architects of the Brooklyn Bridge, Jean Toomer, Samuel Greenberg and the man in the boat below on the East River. Matching Lewy's plea against the authenticity of origins, Posnock argues that, in his conversation with Sam, Hart "articulates an aesthetic of the ineffable, the uncontainable and the 'borrowed' that the novel as a whole will celebrate as a cosmopolitan insouciance regarding ownership and origin."[453] This aesthetic principle can be seen, for example, in Hart's defense of alluding to the words and works of other poets as a legitimate artistic practice: Hart explains to Sam that it is legitimate to use the works of other poets, to "engulf them, digest them, and transform them, *make* them words of my own."[454]

During their conversation on the bridge, Sam finally gets a view of Manhattan and its skyscrapers. Skyscrapers are on his mind during the whole narrative. In fact, the very first sentence refers to his interest in skyscrapers, "Skyscrapers – that's what he was most eager to see."[455] But it is only half a year later that his high expectations are met:

> But the city had changed, astonishingly, while they'd been sitting. The sunlight, in lowering, had smelted its copper among the towers, to splash the windows of the southernmost skyscrapers, there the Pulitzer, in the distance the Fuller, there the Woolworth Building itself.[456]

---

452 Foucault, "Different Spaces," 185.

453 Posnock, 287.

454 Delany, "Atlantis," 91.

455 Delany, "Atlantis," 3.

456 Delany, "Atlantis," 92.

162

While Sam is overwhelmed by the view, Hart starts a multi-layered poetic monologue connecting New York and the myth of Atlantis. In his monologue, Hart suggests that homosexuality might be one way to reach Atlantis, the "truly wonder-filled city."[457] Referring to his work as a poet he states:

> I call up from the impassive earth the whole of the world around you, Sam – stalking the wild nauga and bringing it all down to words, paired phalluses, bridge between man and man. I create and crumble worlds, cities, visions![458]

Encouraged by Sam's "'Wow,'"[459] which he takes as a sign of Sam's being impressed by his artistry of language rather than Sam's being overwhelmed with the sight of Manhattan, he continues with his monologue. His references to his sexual interest in Sam become less and less veiled, for he talks about his male lover, tells Sam that he is handsome and finally explicitly makes a pass at him:

> 'Do you want to come back to the place with me – have a drink? We could be alone. I'm a good man to get soused with, if you like to get soused – and what good self-respecting Negro doesn't? Come on, relax. Spend a little time – come with me, boy – oh – boy, and we'll get boozy and comfortable.'[460]

Despite Hart's explicitness, Sam does not understand Hart's sexual interest, at all. In the first half of the novel Sam's naïveté in sexual matters has repeatedly been made explicit. For example, he is ignorant of his brother's allusions to public homosexual encounters[461] and to masturbation.[462] Sam is even aware of his naïveté. He understands that there is "an area wholly constituted of his ignorance,"[463] an insight he hates but cannot do anything about. In his meeting with Hart, his ignorance is the reason for their misunderstanding. When Sam tells Hart he wants to call the police, Hart gets angry, "His final salvo:

457 Delany, "Atlantis," 92.
458 Delany, "Atlantis," 92.
459 Delany, "Atlantis," 93.
460 Delany, "Atlantis," 97.
461 Delany, "Atlantis," 15.
462 Delany, "Atlantis," 56.
463 Delany, "Atlantis," 56.

'Don't think you'll ever get to it [Atlantis] calling the law on people like *me!*'" [464] Then he leaves out of fear of being reported to the police because of this failed homosexual pick-up. The reader knows that this is not Sam's intention at all; he wants to call the police because he still thinks that the man in the boat has drowned. [465] The two men leave the bridge in opposite directions. [466]

464 Delany, "Atlantis," 98.

465 This supposed suicide by drowning alludes to the suicide of Hart Crane. A parallel column gives
    the details of Hart Crane's suicide "on April 27, 1932, by jumping into the sea from the deck
    of a steamer bearing him from Mexico to the United States" are given (Delany, "Atlantis," 73).

466 Later that night, Sam's relatives meet to celebrate Sam's eighteenth birthday three days
    prior to the day he actually turns eighteen. On that occasion, they talk about Prohibition.
    The conversation leads Sam to think that he understands Hart's motives for getting angry:
    Hart left the Brooklyn Bridge so suddenly out of fear of anti-prohibition laws.

5   Looking for Baldwin and the Protest Era

Next to the Harlem Renaissance, the Protest Era of the 1950s and 1960s is the second important historical point of reference for black gay writers from the 1980s onwards. In the 1980s and 1990s black gay writers in addition to referring to Bruce Nugent, Langston Hughes and their writings, deal with the work and persona of James Baldwin. To this day, there are numerous references to Baldwin in different genres of black (gay) cultural production. Since the early 1980s, black gay men and black lesbians have claimed that Baldwin's work and life are of central importance for their own life and work. The fact that Baldwin was one of the few writers who explicitly wrote about homosexuality even in the 1950s is one reason for his "reputation as an important – perhaps the most important – gay black American writer."[467] There are numerous references to a specifically black gay Baldwin in different genres of cultural production. I will briefly give three examples. As I have shown in the previous chapter, Isaac Julien's film *Looking for Langston* pays tribute to Baldwin on several levels. In the opening credits the film is dedicated to Baldwin, who had died two years before the film was made, and a large photograph of Baldwin is displayed by a black man dressed as an angel. A photograph of Baldwin is printed on the cover of the CD "BourgieBohoPostPostModernAfricanAmericanHomosexual" by the gay black hip hop group DeepDickCollective. In addition, in Rodney Evans's film *Brother to Brother*, the young black gay protagonist Perry fuels a discussion about black maculinity and homosexuality after making a presentation on Baldwin's sexual politics in his literature class.[468]

---

467   Field, "Looking for Jimmy Baldwin," *Callaloo* 27.2 (2004): 457–480, 457.

468   In 1999, the strategy of referring to the black gay Baldwin was taken up and altered by John A. Williams, a black heterosexual writer, but for different reasons. His novel *Clifford's Blues* (1999) is about Clifford Pepperidge, a black homosexual jazz pianist, who is an inmate of the concentration camp at Dachau in Germany at the time of the Nazi regime (John Alfred Williams, *Clifford's Blues*, Minneapolis: Coffee House, 1998). Its title alludes to Baldwin's *Sonny's Blues*. Williams was already an established writer and did not need to refer to a black literary tradition to legitimate himself in the eyes of the black community. Rather, his choice of title and his reference to black gay Baldwin grants him a certain amount of credibility for his black gay narrative. His signifying on Baldwin might even be addressed to the black gay community whose members are probably skeptical of a novel about a black homosexual man written by a novelist whose negative attitude towards Baldwin put forward in his 1967 novel *The Man Who Cried I am* has been compared to that of Eldridge Cleaver (Maria Diedrich, "James A. Baldwin – Obituaries for a Black Ishmael," *James Baldwin: His Place in American Literary History and His Reception in Europe*, ed. Jakob Kollhöfer, Frankfurt a.M.: Peter Lang, 1991, 129–140, 129–130).

In this chapter, I first want to look at the historical contexts of the 1950s and 1960s, paying special attention to the circumstances of Baldwin's life. Comparing the situation to the 1980s, I will then explore why many black gay writers in the 1980s invented a Baldwin much more unambiguous than can be deduced from his writings and interviews. The main part of this chapter consists of an analysis of three longer texts that either directly refer to Baldwin's writings, as is the case with Randall Kenan's A *Visitation of Spirits* and Melvin Dixon's *Vanishing Rooms*, or give an alternative account of the 1950s and 1960s as is the case with Samuel R. Delany's *The Motion of Light in Water*.

One example of how black gay writers have emphasized Baldwin's life and work is a statement Steven Corbin made in an interview with Larry Duplechan for BLK, *The National Black Gay and Lesbian Newsmagazine* in 1992. Corbin emphasizes the impact of Baldwin's writings on his own decision to become a writer:

> Then something profound happened. I don't say that to sound melodramatic, but it really was profound: I read James Baldwin's *Just Above My Head*. My favorite Baldwin novel. [...] And then I said, God damn! And I worked my way back: *Giovanni's Room*, *Go tell it on the Mountain*. And I thought, This man is a black queer, and he's saying 'I am a black queer, and these are my stories and fuck you!' And I thought, that speaks to my anger, speaks to my rage, as both a black and queer man. And he's getting away with that! [...] Baldwin's work said, 'You *must* do this.' [469]

Corbin's quotation indicates the strategy black gay writers employed in the 1980s. He invents a Baldwin who is "saying 'I'm a black queer, and these are my stories and fuck you!'" and connects his own identity directly to Baldwin's writings ("speaks to my anger, speaks to my rage, as both a black and queer man").

Dwight A. McBride characterizes Baldwin as "the first 'openly gay' black writer," because he was "the first to talk publicly about his homosexuality and to purposefully make use of it in his fiction." [470] Baldwin wrote about male

---

469 Larry Duplechan, "Interview with Steven Corbin," *BLK: The National Black Gay and Lesbian Newsmagazine* 4.1 (1992): 11–25, 15–16.

470 Dwight A. McBride, "Straight Black Studies: On African American Studies, James Baldwin, and Black Queer Studies," *Black Queer Studies: A Critical Anthology*, eds. E. Patrick Johnson and Mae G. Henderson. Durham: Duke UP, 2005. 68–89, 72.

homosexuality in his early essays, and he created black male homosexual and bisexual characters in his novels, for example Rufus Scott in *Another Country* (1962) and Leo Proudhammer in *Tell Me How Long the Train's Been Gone* (1968). Consequently, Corbin's statement about the impact of Baldwin's writings on his own decision to become a writer is understandable. But the numerous positive references to a black gay/queer Balwin are also surprising. Baldwin was very skeptical about the concept of gay identity, and he repeatedly distanced himself from the gay sub-culture by criticising drag queens and sissies in both his fiction and essays.

Douglas Field deduces three important points from an interview between Baldwin and Richard Goldstein in 1985: "first Baldwin's repeated rejection of the terms 'homosexual' and 'gay,' (...) his insistence that sexuality is a private matter; and finally, his repeated statement that race is a more important question than issues of sexuality."[471] As all three statements contradict the political agenda of black gay activism since the 1980s, Baldwin's status as a black gay role model becomes ambiguous. Moreover, especially in his early fiction, Baldwin repeatedly depicted male homosexuality and bisexuality as hopeless situations. The suicide of the black bisexual Rufus in *Another Country*, and the failed relationship between David and Giovanni in *Giovanni's Room* are two such examples.

Since the advent of cultural studies, academics have re-examined Baldwin's work from an interdisciplinary perspective that takes into account the intersections of various axes of difference in his texts. One important publication is Dwight A. McBride's critical anthology *James Baldwin Now* (1999). It focuses on the intersectionality of race, sexuality, class, and gender in Baldwin's writings, and it differs significantly from most approaches to Baldwin in the 1970s and 1980s. During these decades, his texts were analyzed from either an African American studies perspective or a gay and lesbian studies perspective. These separate approaches sometimes led to a narrow perspective which granted race or homosexuality primary importance. For example, *Giovanni's Room* and its depiction of the homosexual relationship between two white

---

471 Field, 459.

men in Paris became a canonical text within gay and lesbian studies, whereas it was largely ignored within African American studies. In his essay "White Fantasies of Desire: Baldwin and the Racial Identities of Sexuality," Marlon B. Ross observes that the emergence of a black gay community since the early 1980s was the main reason for regarding Baldwin's novel as part of the African American literary tradition:

> Only with the emergence of a more autonomous gay black sociopolitical consciousness in the early 1980s did a public discourse arise that began to integrate Baldwin's 'gay' novel [*Giovanni's Room*] into an African American context. It is as if only an openly gay black readership could give a valid racial identity to a novel otherwise cut off from black experience, and it is no surprise that Baldwin's work as a whole has been a major cultural resource for people who identify as black and gay.[472]

Ross and the other authors included in McBride's anthology read Baldwin's texts as transgressive regarding the categories race, sexuality, and nation, and this paradigm is reflected in the scholarship on Baldwin from the 1990s onwards.

When considering Baldwin's position towards homosexuality and the gay sub-culture, one has to acknowledge the political climate he worked in. Baldwin repeatedly distanced himself from the homosexual sub-culture for three reasons: first, the persecution of homosexual men and women during the McCarthy era, second, the offensive critique formulated by Black Nationalists, and, third, his public role as a Civil Rights spokesperson. Even after the advent of gay identity and the establishment of coming out as a political strategy, Baldwin remained skeptical of the 1970s and 1980s gay movement and culture. Baldwin's skepticism also included the black gay movement. In 1982, he participated in a forum that was sponsored by the New York chapter of the group "Black and White Men Together" where he publicly talked about his homosexuality. The black gay community interpreted this event as his public "Coming Out."[473] Later, however, he refused Joseph Beam's request for an interview for the 1986 anthology *In the Life: A Black Gay*

472 Ross, 15–16.

473 James S. Tinney, "James Baldwin 'Comes Out' at Gay Forum," *Blacklight* 3.5 (1982): 4.

Anthology.[474] His support of a group whose politics aimed at a conversation between black and white gay men and his rejection of Beam's request for a contribution to a an exclusively black gay project correspond to his repeated depiction of inter-racial relationships in his fiction.

5.1 Baldwin and the Protest Era

In their texts Kenan and Dixon refer to Baldwin's first two novels from the 1950s, and Delany gives and account of the first half of the 1960s. Consequently, this historical context is an important prerequisite for the analysis of the way these writers refer back to this particular period. In the following part, I will establish the historical context necessary to understand Baldwin's aesthetics and sexual politics. I will consider the persecution of homosexual men and women in the 1950s in the US as a prerequisite for reading Baldwin's early Parisian essays on homosexuality, "Preservation of Innocence" (1949) and "The Male Prison" (1954). I will then consider Baldwin's strategy of distancing himself from Richard Wright and the genre of the protest novel in his essays "Everybody's Protest Novel" (1949) and "Alas, Poor Richard" (1960). In conclusion, I will explore his reactions to the attacks by the black power representatives Eldridge Cleaver and Amiri Baraka in the 1960s. The arguments put forward by Cleaver in *Soul on Ice* (1968) reveal that male homosexuality was a difficult topic within the black community during the time when most black gay artists who came out in the 1980s grew up. Cleaver's attack led Baldwin to reformulate his public opinion on male homosexuality.

The decade of the 1950s was determined by the oppressive atmosphere of McCarthyism, but it also saw the rise and political impact of the Civil Rights movement. The 1960s were the decade of the emergence of social

---

474 This pdf-document is available at www.blacklightonline.com, a site maintained by Brinkley to document the six years of the magazine *Blacklight* founded by Brinkley and published in Washington DC between 1979 and 1985. Sidney Brinkley, *The Complete Blacklight*. <http://www.blacklightonline.com>, accessed October 7, 2007.

movements, such as the women's movement and the gay rights movement that took the political strategies of the Civil Rights movement as a blueprint for their own politics. The activists of the Civil Rights movement were engaged in unprecedented means of social protest, including sit-ins, boycotts such as the Montgomery Bus Boycott (1955–1956), marches, and other forms of civil disobedience. With Martin Luther King as its most famous representative, the movement promoted the strategy of non-violent protest effecting the desegregation of public transport and eating establishments in the South. In the mid-1960s, Black Power activists distanced themselves from the integrationist politics of the Civil Rights era. During this decade Black Nationalists and the founders of the Black Arts movement formulated a political and aesthetic agenda that was more radical than the integrationist politics of the Civil Rights movement. Black Power and the Civil Rights movement differed over the question of the legitimacy of violence as a political means and questions of integration and separatism.[475] Baldwin, who was regarded as a representative of the Civil Rights paradigm, became the target of criticism formulated by Black Power representatives such as Cleaver and Baraka. William J. Spurlin states that Baldwin was often called by the name "Martin Luther Queen," a name that combines a devaluation of an integrationist political agenda and a denunciation of Baldwin's homosexuality.[476]

The McCarthy era was an oppressive period for supposed communists, as well as for homosexual men and women. From the 1940s onwards, homosexuality was politicized "as a form of psychopathology that undermined the nation's defenses against Communist infiltration."[477] Consequently, the House Un-American Activities Committee (HUAC) did not merely persecute supposed Communists. It extended its investigations to include men and women suspected of being homosexuals:

---

475 Michael Omi and Howard Winant, *Racial Formation in the United States: From the 1960s to the 1990s*, New York: Routledge, 1994, 99–104.

476 William J. Spurlin, "Culture, Rhetoric, and Queer Identity," *James Baldwin Now*, ed. Dwight A. McBride, New York: New York UP, 1999, 103–121, 109.

477 Corber, *Homosexuality*, 3.

On the basis of testimony from psychiatrists and other medical 'experts' who testified that they were susceptible to blackmail by Soviet agents because they were emotionally unstable, homosexuals and lesbians were officially identified as national security risks. As a result, more homosexuals and lesbians were expelled from the federal government in the 1950s than were suspected Communists and fellow travelers.[478]

One of the consequences was that "in the 1950s sexual orientation became as crucial a determinate as race and gender."[479] In his 1997 study *Homosexuality in Cold War America: Resistance and the Crisis of Masculinity*, Robert Corber shows that stereotypes of homosexual men and women as emotionally unstable and untrustworthy resulted from the politicization of homosexuality as a national security risk. Simultaneously, a new hegemonic "model of masculinity that stressed domesticity and cooperation"[480] evolved that became dominant in American society from the 1950s onwards as a model antithetical to supposed homosexual men who lived in the cities and refused to raise a family or buy a house in the suburbs. These two developments are important origins of the pejorative image of gay men in the American hegemonic discourse.

The Kinsey Reports on male and female sexual behaviors, first published in 1948 and 1953, were the first broad-based investigations of sexual behavior in US society. The data of the Kinsey reports demonstrated that homosexual behavior was common in American society. The Reports were the first influential publication to treat sexual orientation in an unbiased way. The large percentage of persons who had had heterosexual, as well as same-sex encounters indicated that homosexuality and heterosexuality could not be seen as stable, exclusive,

---

478 Robert J. Corber, *In the Name of National Security: Hitchcock, Homophobia, and the Political Construction of Gender in Postwar America*, Durham: Duke UP, 1993, 8.

479 Corber, *In the Name of*, 9.

480 Corber locates the origin of "the postwar crisis of masculinity" in the change of the economic system, namely the "transition to a Fordist regime of capital accumulation." Male identity was now being constructed through qualities that were formerly conceived of as feminine, such as "respect for authority, loyalty to one's superiors, and an ability to get along with others." Men were expected to support their families by consuming capitalist goods and buying a house in the suburbs, rather than by independently working for their own enterprises, a male quality that had formerly been prevalent. Corber states that "promoted by both the culture industries and a set of government programs designed to encourage suburbanization, the domestic model of masculinity gradually became hegemonic" (Corber, *Homosexuality*, 5).

and permanent categories of sexual identity. These findings were supportive of the self-esteem of homosexual men and women because they no longer had to think of themselves as a very small group of pathological individuals. Still, the reports did not immediately lead to a more liberal climate because the insight into the instability of sexual categories cleared the ground for the argument that homosexual men and women "might convert heterosexuals to their 'perverted' practices by seducing them."[481]

In 1962, the year Baldwin's novel *Another Country* was published, Dr. Irving Bieber and his colleagues published the study *Homosexuality: A Psychoanalytic Study of Male Homosexuals* aimed at contesting the Kinsey Reports. This study presents homosexual men as effeminate and pathological figures. Despite the popularity of the Kinsey reports, Bieber's study became "the leading authority and standard pronouncement on male homosexuality until [...] the American Psychiatric Association (APA) decided in 1973 to delete homosexuality as a category of psychopathology from the *DSM III*."[482]

In his essay "Coming/Out," Delany argues that the persecution of gay men and lesbians during the McCarthy era was one of the reasons for the change of meaning of the term "coming out." Before the 1970s, it had been used within the gay subculture to designate one's first major homosexual experience in the sense of "coming out into gay society." Since the 1970s, the term "coming out," whose origins go back to formal society balls where young women came out into society, is understood as a political strategy that was directed at the heterosexual public in the sense of "coming out of the closet." According to Delany, after the Stonewall riots and with the emergence of the gay liberation movement, the term changed its meaning within eighteen months. In response to the negative experiences from the McCarthy era, gay and lesbian activists

---

481 Corber, *In the Name of*, 9.

482 Spurlin, "Culture, Rhetoric, and Queer Identity," 108. *DSM III* refers to the third edition of the *Diagnostic and Statistical Manual* published by the American Psychiatric Association. It is used to diagnose psychiatric disorders. Spurlin presents a short summary of the methodology of Bieber's investigation. He states that "it was Bieber's study that promulgated the by now all-too-familiar view that a high proportion of gay men had 'close-binding mothers,' who demasculinized their sons and thwarted the development of their heterosexual drives, and detached hostile fathers" (Spurlin "Culture, Rhetoric, and Queer Identity," 108).

promoted the strategy of coming out of the closet as a political strategy, arguing that once they were open about their sexuality, they could no longer be accused of being a target of blackmail.[483]

5.1.1 Transatlantic Baldwin

From 1948 to 1957, Baldwin lived in Paris, and he wrote his first accounts of homosexuality in his essays "Preservation of Innocence" (1949) and "The Male Prison" (1954), as well as in his first two novels *Go Tell It on the Mountain* (1952) and *Giovanni's Room* (1956), while living abroad. Even though Baldwin was living in Paris, his writings can be regarded as a commentary on the political situation in the US. For example, his claim that there was no racism in France might be interpreted as a strategic critique of racism in the US. Likewise, his depiction of the Parisian homosexual sub-culture in *Giovanni's Room* can be read as comment on the oppressive situation homosexuals faced in the US.

The editors of *Black Like Us* call "Preservation of Innocence" Baldwin's "boldest declaration of gay identity politics until he published the gay love story *Giovanni's Room* in 1956."[484] However, as Baldwin remained skeptical of the term gay as well as of gay identity politics, their characterization of the two texts is arguably too strong. Still, "Preservation of Innocence" contains some elements regarding the societal construction of homosexuality rather than solely asserting its groundedness in biology. "Preservation of Innocence" was first published in the Parisian magazine *Zero* in 1949. In his essay, Baldwin criticizes the then popular understanding of homosexuality as "unnatural" and unacceptable, and he analyzes some representations of male homosexuals in American literature. Baldwin begins the essay by revealing the meanings of the terms 'unnatural' and 'natural' as relative to the cultural context in which they are used. He shows that in modern societies nature is dismissed as the Other of civilization while at the same time it is used to legitimize certain desirable behaviors (heterosexuality) and banish undesirable behaviors (homosexuality). Because of these double standards, Baldwin rejects the terms 'natural' and 'unnatural' as a basis for

---

483 Delany, "Coming/Out."

484 Carbado, McBride, 2002.

the judgment of human behavior and opposes the common notion that the homosexual "is unnatural because he has turned from his life-giving function to a union which is sterile."[485] He dismisses this criterion by stating that there are heterosexual persons who do not procreate. Moreover, in maintaining that the meaning of homosexuality is historically situated, he further dismantles the connection between sexuality and nature. Though he regards the existence of homosexual behavior as a "phenomenon as old as mankind," and thereby suggests its trans-historical grounding, he observes that the homosexual's "existence did not always invoke that hysteria with which he now contends,"[486] thereby suggesting that attitudes towards homosexuality depend on societal changes. He expresses the same skepticism about a naturalistic discourse in "The Male Prison," his 1954 essay on André Gide, stating that "it does not seem [...] that nature helps us very much when we need illumination in human affairs."[487]

5.1.2 Richard Wright and the Protest Novel

Baldwin's essays show an awareness of the origins and prevalence of racist stereotypes degrading black people. His early essays are preoccupied with questions concerning the representation of African Americans. His critique of his mentor and friend Richard Wright has to be seen from this perspective. The essay "Everybody's Protest Novel" was first published in *Partisan Review* in 1949. It analyzes the genre of the social protest novel and of Richard Wright's *Native Son* (1940) in particular. Baldwin's essay contains a criticism of Wright's notion of black masculinity. He regards it as a confirmation of the hegemonic stereotype of the black man as super-macho. I will give a short account of Baldwin's line of argument because his way of distancing himself from Wright is the basis for the homophobic critique formulated by Cleaver, a critique which caused Baldwin's isolation and silence during the Black Arts and Black Nationalist period (see 5.1.3).

In "Everybody's Protest Novel," Baldwin relates *Native Son*'s protagonist

---

485 James Baldwin, „Preservation of Innocence." *Collected Essays*, New York: Library of America, 1998, 594–600, 595.

486 Baldwin, "Preservation of Innocence, 595.

487 James Baldwin, "The Male Prison," *Collected Essays*, New York: Library of America, 1998, 231–235, 232.

Bigger Thomas to Uncle Tom, the protagonist of Harriet Beecher Stowe's *Uncle Tom's Cabin*. He criticizes both images of African American men and argues that both Bigger Thomas and Uncle Tom are two opposite stereotypes of black masculinity, the black rapist and the emasculated black man (see 3.1.2). Corber argues that, "in locating *Native Son* in the same literary tradition as *Uncle Tom's Cabin*, Baldwin stressed the way in which Wright's novel reinforced the myth of the threatening black phallus."[488] Baldwin states, that in depicting Bigger Thomas as a rapist and murderer, Wright reinforces a racist stereotype of black men: "Below the surface of this novel there lies, as it seems to me, a continuation, a complement of that monstrous legend it was written to destroy."[489] It is especially Wright's characterization of Bigger Thomas that Baldwin rejects:

> Bigger's tragedy is not that he is cold or black or hungry, not even that he is American, black; but that he has accepted a theology that denies him life, that he admits the possibility of his being sub-human and feels constrained, therefore, to battle for his humanity according to those brutal criteria bequeathed him by his birth.[490]

Though in "Many Thousands Gone," he praises *Native Son* as "the most powerful and celebrated statement we have yet of what it means to be a Negro in America,"[491] he believes that the protest novel has lost its revolutionary potential: "The 'protest' novel, so far from being disturbing, is an accepted and comforting aspect of the American scene, ramifying that framework we believe to be so necessary."[492]

In 1961, after Wright's death, Baldwin published the essay "Alas, Poor Richard," a personal memoir of his relation to Wright. In this essay, he refers to his earlier criticism of *Native Son* and claims that he had always admired Wright as an idol:

---

488 Corber, *Homosexuality*, 174. See also Wallace, 55.

489 James Baldwin, "Everybody's Protest Novel," *Collected Essays*, New York: Library of America, 1998, 11–18, 18.

490 Baldwin, "Everybody's Protest Novel," 18.

491 James Baldwin, "Many Thousands Gone," *Collected Essays*, New York: Library of America, 1998, 19–34, 24.

492 Baldwin "Everybody's Protest Novel," 15.

there is probably no greater (or more misleading) body of sexual myths in the world today than those which have proliferated around the figure of the American Negro. This means that he is penalized for the guilty imagination of the white people who invest him with their hates and longings, and is the principal target of their sexual paranoia. Thus, when in Wright's pages a negro male is found hacking a white woman to death, the very gusto with which this is done, and the great attention paid to the details of physical destruction reveal a terrible attempt to break out of the cage in which the American imagination has imprisoned him for so long.[493]

Nevertheless, in this passage, he reinforces his earlier arguments, a criticism of Wright's failure to question the images of black men he (re)produces in his novels.

Baldwin's critique of Wright's representation of black masculinity was rejected by white and black critics alike. The white critic Irving Howe and the later Black Panther activist Eldridge Cleaver praised *Native Son* and formulated their critique of Baldwin by dismissing his way of depicting male homosexuality. Howe reacts to Baldwin's criticism of *Native Son* in two essays titled "Black Boys and Native Sons" (1968) and "James Baldwin: At Ease in Apocalypse." Even though Howe partly agrees with Baldwin's criticism of Wright's one-dimensional characters, he dismisses Baldwin's novels precisely because Baldwin depicts his characters in more than one dimension. As he does not refer to particular examples from Baldwin's novels, the following quotation can be seen as a general rejection of homosexuality as a motif in Baldwin's texts:

As a novelist, Baldwin has always been helpless before the mysteries of heterosexual love, and when he turns to homosexual love he usually drops into a whipped-cream sentimentalism which reminds one of nothing so much as the boy-meets-girl stories in the Saturday Evening Post of twenty years ago.[494] [...] Baldwin slips into the clichés of soap opera, for which he had already shown an alarming fondness in the past when dealing with homosexual love.[495]

---

493 James Baldwin, "Alas, Poor Richard," *Collected Essays*, New York: Library of America, 1998, 247–268, 251. Two of the three sections of "Alas, Poor Richard" originally appeared in periodical form: "Eight Men" in *Reporter* (March 16, 1961) with the title "The Survival of Richard Wright," and "The Exile" in *Encounter* (April 1961) with the title "Richard Wright."

494 Irving Howe, "James Baldwin: At Ease in Apocalypse," *James Baldwin: A Collection of Critical Essays*, ed. Keneth Kinnamon, Englewood Cliffs, N.J.: Prentice Hall, 1974, 96–108, 100.

495 Howe, 103.

With this critique, Howe does not acknowledge differences among African Americans, and he does not take into account that Baldwin's positive depiction of homosexual love was one way to reformulate the sexualized stereotype of black men as rapists.

Despite his critique of Wright's depiction of black men, Baldwin has been criticized for not living up to his own standards. The male protagonists in Baldwin's early novels are often depicted as self-deprecating, suffering black men, a depiction supporting the dominant view of black men as victims rather than autonomous subjects. Rufus Scott, the protagonist of *Another Country* who commits suicide after only one hundred pages is an example of Baldwin's failure in creating a positive black character that would live up to his own ideal. In this respect, Baldwin's early novels are not typical of the consciousness-raising black literature of the 1950s and 1960s that aimed at positive and empowering representations of black characters. Maria Diedrich thus argues that in his own novels, Baldwin did not manage to formulate a positive alternative to Wright's protest literature.[496] Baldwin tried to change his representational politics in his later novels *If Beale Street Could Talk* (1974) and *Just Above My Head* (1980). In *Just Above My Head*, the musician Arthur Montana is depicted as a black homosexual man and artist who does not feel guilty because of his homosexuality. Diedrich states, however, that the interpretation of black musical traditions such as the gospel solely in terms of suffering once again affirms the discourse of victimization.[497]

5.1.3 Black Nationalism and Homophobia

In his essay "Notes on a Native Son" (first published in *Ramparts* in 1966), Cleaver reacts to Baldwin's criticism of Wright. Cleaver's criticism aims at rehabilitating Wright's novel *Native Son*. It confirms the common image of black masculinity by rejecting homosexuality both as a motif in Baldwin's novels and, on a personal level, as a rejection of Baldwin's lifestyle. Moreover, it dismisses

---

496 Maria Diedrich, "Afro-amerikanische Literatur," *Amerikanische Literaturgeschichte*, ed. Hubert Zapf. Stuttgart: Metzler, 1996, 402–426, 418.

497 Diedrich, "Afro-amerikanische Literatur," 418. See also Herman Beavers, "Finding Common Ground: Ralph Ellison and James Baldwin," *The Cambridge Companion to the African American Novel*, ed. Maryemma Graham, Cambridge: Cambridge UP, 2004, 189–202.

Baldwin's political agenda as conservative. In contrast to Baldwin, who states that he "never believed that [Wright] had any real sense of how a society is put together,"[498] Cleaver is of the opinion that "of all black American novelists, and indeed of all American novelists of any hue, Richard Wright reigns supreme for his profound political, economic and social reference."[499]

Cleaver does not consider the main point of Baldwin's criticism, his assertion that Wright confirms racist stereotypes. Instead, Cleaver rehabilitates Bigger Thomas, whom he regards as "Wright's greatest creation, [...] a man in violent, though inept, rebellion against the stifling, murderous, totalitarian white world,"[500] and polemically denounces Rufus Scott, Baldwin's black male character in *Another Country*.

> [Rufus Scott,] a pathetic wretch who indulged in the white man's pastime of committing suicide, who let a white bisexual homosexual fuck him in his ass, and who took a Southern Jezebel for his woman, with all that these tortured relationships imply, was the epitome of a black eunuch who was completely submitted to the white man.[501]

Cleaver argues within the boundaries of racist discourse: his ideal of black masculinity is the hypersexual heterosexual black man, the exact opposite of what he thinks Rufus embodies. The two sexualized images of black men Cleaver employs in order to oppose racism are grounded in racist discourse (see 3.1.2). Cleaver subsequently states that "homosexuality is a sickness, just as are baby-rape or wanting to become the head of General Motors."[502] He regards homosexuality as a disease incompatible with Baldwin's African roots and claims that an embrace of his African heritage would "cure" him of his homosexuality: "the only way out for [Baldwin] is psychologically to embrace Africa, the land of his fathers, which he utterly refuses to do. He has instead resorted to a despicable underground guerilla war, waged on paper, against black masculinity."[503] Cleaver regards homosexuality

---

498 Baldwin, "Alas, Poor Richard," 249.

499 Eldridge Cleaver, "Notes on a Native Son," *Soul on Ice*, New York: Delta, 1992, 122–138, 134.

500 Cleaver, 132.

501 Cleaver, 132.

502 Cleaver, 136.

503 Cleaver, 135.

as a disease and embracing one's African heritage as the only cure. In doing so, he implies that homosexuality and "healthy" blackness are mutually exclusive. This attitude is compatible with the construction of homosexuality as a predominantly white and middle-class identity. However, during that time, (white) homosexual men were an oppressed minority. Rather than criticizing the hegemonic discourse, Cleaver makes use of homophobic stereotypes and directs them against Baldwin. Instead of considering the contents of Baldwin's arguments, Cleaver transposes the origin of Baldwin's critique to the personal level: "Baldwin's essay on Richard Wright reveals that he despised – not Richard Wright, but his masculinity."[504]

Baldwin's and Cleaver's receptions of Norman Mailer's infamous essay "The White Negro," first published in *Dissent* in 1957, are paradigmatic of their different notions of black masculinity and the categories of race and homosexuality. Mailer takes up racist stereotypes connecting black masculinity with *body* and white masculinity with *mind* when he compares the anti-bourgeois hipster with black men.[505] He reinforces the belief that black culture is determined by sex and primitivism, and he ascribes this idea to the existential hipster: "the hipster [...] could be considered a white negro."[506] In his essay, Mailer reproduces stereotypes from the dominant culture to which he himself, as a white man, belonged. Wallace criticizes Mailer for romanticizing racial oppression, and she claims that the black men depicted by Mailer "had never really existed, except in the warped imagination of Western males."[507]

Baldwin points out that "The White Negro" takes up exactly those stereotypes about black men which were prevalent in US American hegemonic discourse. He criticizes Mailer for perpetuating "the myth of the sexuality of Negroes"[508] and sees the cause of Mailer's own identification of black culture with primitivism and sexuality in Mailer's insecurity about his own masculinity.[509]

---

504 Cleaver, 135.

505 Susan Gubar, *Racechanges: White Skin, Black Face in American Culture*, New York: Oxford UP, 1997, 178.

506 Mailer, *Advertisements for Myself*, 341.

507 Wallace, 44.

508 James Baldwin, "The Black Boy Looks at the White Boy," *Collected Essays*. New York: Library of America, 1998, 269–285, 272.

509 Baldwin, "The Black Boy," 269.

Wallace's criticism goes in the same direction. She states that "Mailer exhorted [black men] to return to that brave and noble primitive creature of the jungle."[510]

Cleaver admires "The White Negro" because to him it seems "to be prophetic and penetrating in its understanding of the psychology involved in the accelerating confrontation of black and white in America."[511] He calls it "one of the few gravely important expressions of our time"[512] and praises it for its "solid kernel of truth."[513] Cleaver does not recognize that Baldwin criticizes Mailer for perpetuating racist stereotypes because he does not question his own notion of black masculinity, which is basically in accordance with Mailer's and the dominant culture's stereotype of the black man as hypersexual. Thus, Cleaver names pathological reasons for Baldwin's standpoint:

> The racial death-wish is manifested as the driving force in James Baldwin. His hatred for blacks, even as he pleads what he conceives as their cause, makes him the apotheosis of the dilemma in the ethos of the black bourgeoisie who have completely rejected their African heritage, consider the loss irrevocable, and refuse to look again in that direction. This is the root of Baldwin's violent repudiation of Mailer's *The White Negro*.[514]

Cleaver states that the "racial death-wish" is typical of black homosexual men who are "outraged and frustrated because in their sickness they are unable to have a baby by a white man."[515] Cleaver sees homosexuality as the cause of Baldwin's rejection of Mailer's stereotypes of black men. As Cleaver thinks that "the white man has deprived [the black homosexual] of his masculinity, castrated him in the center of his burning skull,"[516] he contends that it is nearly impossible for Baldwin to embrace what Cleaver and Mailer think is a positive image of black masculinity.

---

510 Wallace, 44.

511 Cleaver, 123.

512 Cleaver, 123.

513 Cleaver, 123.

514 Cleaver, 129.

515 Cleaver, 128.

516 Cleaver, 128.

Even though Baraka does not praise Mailer's essay, Wallace argues that Baraka has "transformed Mailer's 'sexual outlaw' into the role model for the black revolutionary."[517] The following passage from Baraka's essay "American Sexual Reference: Black Male" illustrates Wallace's argument.

> The reason the white woman was supposed to be intrigued by the black man was because he was basic and elemental emotionally (which is true for the nonbrainwashed black, simply because there is no reason he should not be; the black man is more 'natural' than the white simply because he has fewer *things* between him and reality, fewer wrappers, fewer artificial rules), therefore 'wilder,' harder, and almost insatiable in his lovemaking.[518]

Baraka does exactly what Baldwin wants to avoid. He uncritically adopts stereotypes of black men from the dominant culture and reinforces them.

In this essay, Baraka employs several homophobic stereotypes in order to disqualify white men as gay and thus "unnatural," and to re-establish black masculinity as "real." His concepts of sexuality, gender, and race are determined by essentialist categories. Wallace sums up Baraka's ideas and states that "according to Jones [Baraka] the struggle of black against white was the purity of primitivism against the corruption of technology, the noble savage against the pervert bureaucrats, the super macho against the fags."[519] His essay starts with a homophobic passage explicating the author's opinion of (white) gay men:

> Most American white men are trained to be fags. For this reason it is no wonder their faces are weak and blank, left without the hurt that reality makes – anytime. That red flush, those silk blue faggot eyes.[520]

Baraka criticizes white American intellectuals, no matter whether they are representatives of powerful institutions or if they are part of the beatnik counter-culture, as "estranged and alienated from the real."[521] According to Baraka, this estrangement is embodied in the beat artist's ignorance

---

517 Wallace, 64.

518 Baraka, "American Sexual Reference," 221–222.

519 Wallace, 63.

520 Baraka, "American Sexual Reference," 216.

521 Baraka, "American Sexual Reference," 219.

of socioeconomic conditions. For him, the manifestation of the artist's estrangement and alienation is his homosexuality:

> the most extreme form of alienation acknowledged within white society is homosexuality. The long abiding characterization of the Western artist as usually 'queer' does not seem out of place.[522]

Baraka denounces white men in order to emphasize a notion of black masculinity which is just the opposite of white masculinity because it is "real" and heterosexual. By confirming the racist stereotype of the hypersexual black man, he remains within the binary logic of the hegemonic discourse.

In "Brief Reflection on Two Hot Shots," an essay he wrote two years earlier (1963), Baraka presents a similar essentialist view of homosexuality in order to dismiss the writings of Baldwin and Peter Abrahams, a South African writer. In this essay, he accuses Baldwin of integrationism and estrangement from racial struggle. He calls Baldwin "too hip to be *real*"[523] and criticizes him for his claim to be an *individual*. If one takes the essay "American Sexual Reference: Black Male" into consideration, one could argue that the terms "estrangement" and "individualism" refer to homosexuality because in this essay Baraka calls homosexuality "the most extreme form of alienation"[524] and claims that "it is in the 'individualistic' ego-oriented society that homosexuality flourishes most."[525] Consequently, Baraka seems to imply that black homosexual men cannot be trusted because they consider their *individual* and *alienated* "disease" to be more important than the racial struggle. I have argued above that, during the McCarthy era, gay men and lesbians were stereotyped as untrustworthy, as traitors of a common cause. Baraka published his dismissal of Baldwin against the background of these stereotypes. His view of gay men as alienated and self-centered and his pointed criticism of Baldwin's supposed lack of support of racial struggle were guided by the dominant culture's stereotypes of gay men.

---

522 Baraka, "American Sexual Reference," 219.

523 Amiri Baraka (LeRoi Jones), "Brief Reflection on Two Hot Shots," *Home: Social Essays*. New York: Morrow, 1966, 116–121, 117.

524 Baraka, "American Sexual Reference," 219.

525 Baraka, "American Sexual Reference," 230.

In 1970, four years after Cleaver's and Baraka's attack on Baldwin and one year after Stonewall, Huey P. Newton published "A Letter from Huey to the Revolutionary Brothers and Sisters About the Women's Liberation and Gay Liberation Movements." Directed at other members of the Black Panther Party, it critically reflects on their misogyny and homophobia. It aimed at coalition building between the different social movements and was published on August 21, 1970, in the party's newspaper.[526]

5.1.4 Baldwin's Heterosexual Mask

In reacting to Cleaver's homophobic attack, Baldwin partly contradicts the pioneering accounts of homosexuality in his early essays and novels. In 1972, Baldwin published the essay "No Name in the Street," his answer to Cleaver's attack. Even though Baldwin admits that he "didn't like what [Cleaver] had to say about [him] at all,"[527] he does not criticize Cleaver's homophobic rhetoric. Instead, he dissociates himself from gay men, whom he pejoratively identifies as "faggots, punks, and sissies:"

> [Cleaver] seemed to feel that I was dangerously odd, badly twisted, and fragile reed, of too much use to the establishment to be trusted by blacks. I felt that he used my public reputation against me both naively and unjustly, and I also felt that I was confused in his mind with the unutterable debasement of the male – with all those faggots, punks, and sissies, the sight and sound of whom, in prison, must have made him vomit more than once.[528]

Henry Louis Gates, Jr. does not read these lines as an expression of internalized homophobia. Instead, he interprets them as a desperate attempt to be accepted as a part of the Black Power movement. In the 1960s, Baldwin had unwillingly been perceived as a spokesperson of black America despite the notion "that his arguments, richly nuanced and self-consciously ambivalent,

---

526 Huey Newton, "A Letter from Huey to the Revolutionary Brothers and Sisters About the Women's Liberation and Gay Liberation Movements," *We Are Everywhere: A Historical Sourcebook of Gay and Lesbian Politics*, eds. Mark Blasius and Shane Phelan, New York and London: Routledge, 1997, 404–406.

527 James Baldwin, "No Name in the Street," *Collected Essays*. New York: Library of America, 1998, 349–476, 459.

528 Baldwin, "No Name," 459.

were far too complex to serve straightforwardly political ends."[529] When the Black Power movement formulated its radical political program promoting a coherent and stable collective identity as black men, Baldwin "would never be allowed to reclaim the cultural authority he once enjoyed."[530] Gates interprets the passage cited above as an expression of Baldwin's insecurities concerning his political standpoint. As Baldwin did not want to lose contact with the Black Power movement, he emphasized his identity as an African American by rejecting a gay identity. William J. Spurlin assumes that Cleaver's pressure on Baldwin was so strong that Baldwin did not dare to politicize homosexuality:

> Cleaver's attack on Baldwin's work, as well as his attack on Baldwin for being gay, which Cleaver felt alienated him from his African heritage and from his connections to black resistance, while reflecting the homophobia associated with the Black Power movement, did nonetheless have an effect on Baldwin's literary reputation as a black writer and as a potential black leader. [...] Baldwin consistently insisted that homosexuality was a private matter best kept from public view, a position which he embraced even more strongly after Cleaver's attack, but believed that racial relations, unlike sexual ones, were not private, but public matters.[531]

Baldwin's reaction also supports the thesis that he differentiated between "homosexual behavior" and "gay identity." Whereas he considers homosexuality to be a morally legitimate form of expressing love between two human beings, he regards gay identity as a limitation of one's personality.

In his essay "Straight Black Studies: On African American Studies, James Baldwin, and Black Queer Studies," Dwight A. McBride demonstrates that Baldwin even deliberately assumed a heterosexual position when publicly talking as a representative of the race. McBride quotes a passage from a 1973 television interview in which Baldwin states:

529   Henry Louis Gates Jr., *Thirteen Ways of Looking at a Black Man*, New York: Random House, 1997, 9.

530   Gates Jr., *Thirteen Ways*, 15.

531   William J. Spurlin, "Rhetorical Hermeneutics and Gay Identity Politics: Rethinking American Cultural Studies," *Reconceptualizing American Literary/Cultural Studies: Rhetoric, History, and Politics in the Humanities*, ed. William E. Cain, New York: Garland, 1996, 169–185, 178.

I don't know if the board of education hates black people, but I know the textbooks they give my children to read and the schools that we go to. Now this is the evidence! You want me to make an act of faith risking myself, my wife, my woman, my sister, my children on some idealism which you assure me exists in America which I have never seen.[532]

Baldwin's rhetorical strategy of speaking of his (imagined) wife and children implies a black male heterosexual position. McBride states that heterosexual black masculinity was a precondition if a black man assumed the position of representative race man, a fact that Baldwin experienced by way of Cleaver's and Baraka's attacks.

The three aspects I have named, Baldwin's early attempt to address the topic of male homosexuality, his critique of Wright and the Protest Novel, and the attacks by Cleaver and Baraka had grave consequences for his self-representation as a black spokesperson and also for the representation of male homosexuality in his novels. The conflict-laden homosexual desire of John Grimes in *Go Tell it on the Mountain* is rather veiled, the protagonists of *Giovanni's Rooms* are two white men in Paris, and Rufus Scott in *Another Country* is depicted as a black bisexual man. In *Just Above My Head* (1979), Baldwin depicts sexual relationships between black men, but he still does not construct them in terms of gay identity.

Baldwin's sexual politics differ significantly from the political agenda of 1980s black gay activism. As I have shown in the first chapter, many black gay cultural activists discuss an afro-centric gay agenda and seek to strengthen the identity category black gay man. One way of affirming this identity is the reference to a Baldwin who is constructed as black and gay. In their re-writings of Baldwin's texts, some black gay cultural activists of the 1980s alter the equivocal elements in Baldwin's writings (bisexuality, white homosexual protagonists, inter-racial love, and trans-nationalism) and invent a different version of Baldwin, one that is supportive of the black gay political project. In order to support this point, I will put special emphasis on analyzing the representation and critique of gay whiteness in Kenan's and Dixon's texts. The critique of the normative

---

532 Baldwin, qtd. in McBride, 76–77.

construction of gayness as a white identity and the depiction of relationships between black gay men are rooted in the 1980s context of black gay politics that promoted the slogan "black men loving black men is the revolutionary act." It can also be seen as a deliberate reaction to black power representatives like Cleaver and Baraka, who consider male homosexuality as a counter-revolutionary act. In depicting intraracial gay love and in revealing white gay racism, black gay writers like Kenan and Dixon comment critically on an integrationist and assimilationist political agenda while simultaneously reacting to the homophobia inherent in Black Nationalist thought.

5.2 Randall Kenan: *A Visitation of Spirits* (1989)

Horace Cross, the protagonist of Kenan's first novel *A Visitation of Spirits*, is a sixteen-year-old black male adolescent who tries to come to terms with his homosexuality. Parts of the novel are narrated from Horace's perspective, and the first thought ascribed to him is "what to become?"[533] The thought of "becoming" initially suggests a quest narrative, and the reader soon learns that Horace wants to engage in black magic to transform himself into an animal, a bird, in order to escape the sinfulness of his homosexuality. The narration of his transformation will lead to closure, but his quest does not lead to a positive ending, coming out as a black gay man. Instead, it finally results in his suicide. Owing to its setting in the fictitious rural community of Tims Creek, North Carolina, during the 1980s, and to the rather hopeless situation of its black homosexual protagonist, the text differs significantly from many other black gay texts that are set in the 1980s: Horace is not part of a gay and lesbian community, and he is unaware of the existence of an emerging black gay movement in America's urban centers.

Next to *Looking for Langston* and *No Easy Place to Be*, *A Visitation of Spirits* is the third text in my study that was published in 1989. Like Julien, Dixon, Corbin, and

533 Randall Kenan, *A Visitation of Spirits*, New York: Vintage, 1989, 11.

Delany, Kenan is closely affiliated with the academic world. He teaches English at Sarah Lawrence College. Owing to his academic affiliations with literature departments and literary theory, his texts are multi-layered and comment on various literary traditions. *A Visitation of Spirits* signifies on Baldwin's *Go Tell It on the Mountain*, and it stands in a tradition of black feminst/womanist writings. Containing supernatural forces like demons and ghosts, it contains magical realist elements and alludes to the Southern Gothic tradition.

Kenan's *Walking on Water: Black American Lives at the Turn of the Century* (2000) is an ethnographic travel book. In 1994, Kenan wrote *James Baldwin*, a biography of James Baldwin intended for a young adult readership, which puts special emphasis on Baldwin's homosexuality. The series in which it is published is called "Lives of Notable Gay Men and Lesbians," and its general editor is the historian and gay rights activist Martin Duberman. In 2007, Kenan published *The Fire This Time*, a book of personal essays, the title of which is homage to Baldwin's famous essay *The Fire Next Time* which came out 45 years earlier.

In addition to his debut novel *A Visitation of Spirits*, he has published a book of short stories called *Let the Dead Bury Their Dead* (1992). The title story of this collection is a fictional postmodern ethnography that continues the narratives of some of the inhabitants of the fictitious Tims Creek Community started in *A Visitation of Spirits*.[534] Kenan's short story "Wash Me" (1996) narrates the story of Gideon Stone, a character from *A Visitation of Spirits* to whom I will refer below.[535] These additions to and continuations of the narratives begun in *A Visitation of Spirits* go beyond the confined frame of the novel and are transposed to other genres. He uses a fictional ethnographic study in *Let the Dead Bury Their Dead* in which the papers of James Malachi Greene reveal the history of the Tims Creek community, and the genre of the short story that gives an account of the future of one of the novel's protagonists. Raised in the rural South, Kenan is preoccupied with a particular place, a strategy which can

---

534 Lindsey Tucker, "Gay Identity, Conjure, and the Uses of Postmodern Ethnography in the Fictions of Randall Kenan," *MFS Modern Fiction Studies* 49.2 (2003): 277–302, 306–331.

535 Randall Kenan, "Wash Me," *Shade: An Anthology of Fiction by Gay Men of African Descent*, eds. Bruce Morrow and Charles H. Rowell, New York: Avon, 1996, 260–272.

be read as an autobiographical element.[536] He grew up in Chinquapin, a small black community in southeast North Carolina.

In his book *The Queer Renaissance*, as well as in his earlier essay "A Visitation of Difference: Randall Kenan and Black Queer Theory" (1993), Robert McRuer analyzes the implications of the rural setting of the novel for (black) queer theory. In his texts he criticizes what later became known as metronormativity, queer theory's focus on urban gay and lesbian culture.[537] In the chapter "Queer Locations/Queer Transformations" in *The Queer Renaissance*, McRuer exclusively deals with *A Visitation of Spirits*. McRuer offers a reading that considers the way Kenan's novel relates to Baldwin's *Go Tell it on the Mountain* (1952). He analyzes Kenan's references to Baldwin's novel by using Henry Louis Gates's critical theory of Signifying (see 3.5). Apart from McRuer, there are two further essays with a focus on Kenan's references to Baldwin: Sharon P. Holland's "(Pro) Creating Imaginative Spaces and Other Queer Acts," and Sheila Smith McKoy's "Rescuing the Black Homosexual Lambs: Randall Kenan and the Reconstruction of Southern Gay Masculinity." In her essay, Holland asks how Kenan's text "attempts to re-create an imaginative place for black gay experience in the African American tradition."[538] McKoy argues that, in addition to signifying on *Go Tell it on the Mountain*, his *A Visitation of Spirits* can also be read as a signification on Baldwin's novel *Another Country*. Following McRuer's argumentation, McKoy's central thesis is that Kenan's novel demonstrates that "homosexual desire can transform culture and that it can open a space wherein black men can embrace a gay identity, even in the rural south."[539]

In my reading of *A Visitation of Spirits*, I will follow McRuer's, Holland's, and McKoy's approaches to the intertextual references between Kenan's and

536 Susan Ketchin, "Interview with Randall Kenan," *The Christ-haunted Landscape: Faith and Doubt in Southern Fiction*, ed. Susan Ketchin. Jackson: UP of Mississippi, 1994. 277–302, 286.

537 See for example Karen Tongson, "Metronormativity and Gay Globalization," *Quer Durch die Geisteswissenschaften: Perspektiven der Queer Theory*, eds. Elahe Haschemi Yekani and Beatrice Michaelis, Berlin: Querverlag, 2005, 40–52.

538 Sharon P. Holland, "(Pro)Creating Imaginative Spaces and Other Queer Acts," *James Baldwin Now*, ed. Dwight A. McBride, New York: New York UP, 1999, 265–288, 269.

539 Sheila Smith McKoy, "Rescuing the Black Homosexual Lambs: Randall Kenan and the Reconstruction of Southern Gay Masculinity," *Contemporary Black Men's Fiction and Drama*, ed. Keith Clark, Urbana 2001, 15–36, 17.

Baldwin's novels, but I will refute McRuer's and McKoy's arguments that the rural religious community is transformed by Horace's black gay/homosexual presence. Rather, I contend that Horace's suicide can be understood as an inevitable consequence of the repressive situation created by the community's religious and moral standards and of the lack of an alternative model of living as a black gay man. There are two other options Horace might choose: the first is the white gay community, embodied in the openly gay white actors of the theater production he works for the summer prior to his suicide, and the second is identifying as gay within the black community the way his black and openly gay friend Gideon does. As will be shown, neither option is an alternative for Horace.

Kenan uses telling names for the characters of his novel. They signify on Baldwin's texts as well as on the intersections of blackness and gayness. Horace's family name is "Cross," which evokes the title of Baldwin's essay "Down at the Cross" (1962), which describes his religious experiences as an adolescent in Harlem. This essay can be considered an autobiographical companion text to *Go Tell It on the Mountain*. Horace's uncle is called "Jimmy," and he is the minister of Tims Creek. This character is an allusion to Jimmy Baldwin, who was a minister in Harlem. McKoy points out that the literal meaning of Horace's name is "one who marks time." She states that his suicide marks a temporal turning point for the value system of the community.[540] But whereas one can argue that the community members are emotionally affected by Horace's suicide, there is no evidence that the community's value system is changed.

I would rather argue that the name is important for another reason: It consists of two syllables, "Ho" and "Race." If one considers the family name "Cross" as well, one could argue that this name denotes a *cross*over between *ho*mosexuality and *race*, the promise of a black gay identity that Horace is unable to achieve.

A third dimension of his name is the allusion to Horace Walpole. His *The Castle of Otranto: A Gothic Story* (1764) is the foundation text of the genre of the gothic novel, and *A Visitation of Spirits* alludes to this literary form on several levels. As a novel set in the rural South and containing supernatural forces such as demons and ghosts, *A Visitation of Spirits* stands in a tradition of Southern gothic

---

540 McKoy, 20.

writings, a sub-genre of gothic literature which employs stylistic devices of gothic literature in order to depict the essence of Southern culture.[541] In his depiction of Horace's desolate psychic state and his encounter with a demon/ghost, Kenan does not effect suspense or horror in a traditional sense. Instead, these elements reveal the terror effected by the way the Tims Creek community is structured. Literary scholar Cedric Gael Bryant argues for a specific African American gothic tradition which he finds in Richard Wright's short story "Big Boy Leaves Home," his novel Native Son and which "extends back to early 19th-century slave narratives and forward to Toni Morrison's Beloved (1987) and Jewelle Gomez's The Gilda Stories (1991)."[542] Bryant sees the common characteristic of these texts in their repetition and revision of stylistic devices common to the white gothic tradition. In his introduction to Native Son "How Bigger was Born," Wright himself draws the connection between his own novel and gothic literature. He states that

> we do have in the Negro the embodiment of a past tragic enough to appease the spiritual hunger of even a James; and we do have in the oppression of the Negro a shadow athwart our national life dense and heavy enough to satisfy even the gloomy broodings of a Hawthorne. And if Poe were alive, he would not have to invent horror; horror would invent him.[543]

Similar to Bryant, Teresa A. Goddu argues for a black gothic tradition that takes up and revises the conventions used by white gothic writers. She argues that white writers often depict slavery in a gothic mode and states that "the gothic might offer useful metaphors for depicting the historical event of slavery, but its narrative construction could also empty slavery of history by turning it

541 The table of contents of A Visitation of Spirits already points in this direction. Chapter headings such as "White Sorcery," "Black Necromancy" (which possibly alludes to the gothic text The Necromancer: or, The Tale of the Black Forest (1794) by Ludwig Flammenberg aka Carl Friedrich Kahlert), and "Old Demonology" are titles that establish a connection to the genre.

542 Cedric Gael Bryant, "'The Soul has Bandaged Moments': Reading the African American Gothic in Wright's 'Big Boy Leaves Home,' Morrison's Beloved, and Gomez's Gilda," African American Review, 39.4 (2005), 541–553, 541.

543 Richard Wright, "How Bigger was Born," Native Son, New York: Perennial Classics, 1998, 431–462, 462. For an analysis of Wright and gothic traditions, see Joseph Bodziock, "Richard Wright and Afro-American Gothic," Richard Wright: Myths and Realities, ed. James Trotman, New York: Garland, 1988, 27–42. See also Bryant.

into a gothic trope."[544] In her analysis of slave narratives, she demonstrates how black writers used the gothic trope for opposite ends, namely the unveiling of the horrors of slavery:

> The slave narratives's generic conventions seem to be in direct opposition to the gothic's: its documentary form and adherence to veracity announce a refusal of any imaginative rendering. Although the slave narrative might not incorporate the gothic's typical supernatural elements, it does, however, contain, even in its factual form – many gothic characteristics.[545]

Despite the fact that Walker and Morrison reject the label "gothic" for their work because of the "apparent lack of connection to reality and intellectual purpose,"[546] Goddu suggests that "instead of accepting traditional readings of the gothic as unrealistic and frivolous, thereby excluding African-American narratives from the genre, we should use the African-American gothic to revise our understanding of the gothic as an historical mode."[547] Consequently, in using gothic conventions, Kenan does not solely refer to white literary traditions, but he also connects to black strategies of depicting the real horrors of history.

Goddu's revised understanding of the gothic as a mode capable of addressing real historical events through the depiction of supernatural events can easily be connected to magic realist modes of writings that are rooted in Latin American traditions. "Within Anglophone literature, novelists of the African Diaspora (...) have used elements of myth and magic to remember, express, and account for those experiences which Western notions of history, reality, and truth have failed to address."[548] The novels of Morrison are often read as examples of magic realism because they offer a revision of dominant historiography through the inclusion of mythical and magical elements. This function of magic realism is not too far from Goddu's outline of African

---

544 Teresa A. Goddu, *Gothic America: Narrative, History, and Nation*, New York: Columbia UP, 1997, 135.

545 Goddu, 135.

546 Goddu, 140.

547 Goddu, 140.

548 Ajuan Maria Mance, "Magical Realism," *The Toni Morrison Encyclopedia*, ed. Elizabeth Ann Beaulieu, Westport, Conneticut and London: Greenwood, 2003, 197–201, 198.

American gothic as a mode of writing that includes supernatural elements in order to reveal rather than romanticize historical events. Even if they grow out of different traditions, white European and Latin American respectively, gothic conventions and magical realist elements fulfil similar functions in African American literature. In her essay on gothicism in Morrison's novels, Monika Elbert makes the connection between gothicism and magic realism explicit in stating that „The fabulous or miraculous quality of Morrison's Gothic is akin to the magical realism of Isabel Allende's or Laura Esquivel's ghost stories, and in all three cases, these women writers evoke the ghosts in order to connect their protagonists with their histories."[549]

In addition to the allusions to the gothic tradition, *A Visitation of Spirits* is written in an experimental style that contradicts the chronological order of the narrated events. The narrative focuses on two points in time, the day of December 8, 1985, when Jimmy, Zeke, and Ruth make a road trip, and the night of April 29–30, 1984, the night of Horace's suicide. The narrative shifts back and forth between these two days. In addition, there are three passages headed "James Malachi Greene Confessions" and one passage with the heading "Horace Cross Confessions," all of which are written in a confessional mode. Jimmy's confessions contain three dramatized passages that read like a play. Much of the plot is narrated by way of flashbacks of the different characters, who become alternate centers of consciousness.

The combination of narrative modes and the structure as a collage associate *A Visitation of Spirits* with the postmodern novel. The open structure invites the reader to engage actively in the construction of the story. Like the novels of Ishmael Reed, it connects different genres of texts. For example, by alluding to Charles Dickens's "A Christmas Carol" through the ghost that takes the protagonist to important occurrences in the past, it refers to the canon of English literature. High culture is connected with folktales and popular culture. The fusion of popular culture, mythology and folktale is illustrated by the description of various posters in Horace's room depicting pop-cultural icons

---

549 Monika Elbert, "Gothicism," *The Toni Morrison Encyclopedia*, ed. Elizabeth Ann Beaulieu, Westport, Conneticut and London: Greenwood, 2003, 144–147, 146.

such as Hulk, Batman, and the Hobbits.[550] Horace calls them "friends," and they are described as if they were natural allies in possession of supernatural powers. Their names or their pop-cultural origins are never mentioned. Instead, the narrative blends them in with the magical realist elements in the text.

Ishmael Reed calls his strategy of combining such disparate elements "Neo- HooDooism." In his essay "American Neo-HooDooism: the novels of Ishmael Reed," Pierre-Damien Mvuyekure has characterized Neo-HooDooism as a strategy to de-center Judeo-Christian approaches in favor of an affirmation of African-based identities. Myuyekure emphasizes the difference between Reed's approach and those of afrocentrists like Baraka and Molefi Asante, whose aesthetic aim is a return to their African roots. He states that Reed's "writing goes beyond the reconnection to African spirituality in order to create a multicultural space for all cultures and modes of being and thinking."[551] With its collage of rather disparate elements, Kenan's novel follows the same paradigm, at least in a formal sense. However, the world represented in the narrative is not a "multicultural space for all cultures and modes of being and thinking."[552] There is no space for a black gay youth, even if his world consists of myths, folktales, popular culture and the like. The shortcomings of this world are made unmistakably clear in the way Horace's suicide is described. Harshly contradicting the magical realist tone of the novel, the suicide is described in a scientific voice denoting Western rationality. The passage is introduced by explicitly calling the suicide a fact that cannot be explained away by magical realism:

> Whether or not the malevolent spirit existed is irrelevant, in the end. For whether he caused it or not, the boy died. This is a fact. The bullet did break the skin of his forehead, pierce the cranium, slice through the cortex and cerebellum, irreparably bruising the cerebrum and medulla oblongata, and emerge from the back of the skull, all with a wet and lightning crack. This did happen.[553]

---

550 Kenan, *Visitation*, 17

551 Mvuyekure, 204.

552 Mvuyekure, 204.

553 Kenan, *Visitation*, 253.

The detailed description of the suicide does not stop here; it goes on and comprises a full page altogether. On the one hand, the use of scientific language adds one more textual element to the postmodern collage of the narrative. On the other hand, this scientific description can also be read as the finding of a Neo-HooDooist formulation of African American culture that finally fails in granting a space for black gay men.

5.2.1 Baldwin Revisited

There are many references between *A Visitation of Spirits* and *Go Tell it on the Mountain*, and the editors of the anthology *Black Like Us* confirm that Baldwin's "autobiographically based references to race, homosexuality, and his relationship with the black church inspired the content of [Kenan's] book."[554] In addition to the structural similarity of both novels being autobiographical debut novels of writers who can be considered as black homosexual/gay writers, there are also similarities regarding the contents and structure of the novels. The protagonists of both novels are adolescent boys who are part of religious communities and who try to come to terms with their forbidden sexual desires. At the center of *Go Tell it on the Mountain* is John Grimes, a fourteen-year-old boy who, in the course of the novel, experiences religious salvation and becomes a preacher in a congregation. The novel contains elements of irony to the effect that the quest narrative of a boy who is saved by God is undermined. This irony is already contained in the novel's very first paragraph:

> Everyone had always said that John would be a preacher when he grew up, just like his father. It had been said so often that John, without ever thinking about it, had come to believe it himself. Not until the morning of his fourteenth birthday did he really begin to think about it, and by then it was already too late.[555]

The reader witnesses John's quest for salvation and knows from the start that it is "already too late." The name "John Grimes" adds to this knowledge. If one reads his last name as a verb, the full name is changed to the sentence

---

554 Carbado, McBride, 411.

555 James Baldwin, *Go Tell It on the Mountain*, New York: Dial, 2005, 3.

"John grimes," an indication that the protagonist brings filth to himself and the community.

After his conversion, a night he spends on the threshing floor, John does not seem to believe in his salvation himself. He tells the older church pianist Elisha "no matter what happens to me, where I go, what folks say about me, no matter what *any*body says, you remember – please remember – I was saved. I was *there*."[556] There are a few fleeting references to what might be interpreted as John's homosexuality: the way he longs for Elisha and his thoughts of older boys while he is masturbating in the school lavatory. As John's homosexuality is only suggested in these passages, some readers in the 1950s will very likely have missed it.

Compared to Baldwin in 1952, Kenan in 1989 could be more open about the conflict his protagonist experiences because of his homosexuality. McRuer states that Kenan brings Baldwin's story "out of the closet,"[557] to the effect that "*A Visitation of Spirits* in general reads like an openly gay version of *Go Tell It on the Mountain*."[558] The other characters in the two novels form cohesive religious communities. All of them keep their sexual proclivities secret, and none of them lives up to the high religious and moral standards of their respective communities. The narrative techniques of the novels are similar in that they both have shifting narrative centers and reveal the life-stories of the other protagonists by flashbacks.

The way John has internalized feelings of guilt regarding his homosexual desire is mirrored in Horace. In both novels, *Go Tell it on the Mountain* and *A Visitation of Spirits*, the adolescent protagonists' homosexual desires are connected with masturbation. In *Go Tell it on the Mountain*, the masturbatory scene is one of the few passages that directly refer to homosexuality:

---

556 Baldwin, *Go Tell*, 225.

557 McRuer, 80.

558 McRuer, 80.

He had sinned. In spite of the saints, his mother and his father, the warnings he had heard from his earliest beginnings, he had sinned with his hands a sin that was hard to forgive. In the school lavatory, alone, thinking of the boys, older, bigger, braver, who made bets with each other as to whose urine could arch higher, he had watched in himself a transformation of which he would never dare to speak.[559]

Horace is three years older than John. In one passage he remembers the time when he was 12 or 13, an age closer to John's, and recalls his first experiences with masturbation. Like Baldwin in *Go Tell it on the Mountain*, Kenan uses the phrase "to sin with one's hands:"

By the eighth grade he had discovered how to sin with his hands. He knew he was doomed to hellfire and damnation, for try as he might, he could not stop. He would go for days, weeks, without touching himself, only to succumb in delicious fury, and afterwards feel the guilt of a murderer. [...] Is that when the truth uncovered itself and stood naked before him? When the thought of a woman failed to arouse him, and the thought of a man did?[560]

Both passages combine the boys' act of masturbation with homosexual fantasies ("thinking of the boys," "the thought of a man"), the school as a social institution ("in the school lavatory," "by the eighth grade") and a strong sense of guilt inflicted by the church ("In spite of the saints," "doomed to hellfire and damnation"). These passages illustrate the similarities in the power of religion in both communities. Both boys experience guilt and terror, and the fact that John lives in Harlem and Horace in the rural South does not make a difference.

Even though *Go Tell It on the Mountain* is set in Harlem, it has been read as a Southern text that is transposed to the North.[561] The religious community and the value system of the members of the congregation are depicted as belonging to a world isolated from the more liberal options New York has to offer. The

---

559 Baldwin, *Go Tell*, 11. The phrase "a transformation of which he would never dare to speak" evokes the characterization of homosexuality as "the love that dare not speak its name" often ascribed to Oscar Wilde. Henderson states that Lord Alfred Douglas was the first to use this phrase in his sonnet "The Two Loves." Mae G. Henderson, "Notes," *Passing* by Nella Larsen, New York: The Modern Library, 2002, 183–204, 191–192, FN4.

560 Kenan, *Visitation*, 110–101.

561 A. Robert Lee, "The South in Contemporary African-American Fiction," *A Companion to the Literature and Culture of the American South*, eds. Richard J. Gray and Owen Robinson, Malden, MA: Blackwell, 2004, 552–570, 554.

vast difference between John's church and urban New York is illustrated in the description of John's secret trip to a movie theater on 42nd Street. In his essay "The South in Contemporary African American Fiction," A. Robert Lee argues that the way the community and its conflicts are portrayed brings "the South to the North, Dixie's white violence and fervent black Christianity carried echoingly into Manhattan's premier black city."[562] Kenan's text refers to these Southern elements, and his narrative is directly located in the rural South.

The Southern setting also evokes the African American womanist tradition, most prominently embodied by the writings of Alice Walker. In "Oral Culture and Southern Fiction," Jill Terry argues that one key characteristic of black womanist texts is the use of orality to respond to

> negative stereotypes and to assert identity positively – as Southern, as black, as female. In this sense the function of oral forms is [...] a strategy of resistance to master narratives. The claiming of the oral voice is always a controllable literary trope and a political act.[563]

Terry states that orality is introduced by means of representing cultural expressions that are distinctly Southern, such as oral history, folktales, Southern dialect, and music.[564] While these elements are also employed in a *Visitation of Spirits*, I see a crucial difference between the womanist lineage denoted by the early narratives of female slaves, the work of Zora Neale Hurston and Walker signifying on Hurston, and the way Kenan reflects the South. Whereas womanist/black feminist writers of the 1970s and 1980s depicted women's solidarity as a way of countering patriarchal and racist oppression, Horace's quest for an identity ends in his suicide. His growing isolation as a black gay youth stands in stark opposition to the solidarity and love between black women, seen in the relationship between Celie and Shug Avery in Walker's *The Color Purple* (1983). In contrast to this relationship, Horace is depicted as ultimately alone. He cannot reach out to the other

---

562 Lee, 554.

563 Jill Terry, "Oral Culture and Southern Fiction," *A Companion to the Literature and Culture of the American South*, eds. Richard J Gray and Owen Robinson, Malden, MA: Blackwell, 2004, 518–535, 534.

564 Terry, 519.

members of the community. The inability of black men to emotionally bond with other black men is depicted as an effect of the patriarchal and homophobic structure of the Southern black community of Tims Creek. This point becomes clear if one looks at Horace's relations to three black male figures, the minister James Malachai Greene, the novel's other black gay youth Gideon Stone, and the black gay actor Everett.

McRuer's central argument that the Tims Creek community is transformed because of Horace's suicide is supported by his analysis of the personal development the minister James Malachai Greene undergoes after he witnesses Horace's suicide. In three passages with the heading "James Malachai Greene: Confessions,"[565] he reflects upon his own life and his role within the Tims Creek community. McRuer suggests that these confessions are documents Jimmy writes and keeps in a journal. All three confessions are undercut with a dramatized dialogue passage. These are accounts of situations in which Horace's homosexuality is of central importance: the morning he witnesses Horace's suicide, a coming out talk between Horace and Jimmy, and a family conflict because of Horace's pierced earlobe. McRuer argues that these dramatized passages are written by Jimmy, who chooses the dramatized form to emotionally distance himself from the events.[566] I contend that these passages represent Jimmy's memories of crucial situations that, had he acted in a different way, might have saved Horace's life. The dramatized form of these passages has the effect of a direct "reliving" of the situations. The sense of exactness is achieved by way of the stage directions and the direct speech of the persons involved. Jimmy's memories explain his urge to reflect on his life by keeping his journal. The three dramatized passages reveal Jimmy's shortcomings in dealing with Horace's confidence in him.

It is especially the second dramatized passage that demonstrates that Horace and Jimmy do not really connect emotionally. Horace has enough confidence in Jimmy to reveal the secret of his homosexuality. Jimmy, however, cannot cope with this situation. In repeating formulaic phrases

---

565 Kenan, *Visitation*, 31; 107; 171.

566 McRuer, 98.

such as "it's just a phase,"[567] he downplays the topic of homosexuality and Horace's trouble, thus betraying Horace's confidence. In the last dramatized passage, he tries to defend Horace against the other family members' rage effected by Horace's pierced earlobe, but he implicitly rebuilds Horace's closet by suggesting that a pierced earlobe is no longer considered as a sign of gayness. In both situations, Jimmy fails to bond emotionally with Horace and give solidarity and support.

The failure of establishing an emotional bond between two black men is also represented in the relationship between Horace and Gideon Stone. Gideon is a boy from Horace's school. He is the second adolescent black gay character in the novel. Gideon and Horace have a sexual relationship that fails because of Horace's fear. Considering Baldwin's "The Male Prison," his essay on André Gide, one could argue that the name Gideon refers to Gide. Gideon wants Horace to identify as gay but Horace refuses. In "The Male Prison," Baldwin criticizes Gide for the way he dealt with his homosexuality:

> The really horrible thing about the phenomenon of present-day homosexuality, the horrible thing which lies curled like a worm at the heart of Gide's trouble and his work and the reason he so clung to Madeleine, is that today's unlucky deviate can only save himself by the most tremendous exertion of all his forces from falling into an underworld in which he never meets either men or women, where it is impossible to have either a lover or a friend, where the possibility of genuine human involvement has altogether ceased. When this possibility has ceased, so has the possibility of growth.[568]

In Horace's eyes, Gideon embodies the "underworld" Baldwin describes. Gideon identifies as gay, and he wants Horace to do the same. Owing to the pressure of the Tims Creek community, Horace cannot continue his affair with Gideon even if he would like to do so: "he imagined another world, another place, in which he could gladly have complied with Gideon's wish and fallen into lusty, steamy, lascivious abandon – but no."[569] Gideon offers Horace

567 Kenan, *Visitation*, 113.

568 Baldwin, "The Male Prison," 234.

569 Kenan, *Visitation*, 164.

identification as a gay man as the only solution for his conflict, and when Horace rejects this way out he states:

> But remember, black boy, you heard it here first: You're a faggot, Horace. You know? You're a faggot. You can run, you can hide, but when the shit comes down ... you suck cock, you don't eat pussy.' 'You're sickening Gideon.' 'I'm sickening. At least I know what I am.'[570]

This quotation signifies on the critique Cleaver directed at Baldwin. This time, however, it is formulated from a black gay perspective. Cleaver, whose essay "Notes on a Native Son" takes up the title of Richard Wright's novel *Native Son* and connects it with Baldwin, who had distanced himself from the protest fiction of which the very same novel is an example. Likewise, Gideon calls Horace "black boy," evoking the title of Wright's famous eponymous autobiography. In their argument, Gideon obtains the stronger position. He is self-assured and able to re-appropriate the abusive term "faggot" to use it as term of self-identification. Such strategies of re-signification have repeatedly been employed by political groups. For example, it can be seen in the slogan "black is beautiful" or the appropriation of the term "queer" in the early 1990s. From the chosen subject position as a faggot, Gideon can denounce Horace's decision to remain closeted. In calling himself and Horace faggots, Gideon also contradicts Baldwin's fear of the "underworld," which to Baldwin seemed to be the only option for "today's unlucky deviate." In the 1980s, Gideon's black gay subject position has the potential to question the limitations of both identities, blackness and gayness. In the case of Gideon and Horace, Gideon's self-identification as gay is represented as an important stage in his growth, and it is also a prerequisite for his being a lover and a friend. Gideon is capable of "genuine human involvement" precisely because he is not afraid of identifying himself as gay without denying his blackness. Horace, however, is incapable of being a lover or a friend because he denies his gayness. In Baldwin's novels, there are derogatory descriptions of the gay/homosexual sub-culture. For example, in *Giovanni's Room*'s the older homosexual characters Jacques and Guillaume are labeled as "old theatrical sisters."[571] In *A Visitation of Spirits*, as

---

570 Kenan, *Visitation*, 164.

571 Baldwin, *Giovanni's Room*, 31.

Gideon embodies Horace's fear of becoming a gay stereotype, Horace violently terminates their affair and friendship.[572]

Finally, the impossibility of an emotional bond between black men is shown with regard to a third character. In the theater where Horace is working during the summer, he meets Everett, a black gay man whom he idealizes as the person who might have the power to save him. The theater is depicted as a location that reveals different dimensions of racism. The production is a play about the Cross family. Ironically, it is a play about the *white* Cross family who owned Horace's ancestors. Everett is the only black actor in the production. Horace tries to get near Everett three times, and even confesses his love for him, but Everett coldly rejects him. Instead he starts an affair with a white actor who is described as a tall "blue-eyed Georgian."[573] The encounter with Everett shows that it is impossible for Horace to connect to an older emancipated black gay man who comes from a bigger city. In contrast to the singer Shug Avery in *The Color Purple*, who emotionally bonds with Celie and guides her in her quest, Everett is ignorant of Horace's despair. Rather than trying to see the tortured person behind the façade of a self-assured Horace, who boldly tells him he is in love with him, he directs his interest towards a white gay man. In the episode with Everett, the missing solidarity among black gay men becomes clear, and in this respect the relations of black gay men differ from Walker's ideal of womanism. It can also be considered as a criticism of black gay men's sexual desire for white men if it is read in context with the black gay movement's political slogan "black men loving black men is the revolutionary act" (see 2.4).

5.2.2 Constructions of Gay Whiteness

A Visitation of Spirits explores different dimensions of black gayness, white gay racism, and the normative construction of gayness as a white identity. Throughout the novel, coming out as a black gay youth is not an option for Horace. While considering which animal he wants to transform himself into,

---

572 Kenan further elaborates Gideon's character in his short story "Wash Me" (Kenan, "Wash Me").

573 Kenan, *Visitation*, 229.

he thinks "he could not see transforming himself into anything that would not fit the swampy woodlands of Southeastern North Carolina. He had to stay here."[574] Coming out as gay, or transformation into a gay man, would mean to become a subject that does not fit into the social fabric of the region. The reason is the discursive connection of gay identity and whiteness. For example, after Horace's suicide his grandfather Zeke reflects on Horace's alienation and blames it on his white friends:

> Now, in grade school it was all right to have his little white friends, cause they wont friends. They was schoolmates. The way it ought to been. But when he went over to South York High School and commenced to 'hanging out' with them white boys, his 'group' he called it...just messed his mind up. Piercing his ear. I couldn't tell him he couldn't do stuff outside class. That wouldn't a been right either. He was foreign to me. Trying to be like them white folks is what it was.[575]

Zeke's inner monologue implicitly links homosexuality to whiteness. Zeke interprets Horace's behavior as a strategy aimed at becoming like his white friends. His homosexuality, though not directly addressed, is marked by the pierced ear and by Zeke's observation that Horace was "foreign" to him. As I have shown at the beginning of this chapter, black power activists, such as Cleaver and Baraka, stated that black men turn into homosexuals because they really want to become white men (see 5.1.3). Here, Zeke repeats this thought, once again.

Horace himself is also influenced by this figure of thought. There is one passage that links the impossibility of Horace's emancipation as black and gay to the construction of gayness as a white identity. One of the locations the demon guides Horace to is a theater where he formerly worked as one of only a few black persons. In the world of the theater, he was only recognized for his gayness but not for his blackness. In the following quotation he sees himself sitting in front of a mirror:

---

574 Kenan, *Visitation*, 11.

575 Kenan, *Visitation*, 63–64.

He was a black man, dressed in a sun-bright costume, orange and green and blue and red, like a harlequin's. As Horace looked into the mirror, the face appeared more and more familiar, though it was obscured by milky white greasepaint. He realized. Saw clearly. It was him. Horace. Sitting before the mirror, applying makeup. (...) Stunned, confused, bewildered, he could only stare at his reflection, seeing him and him and him.[576]

The white mask Horace is wearing relates to the African American autobiographical tradition. In his essay "Black Autobiography," Roger Rosenblatt states that "in both black autobiography and fiction the final discarding of masks is a character's primary goal because such an act is a demonstration of selfhood and freedom."[577] Horace does not reach this goal. Instead, he sees himself applying and wearing a white mask. This image also evokes the title of Frantz Fanon's *Black Skin, White Masks* (1952), which is a critique of colonialism and the processes by which black persons are made to submit to white norms.[578] The image of the black gay man who is wearing a white mask is once again taken up on the cover of Darieck Scott's black gay novel *Traitor to the Race* (1995). The cover shows a black-and-white-photograph of a black man who is wearing a facial mask consisting of white make-up.

The quotation suggests that the world of the theater, where many of the other actors are white gay men, may grant Horace a certain amount of freedom in his homosexuality, but this recognition can only be achieved if he denies his blackness. In the quotation, this denial is represented as a black minstrel in reverse. Horace becomes a black man in whiteface. He can perceive of himself as a homosexual, but, because of the milky white greasepaint, he perceives of himself as white. As is the case in *Giovanni's Room*, homosexuality, whiteness, and the reflection in a mirror are combined in this one quotation.[579] Henderson calls Baldwin's decision to focus on two white homosexual men in *Giovanni's*

---

576 Kenan, *Visitation*, 219.

577 Roger Rosenblatt, "Black Autobiography," *Autobiography: Essays Theoretical and Critical*, ed. James Olney, Princeton, N.J.: Princeton UP, 1980, 169–180, 176.

578 Isaac Julien's film *Frantz Fanon: Black Skin, White Mask* (1996) reflects on Fanon. His film includes a critique of Fanon's conservative gender politics and homophobic statements.

579 I will elaborate on the use of mirror imagery in *Giovanni's Room* in my analysis of *Vanishing Rooms* (see 5.3.2).

Room "racial drag."[580] This quotation from *A Visitation of Spirits* also demonstrates the connection between gayness and whiteness as a form of racial drag.

Sharon P. Holland observes that the above quotation is the reconstruction of a passage from *Giovanni's Room*. David encounters a man depicted as an androgynous drag-queen and flaming faggot in the bar where he first meets Giovanni:

> Now someone who I had never seen before came out of the shadows toward me. It looked like a mummy or a zombie – this was the first overwhelming expression – of something walking after it had been put to death. [...] It glittered in the dim light [...]; the eyelids gleamed with mascara, the mouth raged with lipstick. The face was white and thoroughly bloodless with some kind of foundation cream; it stank of powder and a gardenia-like perfume. The shirt, open coquettishly to the navel, revealed a hairless chest and a silver crucifix; the shirt was covered with round, paper-thin wafers, red and green and orange and yellow and blue, which stormed in the light and made one feel that the mummy might, at any moment, disappear in flame.[581]

Initially, in not specifying the person's gender, Baldwin underlines the person's androgynous appearance. Like Horace, he is wearing a colorful outfit described by a list of the different colors connected with the additive "and." The drag queen's crucifix is taken up again in Horace's last name "Cross." Similar to Horace's face, which is white from greasepaint, the drag-queen's white face is painted with a foundation cream. Both are constructed as figures that negotiate between the living and the dead. The drag-queen is compared to a zombie and a mummy, and Horace is taken by a demon to witness his own decline shortly before his suicide. Both the white-faced androgynous drag-queen and the white-faced clownish Horace are mediators who reveal the negative aspects of gayness. This passage from *Giovanni's Room* graphically illustrates Baldwin's negative depiction of the gay sub-culture. The white drag-queen is represented as a kind of messenger who prophesies David's coming misery should he become acquainted with Giovanni. The encounter has a strong effect on David, for he becomes aggressive and has fantasies of violently attacking his friend Jacques. In the encounter with the

---

580 Mae G. Henderson, "James Baldwin's *Giovanni's Room*: Expatriation, 'Racial Drag,' and Homosexual Panic," *Black Queer Studies: A Critical Anthology*, eds. E. Patrick Johnson and Mae G. Henderson, Durham, NC: Duke UP, 2005, 298–322, 298.

581 Baldwin, *Giovanni's Room*, 38–39.

white-faced image of himself, Horace experiences negative aspects of gay identity. Unlike Baldwin's derogatory description of a drag-queen as an aberration of masculinity, in Kenan's version the negative aspects of gayness are closely connected to racism. When the white-faced image of Horace encourages him to put on the white paint himself, Horace witnesses a scene in the mirror in which he and a white actor from the theater have sex. Like Metro in *Vanishing Rooms*, the white man uses racist language as sexual stimulation.[582]

The next-to-the-last chapter of the novel is entitled "Horace Thomas Cross Confessions." It consists of seven pages of which each sentence begins with the words "I remember." The last sentence is "I remember me."[583] Like the passage with the mask, this autobiographical passage, seemingly a written document, also refers to the African American autobiographical tradition. As is the case with the slave narrative, the recurrent repetition of the word "I" (written by himself) serves to validate Horace's existence. In Horace's case, however, nobody ever reads his written confessions. At the end of the previous chapter, it says that, directly after writing his autobiography, he destroyed it. He fails in his attempt at self-actualization and self-liberation through writing his autobiography, which is a trope in African American literature:

> So strong was his belief in words – perhaps they would lead him out of this strange world in which he had suddenly found himself. In the end, after reams of paper and thousands of lines of scribble, he had found no answers. In frustration he burned it.[584]

582 Kenan, *Visitation*, 224–225.

583 Kenan, *Visitation*, 251.

584 Kenan, *Visitation*, 239.

5.3 Melvin Dixon: *Vanishing Rooms* (1991)

In contrast to *A Visitation of Spirits*, which signifies on *Go Tell It on the Mountain* and repeats Baldwin's frequent depiction of male homosexuality as a hopeless situation, *Vanishing Rooms* signifies on *Giovanni's Room*. It formulates a critique of gay whiteness while simultaneously offering emancipation to a black gay man as an alternative. In this respect, the novel revises the whiteness of *Giovanni's Rooms*'s protagonists and offers a perspective that Baldwin, the role model of 1980s black gay cultural activism, could not share because of the different political contexts of the 1950s and the 1980s.

Dixon, too, was both a writer and an academic. In 1992, the year he died from AIDS-related complications, he was teaching English at New York's City University. He wrote two books of poetry, *Change of Territory* (1983) and *Love's Instruments* (published posthumously in 1995). His debut novel *Trouble the Water* (1989) is set in the rural south and, like *A Visitation of Spirits*, alludes to the Southern gothic tradition. In 1987, Dixon published a work of literary criticism, which he called *Ride Out the Wilderness: Geography and Identity in Afro-American Literature*, and in 1991 he translated the collected poems of Léopold Sédar Senghor. In 2006, Dixon's eight critical essays and a speech he gave at the 1992 OutWrite-conference were published by Dwight A. McBride and Justin A. Joyce under the title *A Melvin Dixon Critical Reader*. Dixon's second novel *Vanishing Rooms* came out in 1991.

Like Baldwin, Dixon spent many years in Paris. He died only one year after the publication of *Vanishing Rooms*. His inability to promote his book is probably one reason for the relatively few critical responses to the novel. There are two essays that are important for my own analysis of *Vanishing Rooms*, Darieck Scott's "Jungle Fever? Black Gay Identity Politics, White Dick, and the Utopian Bedroom" and Vivian M. May's "Reading Melvin Dixon's *Vanishing Rooms* – Experiencing 'the ordinary rope that can change in a second to a lyncher's noose or a rescue line.'" Both essays put special emphasis on the construction of gay whiteness and the way the intersectionality of differences is dealt with in the novel.

5.3.1 Intertextuality and Intersectionality

Baldwin's second novel *Giovanni's Room* is one of the few novels of the 1950s that explores homosexuality as its central theme. Today it is often discussed from a queer theoretical perspective, and it has become a canonical text in gay and lesbian studies. As it is set in Paris and its protagonists are exclusively white, some critics argue that it illustrates the writer's alienation from the black community and do not pay much attention to it. For example, William A. Cohen maintains that *"Giovanni's Room* was to most critics so foreign in location and so aberrant in subject matter that it practically did not count in an assessment of his reputation."[585] Moreover, the novel has also been seen as cut off from the African American literary tradition.[586] Mae G. Henderson contradicts this point of view in her essay "James Baldwin's *Giovanni's Room*: Expatriation, Racial Drag, and Homosexual Panic." She locates the origin for Baldwin's decision to focus on white homosexual men in the political climate in the USA during the 1950s. She states that Baldwin's

> project not only necessitates a male protagonist, but one defined in terms of racialized whiteness. Further, Baldwin's flight to Paris, along with his 'flight to whiteness,' or "racial drag," may be regarded as a way to open up a space of possibility for subjects at that time not available to black writers in the United States. By literarily crossing the racial divide, and literally crossing the national divide, the author repositions himself at a site that interrogates the borders and boundaries of nation, gender, and sexuality.[587]

Henderson's argument is formulated from a transnational and intersectional perspective that illustrates the approach of many critics working in the field of black queer theory. In his essay "Straight Black Studies," McBride argues along similar lines. Regarding the complexity of the character David, McBride states that he is drawn "at the crossroads of nationality (Americanness), sexuality (or homosexuality or at least bisexuality), and home (or place and social responsibility/respectability)."[588] Black gay cultural activism in the

---

585 William A. Cohen, "Liberalism, Libido, Liberation: Baldwin's *Another Country*," *Genders* 12 (1991): 1–21, 1.

586 For an overview of the critical responses to *Giovanni's Room*, see Ross.

587 Henderson, "James Baldwin's *Giovanni's Room*," 298.

588 McBride, 77.

1980s and 1990s was influential for these black queer theoretical approaches. However, rather than deconstructing categories, the black gay cultural activists in the 1980s aimed at a positive formulation of black gay masculinity located in the US. They outlined an image of Baldwin that was suitable to support this black gay project. As some elements within Baldwin's texts, especially his 'flight to whiteness,' contradicted the black gay political agenda of the 1980s, I want to consider the ways in which black gay writers re-formulated these elements in their own texts.

If, as Henderson argues, Baldwin's text crosses the racial divide by dealing with white homosexual men, and the national divide, by setting the novel in Paris, then one could argue that *Vanishing Rooms* bridges these divides. Since the 1980s, black gay men have established the preconditions for this re-assessment of *Giovanni's Room*. Owing to the achievements of the black gay movement of the 1980s, Dixon had the literary freedom to depict interracial gay sexuality as well as a love affair between two black men set in New York City.

With respect to *Giovanni's Room*, Henderson argues for a "combination of expatriate (or leave-taking) and emergence (or 'coming out') narrative, both [of which] are new genres in African American and American fiction in the 50s."[589] She argues that both narratives are concerned with space and "the crossing of borders and boundaries."[590] I agree with Henderson that the spatial metaphors are central in the depiction of both David's expatriation and the representation of homosexuality. However, *Giovanni's Room* cannot be classified as a coming-out narrative in the post-Stonewall sense of the term. David's hostile attitude towards the homosexual sub-culture and his inability to accept his own homosexual desire remain unchanged up to the end of the story. The narrative offers no resolution to these conflicts.

Like Corbin's *No Easy Place to Be*, Dixon's *Vanishing Rooms* takes up the quest narrative central to many African American novels. The protagonists and narrators, Jesse, Ruella, and to a lesser degree Lonny, experience a process of inner growth. Jesse's and Ruella's quests are clearly influenced by discussions

---

589 Henderson, "James Baldwin's *Giovanni's Room*," 304.
590 Henderson, "James Baldwin's *Giovanni's Room*," 304.

connected with the political movements of the 1980s, especially the black women's movement and the black gay movement. In the end, Ruella emerges as an emancipated black woman, and Jesse comes to a positive formulation of his black gay identity. Jesse's process of coming out as a black gay man is depicted by the way he gradually realizes the oppressive dimensions of the dominant construction of gay identity as white as well as of the way racism has determined his relationship with Metro.[591] He also understands his own part in the perpetuation of the racist structures of that relationship. Against the background of debates surrounding the whiteness of the two main characters in *Giovanni's Room*, one could argue that in *Vanishing Rooms* a gay afrocentric approach is introduced which evokes discussions held among black gay cultural activists of the 1980s, who repeatedly discussed the political slogan "black men loving black men is the revolutionary act." Despite the similarity in depicting the resolution of the inner conflicts of a black homosexual protagonist, *No Easy Place to Be* and *Vanishing Rooms* differ with respect to their didactic function. *Vanishing Rooms* is not a didactic novel in the sense that it aims to inform its readers about homosexuality, to raise the acceptance of a gay lifestyle, or to give an example of a successful coming out process. It is rather a condensed reflection on the debates among black gay activists at the end of the 1990s, which I have outlined in the second chapter.

In the following, I will consider in more detail to what extent *Vanishing Rooms* refers to Baldwin's novel *Giovanni's Room* and how it also alludes to his novel *Another Country*. Considering three subjects, narrative mode, the representation of women, and the construction of gay whiteness, I will demonstrate how Dixon appropriates Baldwin's novels from a 1980s black gay perspective. In my analysis, I will pay special attention to Ruella's quest and her emancipation as a black woman as well as to Jesse's emancipation as a black gay man.

The clearest link between *Giovanni's Room* and *Vanishing Rooms* is a male homosexual relationship around which the plot is organized. In *Giovanni's*

---

591 Several times, a connection to Paris is evoked in the text, for example via the nickname of the white protagonist Metro who has spent some time in Paris prior to the novel's narrated incidents.

Room there are David and Giovanni in Paris who are two white men from Italy and the USA respectively. *Vanishing Rooms* focuses on the relationship between Jesse, a black dancer, and the white journalist Metro, who both live in New York. The nickname "Metro" alludes to the subway in Paris and establishes one more connection to Baldwin's novel. Both couples live in a metropolis where they share a room/apartment which is too small for them. In both novels, one partner reflects on the relationship retrospectively at a moment in time when the other partner is about to die (Giovanni) or is already dead (Metro).

The titles of the novels, "*Giovanni's Room*" and "*Vanishing Rooms*," are phonetically similar. Both titles refer to the spatial metaphor, one that Dixon takes up from Baldwin. However, whereas the room in *Giovanni's Room* is represented as a claustrophobic and closeted space defined by the presence of two white homosexual men, these elements are revised in *Vanishing Rooms*. In *Vanishing Rooms* Jesse's emancipation as a black gay man is repeatedly described in spatial terms; for example, he is the one who takes care of the small apartment he shares with Metro, he calls his female friend Rooms instead of using her real name Ruella, and he visits different rooms on his surreal and dreamlike tour through a gay bathhouse. By restaging his interracial relationship with Metro as a dance performance, he symbolically breaks free from the limited space he and Metro inhabit. Alluding to the actual room of Baldwin's *Giovanni's Room*, the stage is depicted as a room with the audience representing the room's fourth wall. After the performance is over, "the fourth wall burst into light, and the room holding us there vanished."[592] After Giovanni's room vanishes symbolically, Jesse and his new lover Rodney are free to choose the dimensions for their new relationship.

Whereas *Giovanni's Room* is narrated from David's perspective alone, thereby limiting its perspective to that of its white male protagonist, *Vanishing Rooms* is narrated from the perspectives of three of its characters, Jesse, Ruella, and Lonny, a black gay man, a black woman, and a male Italian adolescent. This narrative structure is reminiscent of the narrative structure of Baldwin's

---

592 Melvin Dixon, *Vanishing Rooms*, New York: Cleis, 1991, 213. See also Vivian M. May, "Reading Melvin Dixon's *Vanishing Rooms*: Experiencing 'the ordinary rope that can change in a second to a lyncher's noose or a rescue line,'" *Callaloo* 23.1 (2000): 366–381, 366.

Another Country, whose characters differ with respect to race, gender, and sexual orientation.[593] Like *Another Country*, *Vanishing Rooms* is focused on a small group of people living in New York City. In *Another Country*, the characters react to Rufus Scott's suicide, and those in *Vanishing Rooms* are affected by the murder of the white gay man Metro. Trudier Harris argues that the title of the novel, "Another Country," can be taken as an expression of the characters' inability to transcend the barriers of race, sexual orientation, class, and gender. She states that "Baldwin's metaphor suggests that human beings are isolated from each other by sex, race, culture, and nationality as well as by some existential loneliness of the human spirit."[594]

As early as 1964, in a review of *Another Country*, Norman Podhoretz argues that Baldwin's novel should be understood as a critique of the identity categories "white and Negro" and "homosexuality and heterosexuality."[595] Robert Corber agrees with Podhoretz's thesis that *Another Country* criticizes the limitations of identity categories, but he adds a political dimension. He argues that, in constructing the heterogeneous characters in *Another Country* as "'successive reflectors', or multiple centers of intelligence"[596], Baldwin deliberately adopts a narrative strategy from Henry James in order to overcome the formal limitations of the naturalistic novel, which he had theoretically criticized before in his essays on Wright, "Everybody's Protest Novel" and "Many Thousands Gone" (see 5.1.2).

Corber sees three advantages in the way Baldwin combines a Jamesian mode of narration with the thematic concerns of the naturalistic novel: an emphasis on issues of subjectivity, on multiple axes of difference, and on the presentation of whiteness as a racialized construction. He argues that, "in *Another Country*, whiteness does not indicate an absence of color but is a product of a racialized social formation in which the construction of white and black

---

593 James Baldwin, *Another Country*. New York: Vintage, 1993, 93.

594 Trudier Harris, *Black Women in the Fiction of James Baldwin*, Knoxville: U of Tennessee P, 1985, 98.

595 Norman Podhoretz, "In Defense of James Baldwin," *Five Black Writers: Essays on Wright, Ellison, Baldwin, Hughes, and Le Roi Jones*, ed. Donald B. Gibson, New York: New York UP, 1970, 143–148, 145.

596 Corber, *Homosexuality*, 161.

subjectivity are mutually determining."[597] In narrating the plot on multiple centers of intelligence, the different characters' subjective consciousness rather than the material conditions under which they live, becomes central. This technique also reveals the intersectionality of differences. Corber states that

> by frequently shifting the novel's point of view, Baldwin was able to stage a series of dialogic encounters between characters of different races, classes, and genders which showed that such categories were mutually constitutive and could not be understood apart from one another.[598]

However, Corber's observation is not quite sufficient. First, the point of view of the novel is not shared by all characters equally. Secondly, some of the axes of difference mentioned are depicted as static (especially gender), whereas others appear to be dynamic (sexual orientation). At the beginning of *Another Country*, Rufus Scott, a black male jazz musician in his late twenties, is the focus of the novel. That focus shifts around after his suicide. However, not all of the other characters become temporary centers of consciousness. This function is limited to Vivaldo, a novelist of working-class Italian-Irish origin, to Cass, a white middle-class mother and wife, and to Eric, a white homosexual man. The private thoughts of the other three major characters Ida, Rufus's sister who is a black jazz singer, Richard, a white writer who is married to Cass, and Yves, Eric's French lover, are not revealed to the reader. Their thoughts are only presented in their dialogues with the other characters. The fact that Ida, as the only remaining black character who could testify for black female experiences, is left out as a center of consciousness at least partly contradicts Corber's positive assessment of the way the intersectionality of differences is depicted in *Another Country*.

Like the characters in *Another Country*, those in *Vanishing Rooms* are determined by various lines of difference such as race, class, gender, and sexual orientation. Often, the same incidents are narrated by more than one character. In this way, the reader learns more than one version of the narrated events and sees different facets she might not have thought of otherwise. The results of this

---

597 Corber, *Homosexualiy*, 162.

598 Corber, *Homosexuality*, 162.

stylistic device are a postmodern polyphony of voices and an illustration of the intersectionality of differences. Vivian M. May observes that Dixon

> writes at the intersections of differences, on the boundaries between 'opposites,' delineating how fragile and constructed are the lines that demarcate difference. Reading *Vanishing Rooms* is an experience of seeing, engaging with, and identifying with contradictory subject positions, desires, and psychic boundaries.[599]

None of the characters in *Vanishing Rooms* are represented as either purely innocent or guilty. They are influenced by the positions they inhabit in a complex social structure, but they are not depicted as passive victims. To different degrees, they are also depicted as agents. Metro, for instance, is portrayed as someone who perpetuates racist structures in his relationship with Jesse, but it is he who becomes the victim of a homophobic attack. Jesse is not without contradictions either. After Metro's death he seeks support from his friend Ruella, but soon he egoistically exploits her compassion. Lonny is another example. He is one of Metro's murderers (he is forced at knifepoint to take part in the crime), but his full responsibility for the act becomes questionable when the reader learns his thoughts, worries, and contradictory emotions in those chapters of the novel that are narrated from his perspective. In representing such contradictory character traits, Dixon constructs the protagonists of the novel as multi-dimensional. As most passages that focus on Metro and his relationship with Jesse are retrospectively narrated from Jesse's perspective, the reader sees Metro as he is seen and judged by his lover. Regarding the complexity of Dixon's representation of differences, Scott observes:

> while Jesse's and Metro's conflict is highly charged with and inflected by the most obvious tropes of black/white confrontation, their conflict also has a basis in individual biography and psyche, in social and cultural differences between families and cultures and regions and economic classes – differences which, though permeated by constructs of racial difference, cannot be reduced to a simple racial opposition.[600]

---

599 May, 366.

600 Scott, 316.

The topic of intersectionality is illustrated in the ways in which the characters interact. This formal device appears artificial. In contrast to the didacticism of Corbin's *No Easy Place to Be*, Dixon only partly aims at raising tolerance for black gay men. Instead, *Vanishing Rooms* is laid out as a text that throws light on the intersections of differences and thereby questions political strategies that are based on a monolithic group identity, be it black, gay, or feminist.

By including Ruella's black female perspective, Dixon revises Baldwin's omission of Ida's point of view in *Another Country*. It is also significant that there are no passages narrated from Metro's white male perspective. This inclusion of Ruella and omission of Metro must be seen in the context of Harris's critique of the marginal roles women play in Baldwin's fiction. As Dixon wrote a chapter on Baldwin in his book of literary criticism *Ride Out the Wilderness* (1987), it is likely that he was familiar with Harris's study even though it is not listed in the bibliography of the book. In the introduction to her study *Black Women in the Fiction of James Baldwin*, Harris states:

> However, no woman is ultimately so acceptable to Baldwin that she is to be viewed as equal to the prominent male characters. It is a function of their guilt as well as of their creation that most of the black female characters in Baldwin's fiction have been subordinated to the males; they are in a supportive, serving position in relation to the males and the male images in their lives. [...] they are incomplete without men or male images in their lives because wholeness without males is not a concept the majority of them have internalised.[601]

As there are no black female characters in *Giovanni's Room*, Harris does not discuss this novel in her study. Still, her critique applies to the representation of Hella, David's white fiancée in *Giovanni's Room*. She is depicted as being incomplete without a man; her self-proclaimed aim in life is to get married. She wants to depend on a man. Shortly before she learns that David is sexually attracted to other men, she says: "I want to get married, I want to start having kids, I want us to live someplace, I want *you*. Please David."[602] Likewise, after finding out about David's homosexuality, she loses her aim in life and states:

---

601 Harris, *Black Women*, 9.

602 Baldwin, *Giovanni's Room*, 161.

"But if women are supposed to be led by men and there aren't any men to lead them, what happens then, what happens then?"[603]

In naming the female protagonist of *Vanishing Rooms* "Ruella," Dixon alludes to Hella, because the names sound similar and the second part of the name is spelled identically. Hella's thoughts and emotions are always narrated from David's perspective and seem to be passive reactions to his actions. Ruella, however, is a black female character whose position, development, and inner growth become comprehensible because parts of the novel are narrated from her perspective, a narrative device which stands in contrast to those employed in Baldwin's novels, in which "most of the women are revealed through omniscient narration or through male narrators in a third-person, limited point of view."[604]

At the beginning of the novel, Ruella is dependent on two black men, her brother, whom she has admired since she was little, and Jesse, with whom she falls in love. During the course of the novel, she emancipates herself from both of them and leads a happy life without the need to be validated by a man. Like Metro's name, her name alludes to France. She explains its meaning to Jesse and by saying that it contains the word *rue*, French for street, an indication of movement and progress, and explaining that the second part of her name as the Spanish personal pronoun *Ella*, 'she.'[605] The French part *rue* in her name also evokes the English term route. Gilroy has theorized his concept of the Black Atlantic and focused on the routes black subjects have taken since slavery. Together with its homophone "roots," the term "routes" refers to the construction of diasporic identities that are determined by a reference to cultural origins as well as a specific history of migration. Moreover, the second part of the name alludes to black culture, because it is reminiscent of Ella Fitzgerald, the famous black female artist. Like her, and in contrast to the female characters in Baldwin's fiction, Ruella leads an independent life.

---

603 Baldwin, *Giovanni's Room*, 165.

604 Harris, *Black Women*, 10.

605 Dixon, *Vanishing Rooms*, 46.

Jesse, however, does not respect her autonomy and initially refuses to call her by her first name. He calls her Rooms instead, because he hopes to find in her the quietness and space he needs to recover from the loss of his lover Metro. He thinks of her as "a place to come to, a pier without splinters, a cozy room, not a warehouse."[606] While Jesse is staying in her apartment, Ruella falls in love with him and tries to make him have sex. Later, when she realizes that Jesse is exploiting her affection, she forbids Jesse to call her "Rooms." In the end she tells him to leave when he refuses to call her by her first name "Ruella." By insisting on being called by the name she prefers, she alludes to the significance the naming of the self has as a liberating practice within African American culture. During slavery, white owners invented English names for their African slaves. This determination by the white oppressor is the reason why the practice of naming the self has become an act of liberation among African Americans. For example, during the protest era Black Power activists rejected their slave names and adopted African names. One example is Amiri Baraka who, was called "LeRoi Jones" before he turned towards Black Nationalism.

Even though Ruella's liberation and inner growth are central to the novel, May argues that Ruella and the two other female characters (Lonny's mother and a teenage prostitute) in *Vanishing Rooms* "function within a phallic economy for their livelihood and self-definition. They are relationally defined, stereotypically feminine, and ontologically fixed."[607] In contrast to this critique, I contend that Ruella does not represent the stereotypical image of a self-sacrificing and passive black woman. On the contrary, Jesse's refusal to recognize Ruella's autonomy and to call her by her real name reveals the ways in which men ignore the autonomy of women and subtly try to put them in a passive position. May's criticism of Dixon runs along the same lines as Harris's criticism of Baldwin. She argues that "for Ruella, self-development and finding a man are indistinguishable."[608] This criticism is true for Baldwin's depiction of Hella, but May's criticism is directed at *Vanishing Rooms* and at Dixon's depiction of Ruella, who slowly emancipates

---

606 Dixon, *Vanishing Rooms*, 11.

607 May, 378.

608 May, 378.

herself from the men in her life. Even though she starts a new relationship with her brother's friend Abdul in the end, she does not give up her newly gained autonomy for the sake of the relationship. In fact, she only agrees on the relationship with Abdul if she can continue to dance.[609]

Another point of May's criticism targets the fact that the three female characters are depicted as being exclusively heterosexual. She argues that

> the novel does allow no possibility for the existence or presence of lesbian desire: gay means 'men only' in *Vanishing Rooms*. Ironically, by suggesting that one must have a male body to be gay or to have 'gay' desire, Dixon reinforces oppositional and essentialist dichotomies between male and female bodies.[610]

It is true that there is no representation of lesbian desire in *Vanishing Rooms*, but this fact does not necessarily suggest that a male gender is an inevitable precondition for homosexual desire, and it is unclear why the absence of lesbian desire should result in a reinforcement of "oppositional and essentialist dichotomies between male and female bodies." Still, if one looks at Dixon's novel in connection with Baldwin's work, May's criticism is not unfounded. Baldwin has been frequently criticized for limiting representations of homosexual desire to men. In his essay "The Parvenu Baldwin and the other Side of Redemption," Roderick A. Ferguson approves of Baldwin's challenge of essentialist notions of race and homosexuality, but he criticizes the exclusion of women:

> Baldwin deploys the categories of 'the homosexual' and 'the negro' as if they represent the experiences of all persons who fall into these designations, but in fact, his essays betray a masculinist interest. 'Preservation of Innocence' and 'Everybody's Protest Novel' are really concerned about the racial and sexual discourses having to do with gay and African American men. This masculinist inscription of 'the homosexual' and 'the negro' does not permit Baldwin to ask how lesbians and black women have historically been framed as the antitheses of American domesticity. Moreover, it does not allow him to ask how such representations shaped the contours of American literature by women who were black and/or gay.[611]

---

609 Dixon, *Vanishing Rooms*, 195.

610 May, 379.

611 Roderick A. Ferguson, "The Parvenu Baldwin and the Other Side of Redemption," *James Baldwin Now*, ed. Dwight A. McBride, New York: New York UP, 1999, 255.

Ferguson formulated this critique nearly a decade after the publication of *Vanishing Rooms*. Rather than blaming Dixon for the omission of lesbian desire, I would emphasize the similarities between Ferguson's theoretical approach and Dixon's project of re-writing Baldwin from an intersectional perspective.

5.3.2 White Gay Racism and Black Gay Identity

Jesse's quest and his emancipation as a black gay man are inextricably linked to his growing awareness of the way racist structures determined his relationship with Metro. Throughout the novel, the relationship between Metro and Jesse becomes more complicated because of racism. The separation of the two men is shown on symbolic, social, cultural, and political levels. In the end, even their sexual practices are affected by racist structures.

In describing Metro and Jesse's first encounter in college, Dixon makes their separation clear on a symbolic level. They are on two different sides of two geographically opposed groups of people. As the university would not cancel classes to memorialize the death of Malcolm X, Jesse takes part in a political demonstration of black students who take over a university building. Jesse sees Metro from the inside of the building, and Metro, who is standing outside, looks at Jesse. As Jesse cannot leave the barricaded building and Metro cannot enter, they are not able to talk to each other. These two spaces are characterized by the opposites inside/outside and dark/light, because the brick walls of the occupied building are described as dark, and the outside is light because of the snow.[612] Just as in this first encounter, Metro's whiteness is repeatedly represented by a connection with snow in later scenes. One example is the morning after the first night they spend together: "The next morning we were late for the same class. We ran through the snow covering the ground, slipping and falling along the way. I called him Metro for the fast slippery train we were on."[613]

In the early stages of their relationship, they jokingly acknowledge their different social backgrounds: "'Ghetto kid meets farm boy.' 'Sounds like a

---

612 Dixon, *Vanishing Rooms*, 38.

613 Dixon, *Vanishing Rooms*, 102.

double-feature horror flick.'"[614] But their differences have a cultural and a political dimension, too. Metro criticizes Jesse for his politically outspoken dance performance of "Strange Fruit." He does not realize the importance the performance has for Jesse and argues instead that Jesse presents himself as a victim. Unwilling to acknowledge his privileged position as a white man, he says that he and Jesse are oppressed to the same degree because they are both gay: "'But why do you always act like black people are the only ones oppressed? There are other oppressed people.' 'Like who?' 'Gays, Jews. Even poor boys from the South. Don't you think we have some weight to bear? Don't you think we hurt sometimes?'"[615] At the end of their argument, Metro says: "'And yes, we're faggots. Two faggots. That's what we are.'"[616] Metro's color-blind argumentation emphasizes Jesse's and his gayness and, in doing so, indirectly claims that their shared position in a homophobic society is of central importance and that their different positions in the hierarchy of race relations are less important. His attitude is also typical of the identity politics of the white-dominated gay liberation movement, which focused on gay rights without contesting their whiteness as a "location of structural advantage, of race privilege."[617] In claiming that gays are as oppressed as black people, Metro uses a race analogy. He argues that sexual orientation is analoguous to race and that homophobia and racial discrimination are parallel forms of oppression. This is one of the strategies Alan Bérubé has called the "whitening practices" of the gay movement. It makes gays and lesbians of color invisible and helps to "construct, maintain, and fortify the idea that gay male means white."[618]

After moving to New York, Jesse and Metro become more and more estranged from one another. Their separation is once again symbolically indicated by their different working hours. Whereas Metro works the nightshift for the *Daily News*, Jesse works during the day and pursues a career as a dancer. While he tries to make their shared apartment a home and to maintain their relationship, Metro

614 Dixon, *Vanishing Rooms*, 98.
615 Dixon, *Vanishing Rooms*, 104.
616 Dixon, *Vanishing Rooms*, 104.
617 Frankenberg, 1.
618 Bérubé 237.

explores the gay sub-culture, engages in sadomasochistic sexual practices and experiments with drugs. The relationship is put to a test when their sexual practices are affected by racism. Metro starts to use racist language while he and Jesse have sex and when he wants to meet Jesse in an abandoned warehouse, a gay cruising area, with a view to engaging in racist sexual role play.

On a visit to the Paradise Baths, a gay bathhouse in New York City, Jesse begins to realize the abusive elements of his relationship with Metro. The surreal description of Jesse's trip to the bathhouse is reminiscent of Dante's *Divine Comedy* (1321), particularly its second book "Purgatorio." It depicts a spiral path that leads up a mountain towards light, where the narrator sees those who seek redemption from their sins. On top of that mountain is the earthly paradise from where the bathhouse gets its name. However, when Jesse finally reaches the light on the top floor of the Paradise Baths, he realizes that the gay sub-culture offers no redemption for him.[619]

Like Dante, who is in search of his dead love Beatrice, Jesse enters the bathhouse because Metro went there when he was alive, and Jesse thinks that "maybe being there would bring me closer to him."[620] In the locker room, he meets Clementine, an older black gay man, who introduces him to the place and to the conventions of the urban gay sub-culture. In his function as a guide, Clementine alludes to Virgil. Darieck Scott argues that "Clementine's job in the novel is at least partly to occupy the space of the 'black gay' or Afrocentrist."[621] One of the first questions Clementine asks is whether Jesse is a snow queen. Jesse has not heard of the term before, but their conversation turns upside down the positive connection of Metro with snow that is established in the beginning of the novel.[622] During his visit to the bathhouse, Jesse realizes even more the role whiteness plays in the gay sub-culture, and how his and Metro's relationship was determined by racist structures. The omnipresence of whiteness within the gay sub-culture is illustrated when Jesse comes to the top floor of the Paradise

---

619 I thank Robert McRuer who mentioned this reference to Dante to me.

620 Dixon, *Vanishing Rooms*, 88.

621 Scott, 315.

622 Dixon, *Vanishing Rooms*, 90.

Baths. In a dreamlike passage, he opens different rooms in which gay fantasies become real. In one room, Jesse is confronted with gay whiteness:

> Suddenly light, blinding light from what seemed like a row of high-intensity bulbs against mirrored walls. I staggered and when I could see clearer I saw a king-size bed with disheveled white sheets and two white bodies coupling furiously. On the wall in every direction was the repeated image of the two men coupling, 360 degrees of it. Even the floor was mirrored, and the image kept repeating and repeating as if it extended into infinity. The men locked in each other's arms seemed to be enjoying immortality as much as each other. The multiplication of images and light gave me a headache. I closed the door.[623]

bell hooks maintains that in the black imagination, whiteness is frequently represented as terror,[624] and this quotation visualizes this terror of whiteness. Dixon's language strongly combines the "high-intensity bulbs," the mirrors, the "disheveled white sheets" and the "two white bodies coupling furiously" in order to show the ubiquity of whiteness in the gay sub-culture. The two white bodies blend in with the surroundings. One consequence is Jesse's feeling of displacement. As a black man, he cannot be a part of the scene; he can only be a spectator. What is more, while looking inside the room, he experiences the rather severe physical reactions of blindness and a headache. When referring to this passage, May argues that Dixon makes a statement about "the racial politics of whiteness that structure queer spatiality."[625] One way to show the exclusiveness and omnipresence of whiteness within the gay sub-culture is the use of mirror imagery. All four walls, as well as the floor of the room, are mirrored and thus, the room leaves no space for anything else apart from whiteness.

The combination of mirror imagery and gay whiteness signifies on the protagonist David in *Giovanni's Room*. The way the mirror is connected to white

---

623 Dixon, *Vanishing Rooms*, 106–107.

624 hooks, "Representing Whiteness," 172.

625 May, 369.

gay men evokes Baldwin's use of mirror imagery in *Giovanni's Room*.[626] The quotation is also reminiscent of the passage in *Visitation of Spirits* I have quoted above: Horace sees himself sitting in front of a mirror, his face covered in white greasepaint, and he finds it difficult to recognize himself. Both quotations seem to suggest that gay identity can only be achieved by a denial of one's blackness. Like Horace and Jesse, Baldwin had to turn to whiteness to be able to represent male homosexuality.

Baldwin's novel begins and ends with the white protagonist David looking at his reflection in a windowpane and mirror. He is absorbed by his self-image. In referring to Narcissus and Freud, Henderson argues that Baldwin's white gay protagonist is "forever entrapped in the specular logic of the same."[627] In *Vanishing Rooms*, this thought is extended to the white gay sub-culture as a whole. The two white gay men described in the quotation are absorbed by their own ever-repeating selves. These mirror images leave no space for (racial) difference.

In the 1950s the intellectual discourse was strongly influenced by the psychoanalytical theories of Sigmund Freud. Freud used the myth of Narcissus, who fell in love with his own reflection, as an explanatory model for male homosexuality.[628] Consequently, Baldwin's use of mirror imagery in *Giovanni's Room* is not surprising. Since the 1960s, poststructuralist philosophers, feminists, and gay activists have rejected Freud's theories.[629] His explanations of homosexuality have been criticized for their inherent homophobia because Freud argued that homosexuality was arrested growth. Freud's model of narcissism is based on the myth of a man who loves his own image, and therefore sameness is one precondition of this theory of homosexuality. This sameness is one element of the way Kenan and Dixon combine mirror imagery with their critique of gay whiteness in the two passages I have quoted. They introduce difference (the protagonist's blackness) to a discourse that has been

626 Henderson, "James Baldwin's *Giovanni's Room*," 310. *Giovanni's Room* and the setting of a gay bathhouse are also connected in Hemphill's poem "Heavy Breathing" (Essex Hemphill, "Heavy Breathing," *Ceremonies: Prose and Poetry*, San Francisco: Cleis, 1992, 4–21, 13).

627 Henderson, "James Baldwin's *Giovanni's Room*," 318.

628 Joseph Sandler, Ethel Spector Person, and Peter Fonagy, eds., *Freud's "On Narcissim: An Introduction,"* New Haven: Yale UP, 1991.

629 For a critical discussion of this Freudian theory, see Sinfield, 9–31.

dominated by sameness (white gay identity). However, in order to formulate their critique of the sameness within the white dominated gay sub-culture, Kenan and Dixon uncritically continue Freud's homophobic theory regardless of the critiques that were formulated in the 1970s and 1980s.

Metro's whiteness is linked to his unspoken desire for black men. Jesse reevaluates their relationship and depicts Metro not as a loving and affectionate partner, but as a dinge queen, a white man who is sexually interested in black men because of their blackness:

> What did he care when all he wanted to do was to call me a nigger to my face and say it was love talking that way, that excitement and abuse went together in sexual pleasure like cock and mouth or cock and ass or black and white when he was fucking not me but the image of me and black men like me that he had always dreamed about as he sat on his Louisiana gallery swatting mosquitoes and dragonflies.[630]

At the end of the novel, Jesse starts a new relationship, this time with a black man who is also a dancer. This ending meets Marlon Riggs's plea at the end of the film *Tongues Untied*: "Black men loving black men is the revolutionary act," the slogan frequently quoted and discussed within black gay art of the 1980s (see 2.4). The ending of *Vanishing Rooms* is also similar to the ending of Riggs's poem "Tongues Untied." Alluding to the hymn "Amazing Grace," Riggs writes "I was blind to my brother's beauty/my own, but now I see."[631]

Having shown the negative consequences of the normative construction of gay identity as white, Dixon introduces the 1980s discussions among black gay men around this slogan in Jesse's encounter with the character Clementine, an older black gay man. The two men meet in the gay bathhouse. Clementine, who is rather critical of snow queens, states: "[in the newspapers] we are all subway muggers and rapists and drag queens. Not men. And not men loving other black men. Loving being men and black together."[632] But later, Clementine's ideal of solidarity among black men has rather negative consequences for

---

630 Dixon, *Vanishing Rooms*, 108.

631 Riggs, 205.

632 Dixon, *Vanishing Rooms*, 116.

Jesse. Clementine claims his natural right to Jesse's body and especially to anal intercourse because both are black gay men.[633] This passage is an ironic comment on the black gay movement's afrocentric politics, even if the closure of the narrative, Jesse's new relationship with another black gay man, supports this political agenda.

Dixon's critique of gay whiteness, the depiction of the failure of Metro and Jesse's interracial relationship and the subsequent intraracial relationship between Jesse and Rodney are all linked to an African American tradition that regards interracial sexuality as a sign of integrationism. By denouncing interracial sexuality in favor of intraracial sexuality, Dixon turns against the protest tradition, "a tradition that takes racial integration as a fundamental solution to the problem of racism, the struggle to reconcile black and white into a single egalitarian national culture."[634] Dixon's approach is similar to that of those Black Nationalists who were opposed to interracial relationships and sexuality. However, as I have shown with regard to Cleaver and Baraka, the depiction of intraracial sexuality between two black men clearly opposes the heterosexist political agenda of most Black Nationalists.

5.4 Samuel R. Delany:
The Motion of Light in Water (1988)

5.4.1 Interracial Desire and Interclass Contact

Similar to Julien in his film *The Attendant* (1993), throughout his writings Delany chooses a way of depiciting interracial desire that differs from Riggs's and Dixon's strategy. For example, in his pornographic novel *The Mad Man* (1994), he depicts Pheldon, one of the black gay protagonists in the novel, as a self-confident out snow queen and describes Dave as a dinge queen who explicitly speaks of his desire for black men. In his essays "Times Square Red,

---

633 Dixon, *Vanishing Rooms*, 116. See also Scott, 315.

634 Ross, 21.

Times Square Blue," Delany argues for the emancipating potential of urban gay sex venues and cruising areas to transgress boundaries of race and class,[635] and his almost utopian description of his first visit to the St. Mark's Baths in New York City, in his autobiographical memoir *The Motion of Light in Water*, stands in stark contrast to Dixon's account of Jesse's visit to the Paradise Baths.[636] Delany chooses these places as settings for his novels and deliberately places categories of social power relations in a sexual context.

In *The Mad Man*, the black academic and first-person narrator John Marr writes a letter to his college friend Sally May and describes his sexual experiences in New York City's gay sub-culture. One incident is a sexual encounter with Dave in a porn movie theater where men go to have sex with other men. Dave is described as a white gay working-class "butch looking red-bearded guy about twenty-nine"[637] with rough hands and bad teeth. John and Dave engage in oral sex in the cinema, and, at the same time, Dave articulates his desire for black men.

> Once, he came off me. 'Jesus, man, I hope you don't take offense at this. But I like sucking black dick more than just about anything in the world!' He was down on his knees now, wedged between me and the back of the seats in front of me, holding mine up against his bearded face. 'About the only thing better than sucking one of these things – a nice big black cock – would be sucking on *two* of them! Or maybe three or four... .' I just chuckled, locked my hands around the back of his head, and pulled him forward again.[638]

Again, the construction of gay whiteness works by depicting the white gay man's desire for the black male body. But, in contrast to Karl in *Looking for Langston* and Metro in *Vanishing Rooms*, Dave is the one who talks about his desire. The sexually explicit situation in which he utters his fantasy has an ironic effect on the reader. When asked by John Marr to describe his fantasies in more detail, Dave does so:

635 Delany, *Times Square Red*, 15–16.

636 Samuel R. Delany, *The Motion of Light in Water: Sex and Science Fiction Writing in the East Village*, Minneapolis: U of Minnesota P, 2004, 290–295. The text was originally published in 1988 by Arbor House. An unabridged version was first published in 1993 by Richard Kasak. In 2004 a new edition was published by Minnesota UP.

637 Samuel R. Delany, *The Mad Man*, New York: Richard Kasak, 1994, 131.

638 Delany, *The Mad Man*, 132.

'So what would you like two black guys to do to you?' I whispered to him as
I helped him get up. He shrugged in my arms, rubbing his beard against my
cheek: 'I don't know. Just about anything. Fuck me. Stick it in my mouth.
Piss on me – anything man.' Now he pulled away – just a little: 'I don't mean
it in any SM way. I mean friendly-like – the way we're doin'. Doin' it because
they liked doin' it – because it got them off too, you know?' [639]

Later on that night, his sexual fantasies come true when he has sex with
John Marr, Pheldon, and a third black man at The Mineshaft, a gay sex
venue in New York. Delany's description of the sex scene involves the use of
racist language and an eroticisation of racist stereotypes. In contrast to the
representation of Metro's hurting racist insults in *Vanishing Rooms*, and the
racism Horace experiences in *A Visitation of Spirits*, it is clear in this scene
that all four men are consenting adults who have agreed on the type of sex
they are engaging in.

Rather than rejecting the white gay sub-culture altogether because
of white gay racism and calling gay whiteness "a curse," John Marr shows
compassion for Dave, who gave him a wrong phone number when he left
the Mineshaft:

An alcoholic working-class white guy from New Jersey, who, at twenty-nine
or so, realizes he's turning gay, that he likes to make it with black guys,
and that he wants them to piss all over him, well – especially if he's also
basically a nice, affectionate guy – in this country that guy has lot to be
scared of! And I don't mean big, obliging niggers, either.[640]

Delany is aware of the effects the representations of sexual encounters across
boundaries of race and class might have. Asked in an interview about the
political implications of his strategy to eroticize class relations, Delany explains
that anything which is perceived as erotic depends on class because "all human
signs have their class associated aspects." [641] Sometimes the eroticisation of
class relations is easy to name and sometimes it is more difficult to see. "The

639 Delany, *The Mad Man*, 132.

640 Delany, *The Mad Man*, 147.

641 Samuel R. Delany, "Sword & Sorcery, S/M, and the Economics of Inadequation: The Camera
Obscura Interview," *Silent Interviews: On Language, Race, Sex, Science Fiction, and Some Comics*,
Hanover, NH: Wesleyan UP, 1994, 127–163, 136.

easier it is to name, survey, and pathologize the eroticisation of any particular set of class relations, then the more dangerous that set of relations – and their eroticization – is to patriarchal status quo phallocentric society."[642] In *The Mad Man*, the repeated eroticisation of class relations is easy to see. Delany chooses this strategy to represent them positively as interracial and interclass contacts in order to oppose an attitude which regards them as pathology.

Metro's and Dave's whiteness, as well as Karl's in *Looking for Langston*, is constructed by a depiction of their sexual desire for black men. hooks argues that one way to construct whiteness in the black imagination is to use the stereotypes black people maintain about white people. She adds that these stereotypes "emerge primarily as responses to white stereotypes of blackness."[643] The way Metro, Dave, and Karl are marked as white by depicting their sexual desire for black men is clearly a response to stereotypical representations of black men within the white gay sub-culture. This connection is most clear in the scene from *Looking for Langston* I referred to in the previous chapter. Still, they are not to the same degree stereotypically depicted as white supremacists – in hooks's sense of the term. As white men, they obtain a privileged position in the racial hierarchy, but whereas the way Metro pursues his desire is depicted as abusive because he is unaware of or closes his eyes to his privileges, Dave is represented as an affectionate and modest white gay man who explicitly utters his interracial sexual desires. What is more, Dave is clearly marked as a white working-class man whose class status is eroticized by the black academic Marr. Delany's positive representation of their sexual encounter is directed against a position that judges such encounters as undesirable per se.

In his essay "Dinge," Reid-Pharr observes that there are hardly any articulations of white gay desire for black men to be found in texts by white gay writers, and he argues that this silence about interracial desire has a distinct purpose: it is one way to maintain the idea of whiteness as universal. According to Reid-Pharr, "the tendency to insist upon the innocence of our sex,

---

642 Delany, "Sword and Sorcery," 136.

643 Hooks, "Representing Whiteness," 170.

the transparency of desire at the moment of penetration, is itself part of the complex ideological process by which whiteness is rendered invisible."[644]

Even though Dixon and Delany use different strategies in the ways they connect gay whiteness with interracial sexual desire, both texts destroy the myth that sexuality is an innocent realm unaffected by social power relations. Metro's and Dave's whiteness becomes visible because of the different ways their desire for black men is represented. One important effect is the exposure of the particularity of gay whiteness.

Delany's and Dixon's strategies differ with respect to their representations of interracial relationships and gay whiteness, as well as with respect to the ways in which they refer to the black gay political agenda of the 1980s. In *The Mad Man*, Delany pushes the critique of the political slogan "black men loving black men is the revolutionary act" further than Dixon in *Vanishing Rooms*. When John Marr meets Mad Man Mike for the first time, they have sex which involves the consumption of excrements and dirty talk. In this sexual encounter, Mad Man Mike addresses John Marr by saying: "'I'm just pissin' on you, nigger – it ain't nothin'. That's good nigger piss – a nigger pissin' on a nigger. A fuckin' revolutionary act!'"[645] This quotation shows Delany's awareness of the debates about the slogan and the black gay political discourse of the late 1980s. However, instead of formulating a political standpoint in this debate, he humorously signifies on Beam's slogan. One recurring topic in *The Mad Man* are the intersections of race, class, and sexuality, and the dialogue between Mad Man Mike and John Marr humorously demonstrates that the politics of race, class, and sexuality are more complicated than can be addressed in a formulaic slogan.

5.4.2 Experimental Self-Reflections

Corbin, Julien, Kenan, and Dixon started their careers in the 1980s when they were in their twenties. Delany belongs to an older generation. Born in 1942, he experienced the major changes within US society after World War II. Among

---

644 Reid-Pharr, "Dinge," 88–89.

645 Delany, *The Mad Man*, 417.

these changes was the radical politicizations of the categories homosexuality and race: Delany states, for example, that "at that time, the words 'black' and 'gay' (...) didn't exist with their current meaning, usage, history."[646] Delany witnessed the emergence of the new social movements, as well as new (postmodern) developments in literature, art, and popular culture. He states in *The Motion of Light in Water*, "Remember: this was pre-Beatles; pre-wraparound skirts. And phrases such as 'women's liberation' or even 'women's rights' were never uttered."[647] In *Motion*, Delany gives an account of these developments and relates his experiences to the situation of the 1980s, the time he was writing his autobiographical memoir.[648]

From the 1950s to the 1980s, Delany published more novels than Baldwin. The content of his writings differs from Baldwin's work when it comes to the topics of race, gender, sexuality, and class. As he wrote his novels and short stories in the field of science fiction, his texts simply did not receive the same amount of academic attention that Baldwin's novels, essays, and plays did. Rather than drawing on Baldwin as a point of reference, Delany reconsiders his own memories of the protest era of the 1950s and 60s in order to reflect on societal changes, as well as on contemporary constructions of race, gender, sexuality, class, and their intersections. Moreover, his aims differ from that of the majority of black gay writers of the 1980s. Whereas they wanted to form a community based on a black and gay identity legitimized by notable black homosexual "forefathers," Delany aims at an analysis of the role of discourse for constructions of racial and sexual identities, a project which questions

---

646 Delany, *Motion*, 399.

647 Delany, *Motion*, 116.

648 In order to refer to his own experiences as a black gay writer in the 1960s, Delany chooses the genre of autobiographical memoir. Ross Posnock, Hazel Carby, and Jeffrey Tucker, all of whom devoted a book-chapter to The Motion of Light in Water, use different generic terms for Delany's text. Whereas Posnock calls it a memoir, Tucker and Carby refer to it with the term "autobiography." Their use of the term makes it easier to connect Motion to the African American autobiographical tradition, which is the main purpose at least of Tucker's analysis. None of the three writers give reasons for the decision to choose the particular generic term. I combine both terms and use the term "autobiographical memoir." I am reluctant to use the term "autobiography" alone, because the text is consciously limited to a certain period. It does not cover Delany's life span up to the time when he wrote the book. Even if Delany also refers to childhood experiences and later events, the restricted time-period referred to in Motion centers on the years 1960–1965. It seems to me that these accounts of Delany's memories have the function of explaining certain changes within

the basis of 1980s black gay identity politics. The degree to which Delany philosophically reflects on an anti-essentialist approach towards identities and identity politics and the way in which these reflections are mirrored in his postmodern aesthetics distinguish his writings from the writings of Corbin, Dixon, Beam, and Hemphill.

In my reading of *Motion*, I will first consider the extent to which Delany's autobiographical memoir can be read as a commentary on the African American literary tradition. I will pay special attention to the way the African American autobiographical tradition is reflected on a formal level. In a second step, I will analyze the way Delany theoretically reflects on identity categories and the politics connected to them, especially the political strategy of coming out. Finally, I will argue that the irony Delany uses when he refers to Baldwin aims at deconstructing the myth of a distinct black gay tradition that is prominent in the black gay literature of the 1980s.

Similar to his approach in "Atlantis: Model 1924," in *Motion* Delany uses metafictional elements to reflect on the genre in which he writes. He thereby undermines his own authority as the author/subject of his autobiographical memoir. Moreover, he signifies on the conventions of the black autobiographical tradition that evolved with the early slave narratives. Delany's autobiographical accounts are not limited to *Motion*. Apart from numerous autobiographical references in his fictional texts, he has published a variety of autobiographical texts, the earliest of which is *Heavenly Breakfast: An Essay on the Winter of Love* (1979), which is an account of living with the commune and music group "Heavenly Breakfast" in New York in the late 1960s. In addition, many of his numerous essays and interviews contain

---

US-society that took place during these years. I will argue below that Delany's personal experiences are the starting point for societal analysis, an analysis that implies questioning the categories race, gender, sexuality, and class. This purpose and the restricted period of time referred to contradict the aim of other autobiographies that cove r the author's life from childhood to old age and tell of a discovery and maturation of the self. As Delany connects his text to the African American autobiographical tradition, and as his text reveals why he did not arrive at a selfperception as an authentic black gay subject, I decided to keep the term "autobiographical" when referring to The Motion of Light in Water. There is one further reason why the term "autobiographical memoir" is appropriate: In the introductory chapter, Delany himself uses this term when referring to the texts that have most influenced him (Delany, *Motion*, 15).

autobiographical passages, which are the starting point for elaborate theoretical reflections.[649] The book *1984* (2000) is a collection of letters he wrote to friends and colleagues in the years 1983–1985.

Motion is an example of a postmodern approach towards identity categories, which is reflected on the level of content as well as on a formal level. Right at the beginning, in the introductory chapter "Sentences," Delany reflects on autobiography as a genre and on the roles of memory and "facts." He gives examples of events of which he has clear memories, such as the year of his father's death. His memories of these events obviously contradict the historical records, but Delany nevertheless states that such incorrect memories are meaningful and should not be omitted from any autobiography. He thus argues against a conception of history that gives privilege to historical "facts" and then states:

> I am not about to try here for the last word on event and evidential certainty. [...] I hope [...] to sketch, as honestly and as effectively as I can, something I can recognize as my own, aware as I do so that even as I work after honesty and accuracy, memory will make this only one possible fiction among the myriad – many in open conflict – anyone might write of any of us, as convinced as any other that what he or she wrote was the truth.[650]

In this passage, Delany considers his version of his autobiography "one possible fiction among the myriad." In this regard, Delany's approach mirrors George Bernard Shaw's statement that "all autobiographies are lies."[651] Delany presents the undermining of authority and truth as structuring principles of *Motion*. His approach towards the "facts" of his life is reminiscent of Hayden White's theory put forward in *Metahistory: The Historical Imagination in 19th Century Europe* (1973) about the process of writing history. According to White, historiography and fiction are not clearly separable, and fictional elements are

---

649 See for example Samuel R. Delany, *Shorter Views: Queer Thoughts and the Politics of the Paraliterary*, Hanover, NH: Wesleyan UP, 1999 and Samuel R. Delany, *Silent Interviews: On Language, Race, Sex, Science Fiction, and Some Comics*, Hanover, NH: Wesleyan UP, 1994.

650 Delany, *Motion*, 15.

651 George Bernard Shaw, *An Autobiography 1856–1898: Selected from his Writings by Stanley Weintraub*, London, Sydney, Toronto: Max Reinhardt, 1970, 1.

used when writing history.[652] White's approach became a major influence for New Historicism.

Delany deliberately undermines his own authority even further. In frequently citing poems that the poet Marilyn Hacker, Delany's former wife, wrote about the time Delany's autobiographical memoir covers, he includes a second voice, which sometimes contradicts his own memories. As Delany states in the introduction that some of his memories contradict the historical records, the reader is left to wonder whether the question of adequacy is the most important after all more than whether Hacker's or Delany's texts are adequate. In inserting a second (poetic) voice, Delany generally criticizes the idea of an authoritative voice claiming direct access to historical and even autobiographical truths. Instead, he stresses the relevance of subjective memories for accounts of the past.[653]

The undermining of authoritative voice and the possibility of alternative accounts of the time period covered in *Motion* are continued in Delany's latest novel. In *Dark Reflections* (2007), Delany does more than merely narrate the life story of Arnold Hawley, a black gay poet living in New York's Lower East Side from the 1960s onwards. One could argue that *Dark Reflections* is, in fact, a companion text to *Motion*. A connection between the two texts is already established in the titles, both of which contain the opposites dark and light, and the name of *Dark Reflections'* protagonist Arnold Hawley contains all the letters that comprise the name "(R.) Delany." To some degree, Delany in *Motion* and Hawley in *Dark Reflections* live in similar circumstances. Both of them are black gay writers living in New York's East Village. This location is indicated by the subtitle "Sex and Science Fiction Writing in the East Village" in *Motion* and the photograph on the cover of *Dark Reflections* showing Tompkins

---

652 Hayden V. White, *Metahistory: The Historical Imagination in Nineteenth-Century Europe*, Baltimore: John Hopkins UP, 1973.

653 In his autobiography *My Life: Poetry and Truth*, Johann Wolfgang von Goethe also draws on various sources, among them letters, notes made by Bettina von Arnim, his mother's accounts of his childhood, and academic texts. Goethe's autobiography is not written from the perspective of an historian. Instead, he reflects on his role as a writer and artist, hence the title *Poetry and Truth* (Johann Wolfgang von Goethe, "Dichtung und Wahrheit," *Poetische Werke*. Vol. 8. Essen: Phaidon, 1999. 9–536.)

Square Park. *Dark Reflections* once again raises questions regarding the black autobiographical tradition; the coming-out narrative; the intersections of race, gender, sexuality, and class; the profession of the writer; and the significance of black cultural traditions. The topics both works have in common are New York and the East Village, marriage, the change of political climate in the 1960s, gay liberation, black politics, living as a writer, psychiatric treatment, and comments on HIV/AIDS. However, the two texts approach these questions in different ways, for example in the way Delany depicts his own and Hawley's processes of emancipation as black gay men. Whereas in *Motion* Delany reflects on the processes of interpellation and subject formation and disidentifies with the dominant discourse represented by scientific texts as well as literature, Hawley believes the words of a doctor who tells him that there are hardly any homosexuals and that blackness and homosexuality are mutually exclusive categories,[654] a belief that is also uttered by Sally May in *The Mad Man*.[655] Arnold's life decisions and his reluctance to have sex with men are strongly determined by the negative attitudes towards homosexuality he encounters in childhood.

Dark Reflections narrates the life story of a black gay poet with obvious parallels to the events narrated in Delany's autobiographical memoir twenty years after the publication of *Motion*. This account can be interpreted as the addition of an alternative voice that is also a comment on the narrative Delany presents in *Motion*. There is one more postmodern twist: In *Dark Reflections* Hawley is the author of the anonymously published "gay pornographic novel about the adventures of some Sicilian youth in the reign of the emperor Hadrian."[656] Delany's 1994 novel *Phallos* is about the search for this very same fictional gay pornographic novel, which is called "Phallos." Like Hawley's fictional novel, it was written in 1969 and consists of 51 chapters. In *Phallos*, the anonymous author is believed to be "a black southern writer, currently

---

654 Samuel R. Delany, *Dark Reflections*, New York: Caroll & Graf, 2007, 216–219.

655 Delany, *The Mad Man*, 16.

656 Delany, *Dark Reflections*, 42.

living in New York City."[657] In *Phallos*, the blackness of the anonymous author is questioned because his or her style of writing differs from those texts constituting the black literary tradition:

> But at the risk of sounding hopelessly racist, *Phallos* just does not seem the sort of book I would imagine from a black man (or woman). Though many of the main characters are, indeed, black […] the string of unsatisfactory lovers (all except the last) makes it much closer in feel to say, to, say *Sentimental Education* or something by Jean Rhys than to *Invisible Man*, *Roots*, or *Beloved*.[658]

This quotation resonates with those passages in *Dark Reflections* in which Hawley reflects on his own relation to black poetic and black musical traditions,[659] and to those in *Motion* when Delany does the same.[660] Moreover, Delany's blackness has sometimes been disregarded, because the genres he writes in are believed to be detached from "authentic" black traditions.[661]

The most striking formal characteristic of *Motion* is the fact that it does not consist of ordinary chapters. The narrative is divided into 61 numbered passages, which again are sometimes, but not always, subdivided.[662] At first glance, this division suggests that Delany establishes a hierarchy according to which he organizes his memories. It also reflects the style of academic writings, and it is especially reminiscent of the form Ludwig Wittgenstein used in *Tractatus Logico-Philosophicus*. Delany reflects more than once on the effects of this decimal enumeration. For example, regarding October 1962, he remembers three events and writes about them in numerical order. First he writes about his fear of the atomic bomb, he gives an account of two media broadcasts of a speech by the Cuban ambassador delivered to the UN, and third he records a meeting with an artist. In between the first two incidents, Delany states, "I'm not sure which of the above two incidents, the false bomb scare, or the US General assembly session, came first. I don't know whether both, one

---

657 Delany, *Phallos*, Whitmore Lake, MI: Bamberger, 2004, 94.

658 Delany, *Phallos*, 94.

659 Delany, *Dark Reflections*, 270–278.

660 Delany, *Motion*, 376.

661 Stephanie A. Smith, 568.

662 For example 10., 10.1., 10.2., 10.21., 10.22..

or neither came just before (or just after) the incident below."[663] And having written about all three incidents, Delany directly addresses the reader of his autobiographical memoir and states:

> For a moment, release these three incidents from their decimal enumeration and consider them – the false bomb scare, the media distortion, the aesthetic demonstration – as objects to be arranged or rearranged on the stage called 'October 1962.' Which orders are most pleasing? Which orders are not? And why?[664]

In this passage, he advises his readers about how to read his autobiographical memoir. As Delany's whole autobiographical memoir is divided into numerical passages, the questions he asks can be applied to them, too. The incidents in *Motion* are quite clearly not arranged in chronological order because Delany admits to have no objective access to the correct order of events and, what is more, the book starts with the events surrounding Delany and Hacker's marriage, which chronologically would have to be narrated after the accounts of his time in school, which are described only later in the book. Rather than wanting to establish a fixed order of the events he recounts, Delany wants his readers to "release the incidents from their decimal enumeration [...] and consider them as objects to be arranged or rearranged" and thereby subverts expectations about the use of time and space. Posnock argues along similar lines:

> The form of Delany's memoir affirms this autotelic trajectory: though the text is broken into numbered sections, the numbering is full of gaps that serve to undercut the appearance of numerical precision.[665]

One further effect of the numbered passages is the fractured layout of the page, which frequently undercuts the wholeness of the text. This device visually works against the expectation of closure and is comparable to the gap between the splitting of the textual body of "Atlantis: Model 1924" into two separate columns.

The two parallel columns that are visible on the pages of "Atlantis: Model 1924" also play a role in *Motion*. However, in *Motion*, the two columns are not

---

663 Delany, *Motion*, 229.

664 Delany, *Motion*, 231.

665 Posnock, 283.

visible on the page. Instead, Delany frequently reminds us of the simultaneous presence of a second strand of narrative. The double columns are introduced in "The Motion of Light in Water," the title of the book, which Delany calls the "running metaphor" of the book.[666] This metaphor is introduced when Delany looks outside his apartment window splattered with drops of water from a hydrant in the street:

> I'd wander into the front bedroom – just as another arc from the hydrant below broke between the black fire escape slats to sing across the glass, and five hundred purple crescents would gem and drool the pane, while I stood watching the motion of light in water.[667]

This passage stands in contrast to David of *Giovanni's Room*, who looks at a windowpane and sees nothing but his own reflection. Rather than seeing himself, Delany is interested in the underlying structure, the way two different and disparate realms (light/water) interact. In order to grasp these different realms Delany repeatedly reminds us to imagine

> a second column of type that doubles the one that makes up this book, a parallel column devoted only to those elements that are repeated and repeated throughout any day, any life, incidents that constitute at once the basal and quotidian – waking up, breakfast, lunch, dinner, washing, elimination, drifting off to sleep – as well as the endlessly repeated risings and fallings of desire.[668]

Delany is particularly interested in the gap between these columns because he contends that this gap is what finally constitutes the subject:

> the gap between them, the split, the flickering correlations between, as evanescent as light-shot water, as insubstantial as moonstruck cloud, are really all that constitutes the subject: not the content if you will, but the relationships that can be drawn out of that content, and which finally that content can be analyzed into.[669]

---

666 Delany, *Motion*, 357.

667 Delany, *Motion*, 122.

668 Delany, *Motion*, 47.

669 Delany, *Motion*, 356.

Tucker states that the idea of the double columns in *Motion* takes up a motif from the African American tradition, what Werner Sollors calls the double-voicedness of Equiano's *Interesting Narrative*, the African and the European voice. It also reflects W.E.B. DuBois's concept of Double Consciousness.[670]

5.4.3 Black Autobiography and the Coming Out Narrative

In addition to these formal devices that work against the impression of wholeness and closure, the text also reflects on these topics on the level of content. It particularly reflects on the African American autobiographical tradition and the genre of the coming out narrative. Carby states that *Motion* is "absolutely central to any consideration of black manhood" because it offers "incisive and informative reflections upon the formation of black male subjectivities in the 1950s and 1960s in the United States."[671] Carby argues that central to Delany's autobiographical memoir is socio-linguistic "reflections" rather than solely personal anecdotes. The narrated events are not solely depicted as personal experiences. Even experiences which are commonly considered to be personal. For example Delany and Hacker's open marriage, their polyamorous affair with Bob Folsom, and Delany's numerous homosexual encounters are taken as examples of social formations and as indicators for social change during the 1960s.

The title of the book itself already indicates Delany's concern with societal processes. Rather than choosing a title like "My Life in the East Village," or "My Formative Science Fiction Years" Delany chooses a title that is impersonal. "The Motion of Light in Water" is a recurrent image throughout the text, and it is already introduced in the title. The subtitle "Sex and Science Fiction Writing in the East Village" only hints at the fact that the book is Delany's autobiography. The impersonal title is an ironic stylistic device that signifies on the genre of the slave narrative. The titles of slave narratives always include the name of the author and a direct reference to his or her persona, for example Olaudah Equiano's *The Interesting Narrative of the Life of Olaudah Equiano, Written by*

---

670 Tucker, 181.

671 Hazel Carby, *Race Men*. Cambridge Mass. and London: Harvard UP, 1998, 135–136.

Himself, from which Delany chooses a quotation as an epigraph for his own text. In "Sentences," the introductory chapter of *Motion*, Delany states that Frederick Douglass's *Narrative of the Life of an American Slave* is among his favorite autobiographical memoirs.

The autobiographical tradition within African American literature starts with the slave narrative, the earliest African American literary genre. Aiming at the abolition of slavery, slave narratives were largely written for moral and didactic goals. Each particular slave narrative had to prove the authenticity and the reliability of the narrator, often by the inclusion of written documents. As the authentication of the writer's existence depended on such documents, scholars argue for a crucial link between literacy, identity, and freedom. According to Rosenblatt, the tropes of self-authentication used by black writers and the quest for an identity are repeated in later black autobiography and fiction.[672] Asserting the significance of the African American autobiographical tradition for writings by black women, hooks states:

> Though autobiography or any type of confessional narrative is often devalued in North American letters, this genre has always had a privileged place in African American literary history. As a literature of resistance, confessional narratives by black folks were didactic. More than any other genre of writing, the production of honest confessional narratives by black women who are struggling to be self-actualized and to become radical subjects are needed as guides, as texts which affirm our fellowship with one another.... Even as the number of novels by black women increase this writing cannot be either a substitute for theory or for autobiographical narrative. Radical black women need to tell our stories; we cannot document our experience enough.[673]

hooks' plea for "honest confessional narratives by black women who are struggling to be self-actualized and to become radical subjects" mirrors the observation that black autobiographies aim at self-authentication. The choice of words indicates a truth that can be revealed by honesty, confession, and revelation of the self.

hooks's plea cannot easily be applied to Delany's work. He fundamentally questions the concept of identity on a theoretical/philosophical level. Delany's

---

672 Rosenblatt 1980.

673 bell hooks, "Revolutionary Black Women," *Black Looks: Race and Representation*. Boston: South End Press, 1992, 41–60, 59.

experiences as a black gay man, his encounters with racism and his strategies in coping with the threat of AIDS are always accompanied by a questioning of the very concept of identity and a deconstruction of the idea of authenticity itself. Such a fundamental critique of identity and identity categories can be found in *Motion*, too, and this critique is the reason for Posnock's argument that Delany distances himself from African American cultural traditions and especially from the concept of identity politics. Posnock argues that "one reason Delany's meanings remain fluid is that they are unconstrained by the grimly weighted signifieds of black autobiography." Later he states that "in Delany's book the generic expectations of black autobiography are subtly raised then left unfulfilled."[674] According to Posnock, Delany raises the generic expectations of black autobiography by quoting Equiano and by stating that Douglass's narrative is among his favorite autobiographies. The expectations that are not met are "tropes of anguish, self-hatred, victimization, redemption, and uplift, themes that would not be unexpected in a memoir of a black bisexual in fifties America."[675] In his reference to black cultural traditions, Delany frequently uses humor and irony and, by doing so, distances himself from the expectations of the black autobiographical tradition.

One example of Delany's ironical distance to the African American autobiographical tradition and the trope of gaining liberation and emancipation through literacy is a long passage that refers to his early years in school. Delany gives an account of what is perceived as his inability to spell words correctly and put them in the correct order. Only later is this condition diagnosed as dyslexia. Another striking example is the passage in which he describes how, as a young boy, he invented his own nickname "Chip" while he was in summer-camp. It is a passage that ironically signifies on the African American autobiographical convention of the naming of the self as a means of gaining autonomy and liberation. The use of the nickname "Chip" in references to Delany has become so common that it is sometimes even used in academic writing.

Two other elements prominent in African American autobiography and fiction that are taken up and treated ironically in *Motion* are the trope of the

---

674 Posnock, 285–286.

675 Posnock, 285.

journey north, which is reversed and narrated as Delany's hitchhiking trip to work on the shrimp boats in Aransas Pass in Texas, as well as several accounts of Delany's passing for white while staying in the South. The journey south is neither represented as a means of connecting with the southern origins of Delany's ancestors, nor is it connected to African American culture in particular. On the contrary, Delany decides to take Theodore Sturgeon's *E Pluribus Unicorn* with him. Delany wants to read it in the south because parts of its last story, "A Way of Thinking" are set on the Gulf, and he is curious of the effects of reading the story in this setting.[676] For Delany the personal connection to the South is established by a science-fiction text rather than by texts from the African American literary tradition or even his family history.

Delany's accounts of passing while staying in the South reveal that the concept of race is "grounded on a biological fantasy."[677] These passing situations do not represent areas of conflict for Delany. There is neither concrete danger involved in Delany's ignoring the segregation laws, nor do these situations inflict a moral dilemma on him. For example, when entering a segregated eating establishment for the first time in his life, Delany uses "the unmarked (so presumably white)"[678] entrance because, as he writes, he did not want to make a statement but he wanted something to eat. The inside of the place is described in terms of cultural hybridity rather than racial purity: there are "two Hispanic workmen (...) both substantially darker than [Delany]," a "redheaded waitress," and Delany's meal consists of enchilada, tacos, rice, and beans.[679] The passage concludes with an observation on the high quality of the food, rather than an accusation of Jim Crowism.

In another passage, Delany ironically signifies on Richard Wright's novel *Native Son* and the protest tradition. When Delany and Hacker first move to Manhattan's Lower East Side in 1961 as a young couple, they rent an apartment in a

---

676 Delany, *Motion*, 475.

677 Samuel R. Delany, "Introduction: Reading and the Written Interview," *Silent Interviews: On Language, Race, Sex, Science Fiction, and Some Comics*, Hanover, NH: Wesleyan UP, 1994, 1–17.

678 Delany, *Motion*, 503.

679 Delany, *Motion*, 503.

building into which the landlord, who owned a goodly number of apartment houses in the neighborhood, just *happened* to put all the interracial couples who came to his dim, store-front office out on Avenue B, looking for a place to live [680]

The apartment they rent is in an awful condition, and after having cleaned the place, Delany and Hacker discover that it is rat infested:

> At home now and again the apartment rat would jump up on the back of the kitchen sink, while one or the other of us was brushing our teeth – shocked paralysis holding a moment between human and rodent, before one of us shrieked and the other fled: or it skittered out from under the tub to dash toward the toilet and leap to the rim for a drink – halting only because I was sitting there.[681]

But instead of elaborating on the connection between racism and their living conditions and instead of killing the rat, as Bigger Thomas does in the opening chapter of *Native Son*, Delany uses humor to resolve the situation: "We named him Gregor, after Kafka's giant waterbug."[682] In this episode, Delany ironically signifies on the black literary tradition without fulfilling the generic expectations of a black autobiography as laid out by Rosenblatt and hooks. In his use of humor and irony when signifying on *Native Son*, he also distances his own approach from the protest tradition embodied by Wright, but he employs a strategy that is different from Baldwin's theoretical critique of Wright (see 5.1.2).

Delany refers to Wright's novel as one of numerous texts of different origins that comprise his system of cultural references. Accordingly, among Delany's favorite autobiographical memoirs, he does not name only slave narratives. He also refers to *Barthes* by Roland Barthes, a paradigmatic example of poststructuralist thought, and in doing so, he positions himself in a line of postmodern thought and writing.[683] Similar to Lewy, who claims his multiple origins in "Atlantis: Model 1924," Delany, throughout *Motion*, draws on disparate cultural influences,

---

680 Delany, *Motion*, 20.

681 Delany, *Motion*, 117.

682 Delany, *Motion*, 117.

683 See also Posnock, 281.

such as Latin, classical Greek, Hebrew, opera, and canonical as well as sub-cultural literature. Black cultural works are mentioned as one influence among others. In referring to these various cultural sources, Delany does not claim to obtain the position of a spokesperson for African Americans alone.

Posnock and Tucker interpret Delany's references to the slave narrative and to postmodernism in two opposing ways. Whereas Posnock states that Delany distances himself from African American cultural traditions, Tucker, in arguing that Delany combines the African American autobiographical tradition with postmodernism, calls *Motion* "one of the most important texts in the tradition of African American autobiography to appear in the last two decades."[684] *Motion* contains passages to support both readings. Rather than arguing in one of these two directions, I contend that Delany's text makes it clear that American culture is determined by disparate elements which influence each other and are not clearly separable. Rather than distancing himself from one of these elements or supporting others, Delany shows his affiliations with all these different cultural sources in order to reveal the interrelatedness of different aspects of culture. For example, he alludes to high culture, popular culture, African American culture, gay and lesbian culture, Science Fiction, graphic novels, and pornography.

5.4.4 "Coming/Out"

Posnock quotes several passages in which Delany criticizes the idea that there might be a biological truth to the concepts of race and sexual orientation and states that

> since the early seventies Delany has been a devoted student of antifoun-
> dationalist thought [...] and a skeptic of identity politics. Group identity, he
> observes, disciplines and confines one even as it may grant political efficacy.
> Delany distrusts 'Gay Identity' regarding it as a policing device when it is
> anything more than a 'provisional or strategic reality.'[685]

Even if Delany has a constructionist rather than an essentialist approach to

---

684 Tucker, 3.

685 Posnock, 266.

identity categories, I contend that Posnock underestimates the importance that the strategic usage of the terms black and gay can have for those interpellated as black and gay. For Delany, the "provisional or strategic reality" of the term "gay" is what grants certain people, those who are oppressed as a group, the political power to act up against discrimination. I will illustrate my point by referring to Delany's reflections on the political strategy of coming out.

The strategy Delany uses with regard to the black autobiographical tradition can also be seen in his references to the coming out narrative prominent in many gay and lesbian novels and autobiographies since the 1960s. Tucker observes that "*Motion* subverts the reader's expectations of a gay autobiography in that it features no great conflict of 'coming out.'"[686] Delany's decision to resist such a coming out narrative becomes clear if *Motion* is read together with Delany's essay "Coming/Out," which also contains long autobiographical passages. Delany is highly critical of coming out understood as a singular event dividing one's biography into two phases, and he doubts that coming out defines somebody as gay. But he nevertheless stresses the strategic political use of the term. As can be deduced from the essay "Coming/Out," there are many situations in which Delany decides to make a strategic use of the category gay. For example, he comes out as a gay man to each new group of students when he teaches university courses, not because he wants to reveal an authentic core of his personality to them, but because he wants to raise the awareness of the effects the different subject positions have for the interpretation of literary texts. Delany, who spent the first thirty years of his life without the existence of the political strategy of coming out, has mixed feelings about it:

> While I approved vigorously of "coming out" as a necessary strategy to avoid blackmail and to promote liberation, there seemed to be an oppressive aspect of surveillance and containment intertwined with it, especially when compared to the term's older meaning.[687]

In *Motion*, as well as in "Coming/Out," there are several episodes in which Delany openly declares his homosexuality. These episodes include a conversation

---

686 Tucker, 186.

687 Delany, "Coming/Out," 90–91.

about his homosexuality during summer camp in the 1950s, addressing his homosexuality in a therapy group in the 1960s, writing about homosexuality in his first two SF stories, participating in the first-ever panel on gay SF at a SF convention in 1977, and being referred to as a gay black SF writer in the media afterwards. Still, he rejects the idea that a single event, the decision to define oneself as gay, can "carry the explicative strength 'definition' and 'identity' denote,"[688] even though he does believe that some events are more important than others. For Delany "the rhetoric of singular discovery, of revelation, of definition is one of the conceptual tools by which dominant discourses repeatedly suggest that there is no broad and ranging field of events informing the marginal."[689] This idea is highlighted in some of the episodes in which he "reveals" his homosexuality to others.

In one such coming out situation Delany depicts in *Motion*, he tells his therapy group about his homosexual experiences and realizes later that the way he formulated what he calls his confession was the result of the way homosexuality was pathologized in medical as well as literary discourse in the 1950s. Here, the normative element of coming out becomes quite clear. His coming out is determined by the dominant discourse which narrows the possibilities of presenting and perceiving who he is. Later Delany says the following:

> When you talk about something openly for the first time – and that, certainly, was the first time I'd talked to a public group about being gay – for better or worse, you use the public language you've been given. It's only later, alone in the night, that language reflects your experience. And that night I realized that language had done nothing but betray me.[690]

This betrayal by language is once again illustrated in an episode from the essay "Coming/Out." Delany describes what he ironically calls his first major homosexual experience, his "coming out into gay society." Afterwards, he writes about this experience in a letter to his friend Gale which he never sends. One year later, however, when he reads the letter again, he realizes: "I

---

688 Delany, "Coming/Out," 68.

689 Delany, "Coming/Out," 74.

690 Delany, *Motion*, 405.

was astonished by how many stock phrases of despair and disgust I'd used, as though the entire vocabulary for describing the incident had been lent me by some true-confessions magazine (that didn't exist) devoted to degrading homosexual encounters."[691]

Both incidents show that someone who self-identifies as a gay man starts to describe himself in the same vocabulary that is used within the dominant discourse. What is more, he starts to perceive himself as belonging to a unified group of persons who share certain character and personality traits, even if these are considered negative. Through dominant discourses, the discourses of education, psychology and through literary discourse, these negative characteristics are naturalized and inextricably linked to the identity category homosexual, a process Michel Foucault has analyzed in *The History of Sexuality: An Introduction* (1976). Foucault analyzes how homosexuality was constructed as an identity category[692] in the nineteenth century in Western Europe:

> This new persecution of the peripheral sexualities entailed an *incorporation of perversions* and a new specification of individuals. [...] The nineteenth-century homosexual became a personage, a past, a case history, and a childhood, in addition to being a type of life, a life form, and a morphology, with an indiscreet anatomy and possibly a mysterious physiology. Nothing that went into his total composition was unaffected by his sexuality. It was everywhere present in him. [...] The sodomite had been a temporary aberration; the homosexual was now a species.[693]

Foucault supports his thesis with a combination of examples from sources as different as Catholic confessions, medical case histories, psychiatric clinics, psychological discourse, and the regulations and architecture of boarding

---

691 Delany, "Coming/Out," 84.

692 In his essay "Gay Politics, Ethnic Identity: The Limits of Social Constructionism," Steven Epstein presents an overview of the theoretical foundations of constructionism. He differentiates between "symbolic interactionists," like John Gagnon and William Simon and "labeling theorists," like Mary McIntosh ("The Homosexual Role," 1968) and Kenneth Plummer ("The Sexual Stigma," 1975) and then discusses their approaches. Though some of these texts were published before Foucault's *History of Sexuality: An Introduction*, most queer theorists refer to Foucault because of his emphasis on the connections between discourse, knowledge and power (Steven Epstein, "Gay Politics, Ethnic Identity: The Limits of Social Constructionism," *Social Perspectives in Lesbian and Gay Studies*, eds. Peter M. Nardi and Beth E. Schneider, London: Routledge, 1998, 134–160).

693 Foucault, *History of Sexuality*, 43.

schools and prisons. His interdisciplinary way of investigating the history of sexuality and the history of homosexuality in particular is part of his broad research program about the way discursive and non-discursive practices situate the modern human being. Far from being a singular historical event, the construction of male homosexual identity is a complex process of interactions.

Delany's examples reveal that these institutions and discourses remain influential in defining the personality of "the homosexual." Consequently, he is very doubtful about the extent to which the political strategy of "coming out" contributes to liberation from oppression. He has experienced events in which he "came out into gay society," as well as events when he "came out of the closet", and states that "both showed me much and changed my life in ways I can only celebrate, I cannot claim that either identified or defined anything of me but only illuminated parts of my endlessly iterated (thus always changing) situation."[694] Delany thus rejects the normative tendencies inherent in the terms "gay identity" and "coming out." As an alternative, he suggests a new meaning of the term:

> an aware attitude, a vigilant disposition, an open mood (or even a discursive apparatus) that could beneficially inform all our behavior and discussions involving the sexual, and even, at some points, for any number of considerations, contain its presumed opposite – not coming out to someone – as long as the reason involved choice and not terror, not intimidation, not victimization, nor any of the range of attitudes that fall under the umbrella of oppression.[695]

Inherent in this new meaning of the term is the potential to escape the "obligation to confess,"[696] which, according to Foucault, is "the effect of a power that constrains us."[697]

694 Delany, "Coming/Out," 97.

695 Delany, "Coming/Out," 97.

696 Foucault, History of Sexuality, 60.

697 Foucault, History of Sexuality, 60.

5.4.5 Differences and Intersections

In spite of realizing the importance of Delany's participation in 1960s gay culture, Posnock, throughout his study, calls him "bisexual" and never elaborates on sexual orientation as an axis of difference to the same degree he considers class and race. Moreover, as far as the relation between race and class is concerned, Posnock does not put forward an intersectional analysis, either. Instead, his analysis of racism is largely based on class. Posnock partly derives his argument for the central importance of class from a statement of the introduction of Delany's book *Silent Interviews: On Language, Race, Sex, Science Fiction, and Some Comics*. I will quote Delany's statement and offer an interpretation which contests Posnock's reading. In my reading of the quotation, I will argue for Delany's emphasis on the interconnections between race, class, gender, and sexuality:

> the realities of race – if that is the proper term for what I take to be in all of its manifestations a system of political oppression grounded on a biological fantasy – also comes up [in this book], now and again, as they must, in the discussion of any black man or woman carried out extensively enough, in this or such a nation. (Anything 'positive' in the system associated with 'race' can be translated into terms of class – as class conflicts alone can explain the obfuscation, lies, and unspeakable cruelties that are the oppressive system itself.)[698]

Delany's characterization of race as "a system of political oppression grounded on a biological fantasy" is consistent with his anti-essentialist approach towards identity categories. The fact that race is socially constructed and historically situated does not deny the real material consequences of race and racism for those identified as black. The second part of the quotation, however, is more complicated. The statement "everything positive in the system associated with 'race' can be translated into terms of class – as class conflicts alone can explain the obfuscation, lies, and unspeakable cruelties that are the oppressive system itself" evokes traditional Marxist modes of social analysis. It seems to imply that, once capitalism is abolished, there will be no racism, no sexism, and no homophobia. Black activists, as well as feminists, have often criticized this one-dimensional mode of social analysis by claiming that it does

---

698 Delany, "Reading and the Written Interview," 8.

not pay sufficient attention to other forms of oppression. Such critiques have led to intersectional analyses of race, class, gender, sexual orientation, and other axes of difference (see 3.1).

Posnock takes Delany's quotation as a proof of "how intensely and persuasively Delany here and throughout focuses on class rather than race."[699] However, by repeatedly focusing on race, gender, and sexual orientation in his fiction as well as non-fiction, Delany renders such a reading reductive. After all, he says that everything *positive* in the system associated with 'race' can be translated into terms of class, rather than everything in the system. By "positive" he surely does not mean affirmative, constructive or pleasant because such a meaning would contradict his characterization of the oppressive system with the terms "obfuscation, lies, and unspeakable cruelties." Instead, the term "positive" should rather be understood in the sense of the term "positivism," as the "hard facts" which are directly evident. These could imply different forms of discrimination, such as housing discrimination, the disproportionally high number of black male prison inmates, restricted access to health care and education. These aspects of racism might arguably be translated into terms of class. Other aspects of racism, such as the stereotypical representation of black persons in the media, the obstacles a black person has in coming to a positive self-perception, the interpellation as a black subject, would not fall under Delany's definition of "anything positive in the system," and yet, they constitute racism. Moreover, Delany uses the term "translate" when he states that "anything positive in the system [...] can be translated into terms of class." Someone who considers race irrelevant might have used the words "must" and "reduced" instead of "can" and "translated."

I suggest that what can be legitimately derived from the quotation is Delany's claim that class is inextricably linked to race, gender, and sexual orientation. In *Motion*, he always relates his personal experiences of racism and homophobia to larger structures determined by a capitalist society. Rather than granting class primary importance in his memoir, Delany specifically focuses on the intersections of race and sexual orientation. At the beginning of *Motion*, he establishes three questions to guide the reader through her reading of the

699 Posnock, 282.

text: "a black man? a gay man? a writer?" These questions explicitly concern his sexual and racial identity, and his profession as a writer and can be interpreted as the guiding questions of Delany's autobiographical memoir:

> The previous summer, [...] I'd begun what I'd since planned out as a huge novel. Why wasn't I working on it? Just who was I? Where was I going? Through my tiredness, questions glimmered. I was a young black man, light-skinned enough so that four out of five people who met me, of whatever race, assumed I was white. [...] I was a homosexual who now knew he could function heterosexually. And I was a young writer whose early attempts had already gotten him a handful of prizes, a few scholarships [...] I spread my arms out on the back of the bench. So, I thought, you are neither black nor white. You are neither male nor female. And you are that most ambiguous of citizens, the writer. There was something at once very satisfying and very sad, placing myself at this pivotal suspension. It seemed, in the park at dawn, a kind of revelation a kind of center, formed of a play of ambiguities, from which I might move in any direction.[700]

Delany's insecurities about his identities are resolved in the end, but not in the traditional way of the black and gay subject who discovers, accepts, and is proud of his black gay identity. The resolution takes a different turn, one that reflects on postmodern theories.

In an interview with a member of the St. Mark's Poetry Project,[701] Delany is asked about the identity categories black man, gay man, and writer. The person who formulates the question directly refers to the above quotation without considering a later passage in *Motion* that approaches the question of identity from another direction. Rather than stating that he is "neither black nor white...male nor female...and that most ambiguous of citizens, the writer," Delany comes to the opposite conclusion in this later passage of the book when he accepts that his subject position has been determined by all of these categories all along. Near the end of *Motion*, he has developed a different perspective concerning questions of race, sexuality and the profession of a writer, and he simply writes three phrases: "A black man. A gay man. A writer."

---

700 Delany, *Motion*, 111.

701 The interview is collected in *About Writing*, Delany's most recent volume of essays, letters, and interviews. Samuel R. Delany, *About Writing: Seven Essays, Four Letters, and Five Interviews*, Middletown, CT: Wesleyan UP, 2005.

In his answer to the interview question, Delany explains the shift in thinking about these categories, which is central to *Motion*:

> [I did] realize that I *was* a 'black man, a gay man, a writer'; that these were specific, if complex categories. As categories they were social impositions – not essences. They were what had always already *given* me my identity, and an identity was something to be examined, interrogated, analyzed: vigilance and often, resistance, were the *conditions* of being able to function. [...] What I learned is that precisely when one says, 'I'm not a part,' one is most trapped by one's identity, most paralyzed and most limited by the greater society, and that is the sign one has given up, given in: that one is precisely *not* in a condition of freedom – but of entrapment. Saying 'I am not a part' is very different from saying, 'Because I *am* a part, I will not participate in *that* manner.' The first is delusion. The second is power – which is inimical to the cry of powerlessness that you quote and is the other way discourses are changed.[702]

Delany's statement that identity categories are social impositions, not essences, matches with poststructuralist thought. His recognition of the constructed character of every identity category does not lead him to believe that categories have no real consequences for human beings if they are merely socially constructed, a frequent critique uttered by skeptics of poststructuralism. On the contrary, he recognizes the fact that everyone is confined by the way the dominant discourse operates. He sees a potential for examination, interrogation, analysis, vigilance, and resistance by operating from within discourse rather than giving in to the illusion that one can position oneself outside of it. Hence, he utters skepticism towards identification as well as counter-identification.

Delany's approach towards identity categories differs from strategic essentialism and strategic identity politics. As he is critical of all forms of essentialism, he rejects the notion of strategic essentialism, too, because this strategy has the tendency to support the way the dominant discourse operates. In order to function effectively, it has to rely on categorizations implemented by the dominant discourse. His own project is rather to shift the boundaries of identity categories. He states that he is 'a black man, a gay man, a writer,'

---

702 Delany, *About Writing*, 303–304.

in order to be able to act and write in unexpected ways and support the slow process of changing the oppressive discourse.

Delany comes to what might be called a poststructuralist understanding of his identity as a black gay artist by reflecting on his own experiences a decade before these questions were addressed by the political movements of the 1960s. He claims that before the 1960s

> there were only Negroes and homosexuals, both of whom – along with artists – were hugely devalued in the social hierarchy. It's even hard to speak of that world. But looking back on that morning and the mystical ambiguities that seemed so important to it, I saw that such moments were themselves largely social and psychological illusions – unless you realized that what they meant was that forces both social and psychological were at work to pull you toward the most conservative position you might inhabit, however poorly you might be suited for it.[703]

This conservative position might be described as an uncritical universalism, a strategy to counter devaluing terms such as black and gay.

In paragraphs 40–45, Delany describes his experiences during treatment at Mount Sinai's Day/Night psychiatric program, in which he participates because of his acrophobia and fear of subway trains. In paragraph 41, he writes:

> It's hard to go into a hospital situation and not spend a good deal of time wondering what exactly brought you there, figuring out who you are, or why this is where you've ended up, reflecting on the select elements of the past that led to this particular present.[704]

This passage evokes Foucault's critical project of analyzing the significance the human sciences, in this case psychiatry, have had in situating the modern human being. Even though the therapy program was "firmly centered towards the present, rather than toward the historical retrieval of psychic minutiae more orthodox Freudian approaches encourage," [705] in the hospital Delany reflects on those childhood memories he considers significant for his problems. The memories revolve around homosexuality, blackness, and art. Delany's memories of his childhood and youth are not narrated

---

703 Delany, *Motion*, 399.

704 Delany, *Motion*, 339.

705 Delany, *Motion*, 343.

at the beginning of the memoir, in a chronological order, but as a part of his thoughts during the days of his psychiatric treatment. Because of this narrative structure, there is already an established interpretative context in which these episodes are told.

Thus, *Motion* does not fulfill the expectations of those readers of autobiography who want to gather information about Delany's past in order to explain his present condition or even find out the reasons why he became a black gay writer. While reflecting on blackness, gayness, and the profession of the writer during the course of his therapy, he puts his childhood experiences in a psychological context. However, at the end of his therapy, Delany arrives at no such thing as a linear explanation starting with childhood and ending with his identity as a black gay writer. On the contrary, what he understands during therapy is the connection between power, language, discourse, and the self. He understands that there are silences around areas like sexuality and homosexuality that limit the possibilities of human beings. The public language in which it is permitted to talk about these things is formalized and restrictive, a point Delany makes by describing his memories of Herman, a black man who played the organ in his father's funereal parlor. Herman is described as a black homosexual, a flamboyant man whose campy but closeted behavior is tolerated by those who know him. Delany observes that "Herman had a place in our social scheme – but by no means an acceptable place, and certainly not a place I wanted to fill."[706] Delany concludes that Herman's identity was limited by the discursive silences surrounding homosexuality: "I always treasured the image of Herman's outrageous and defiant freedom to say absolutely anything.... Anything except, of course, I *am* queer, and I like men sexually better than women."[707]

5.4.6 Delany and Baldwin

As I have shown in the first part of this chapter, the strategy of coming out of the closet became prominent in the late 1960s and early 1970s, and it is nowadays inextricably linked to fixed notions of gay and lesbian identity. This

706 Delany, *Motion*, 367.
707 Delany, *Motion*, 369.

coming-out paradigm has also influenced the theoretical framework of gay and lesbian studies. One example is Emmanuel S. Nelson's 1985 essay "The Novels of James Baldwin: Struggles of Self-Acceptance." Nelson argues that Baldwin's six novels can be chronologically divided into three stages, each of them defined by two novels, that indicate his growing acceptance of his homosexuality and correspond to his coming out as a homosexual man.

> Nearly three decades ago, in *Go Tell*, [Baldwin] voiced his hesitant sexual rebellion, while largely hiding in the closet. Since then he has defiantly kicked open the closet door to march out and polemically confront the American sexual Establishment. More recently he has achieved complete liberation through healing sexual self-acceptance. The development of his art testifies to his growing personal maturity.[708]

I have demonstrated Delany's skepticism towards the language of sexual liberation and coming out Nelson employs in his essay. Delany wrote *Motion* during a period when black gay scholars like Nelson and a new generation of black gay writers appropriated Baldwin's work and persona for the construction of a black gay identity and lineage. The way Delany includes Baldwin in his autobiographical memoir can be read as strategy to counter such appropriations.

Posnock argues that Delany's autobiographical memoir reminds the reader of Baldwin on several levels. It is true, a person who reads the autobiographical memoir of a black gay writer who started his career in the early 1960s would probably expect some connection to Baldwin, either personal or in terms of aesthetic influences. Posnock, however, argues that Baldwin and Delany are linked exactly because there are no connections between the two writers on a personal or aesthetic level. He states that

> as one reads Delany's memoir of the Harlem childhood of a brilliantly precocious black bisexual writer in a tense household headed by a hostile father and a protective mother, it is difficult not to be continually reminded of Baldwin. And it is just as difficult not to be struck by the vast difference within superficial similarities.[709]

---

708 Emmanuel Nelson, "The Novels of James Baldwin: Struggles of Self-Acceptance," *Journal of American Culture* 8.4 (1985): 11–16, 16.

709 Posnock, 282.

Posnock points out three differences between Baldwin and Delany: their class backgrounds, their skin color, and their literary ambitions. Delany's upper-middle-class background "bred a confident ease of access to Western culture,"[710] which made it comparatively easy for him to become a writer. Posnock describes this as "the pivotal difference that constitutes the Delany/Baldwin connection: whereas for Baldwin in the ghetto, *black intellectual* was an oxymoron that he first had to disown and then to reinvent on his own terms, Delany appropriated 'intellectual' as an unproblematic, deracialized description of his immersion in cultural life."[711] In addition to this difference in class, there is a difference in skin color and literary ambition. Delany is light-skinned and repeatedly perceived as white. Rather than writing fiction, Delany starts his career in the pop-cultural genre of science fiction.[712] Adding to the three reasons put forward by Posnock, there is a fourth reason for the distance between Baldwin and Delany: their different approaches towards homosexuality and gay identity.

Opposing Posnock's approach, Tucker argues that, throughout Delany's autobiographical memoir, Baldwin is present even if there are only a few direct references. Tucker's study is based on the assumption that there is a strong connection between Delany and black cultural traditions, one prominent example of which is Baldwin's work. In one direct reference to Baldwin's work, Delany states that *Giovanni's Room* shaped the public discourse that contributed to his own inability to express his own pleasant homosexual encounters adequately. In addition to *Giovanni's Room*, he names texts by Gore Vidal, André Tellier, Theodore Sturgeon, Jean Cocteau, and André Gide. In the 1950s, these texts were part of the discourse that connected male homosexuality with guilt, fear and death. Delany realizes that these texts contributed to the public language in which conversations about male homosexuality were possible. At the same time, he felt that his own homosexual experiences differed immensely from those described in the texts, and he explicitly distances himself from Baldwin's work. Referring to Baldwin and the other writers, he writes, "however full of

---

710 Posnock, 281.

711 Posnock, 282.

712 Posnock, 282.

death and darkness their accounts had been, they'd at least essayed a certain personal honesty. And the thing about honesty is that all of ours is different."[713]

Baldwin's persona is included in *Motion* in what Posnock calls a "brief but telling appearance"[714] near the very end of the text. Delany describes a telephone conversation with Baldwin one day before Delany left New York for a long stay in Europe. As the conversation is very short and as Baldwin does not say anything other than "yes," "that's right," "I see," and "good-bye," Delany calls this phone call a "non-conversation."[715] Posnock describes it as "a resonant moment because it makes visible the disconnection that is the most striking link between them [Baldwin and Delany]."[716] Given the degree to which other black gay writers refer to the importance of Baldwin for their life and work, the way Baldwin is included in *Motion* is striking and ironic. The awkward conversation is mentioned in one of the last paragraphs in which Delany recounts "some incidents from the seventy-two hours before [he] actually took off" to Europe.[717] In total, it does not even comprise a whole paragraph. Another incident described in the same paragraph as equally or possibly more important is an anonymous sexual encounter on a subway toilet which leads Delany to rethink his motifs for his trip to Europe. The conversation with Baldwin, however, whose persona is closely connected to the notion of the black intellectual expatriate in Europe, does not seem to affect Delany's decision to go abroad, at all. Delany insists on the importance and ubiquity of (homosexual) desire. He is skeptical of all forms of essentialism and humorously comments on the way black gay identity is constructed in texts by some black gay writers of the 1980s. All of these factors contribute to the anticlimactic account of his telephone conversation with Baldwin.

713 Delany, *Motion*, 406.
714 Posnock, 280.
715 Delany, *Motion*, 563.
716 Posnock, 280.
717 Delany, *Motion*, 556.

6 Conclusion

The voice-over narrator of *Looking for Langston* criticizes the fact that the success of many Harlem Renaissance writers depended on the approval of white people. Indeed, using a phrase from Chaucer, the narrator calls history "the smiler with the knife under the cloak."[718] During the Harlem Renaissance, black literature was determined by an ambivalent situation characterized by insidiousness and recognition. In fact, after the Great Depression, there was a demise of black literature and art. Since the 1970s, the black studies movement has brought those texts by black writers to critical attention that were in danger of being forgotten. Black (lesbian) feminists and black gay men added two further perspectives, particularly focusing on texts by black (homosexual) women and black homosexual men. The black gay cultural activists whose texts I have analyzed in my study excavated the hidden black gay dimensions of the Harlem Renaissance and thereby tried to defeat the smiler with the knife.

In analyzing the key texts constitutive of the black gay cultural activism of the 1980s and 1990s, I have focused on their references to black cultural traditions, specifically to the Harlem Renaissance of the 1920s and 1930s, and to the Protest Era of the 1950s and 1960s. On the textual basis of four black gay anthologies and six longer texts, one film, four novels, and one autobiographical memoir, I have investigated the effects of these historical references. I have shown that many texts collected in the early black gay anthologies aimed at the empowerment of black gay men by constructing a black gay heritage. Moreover, I have demonstrated that the references to black cultural traditions have two other important functions: the legitimization of black gay identity within the larger black community and the critique of the normative construction of gayness as a white identity.

Like black feminist writings of the 1970s and 1980s, the texts of the early black gay anthologies had a huge impact on political debates surrounding

---

718 Geoffrey Chaucer, "The Knight's Tale," *Canterbury Tales*, London: Penguin, 1969, 37–103,
    line 1141.

identity politics, and they strongly influenced academic discussions concerned with the deconstruction of identities in the fields of queer studies, black studies, cultural studies, and gender studies. The recent formulation of a distinct black queer theory is directly connected to the black gay cultural activism of the 1980s and 1990s. In my theoretical outline, I have connected approaches from sociology, African American studies, queer studies, literary studies, and performance studies. I have used Crenshaw's concept of representational intersectionality in analyzing stereotypical images of black masculinity. I have referred to Johnson's concept of quare and Muñoz's concept of disidentification used for the analysis of performances by subjects whose identity is constructed by antagonistic categories, such as blackness and gayness. I have argued that the concept of disidentification is comparable to strategies of resistance during slavery. I have linked these strategies of resistance to Gates's literary theory of Signifying and, with the help of Nero's analysis of the signifying strategies within black gay literature, transferred it to the analysis of black gay texts.

The six longer texts analyzed in this study, *Looking for Langston, No Easy Place to Be*, "Atlantis: Model 1924," *A Visitation of Spirits, Vanishing Rooms*, and *The Motion of Light in Water*, continue and critically reflect on the work begun by those black gay writers who contributed their writings to the early anthologies, but these longer texts follow different political and aesthetic aims. Isaac Julien, Steven Corbin, Randall Kenan, Melvin Dixon, and Samuel R. Delany have all been teaching at university level. Their texts mirror and contribute to the academic discourse about identity and identity politics. The five authors work in different genres, such as avant-garde film, historical novel, historiographic metafiction, the southern gothic novel, and experimental autobiographical memoir. These genres correspond to the political aims and aesthetic strategies the texts pursue. All of the texts depict or question identities with regard to the intersections of two or more lines of difference. The degree of openness regarding the identity category "black gay man" is reflected in the style of writing. Those texts written and filmed in an experimental mode tend to represent identities as complex and open formations, whereas more traditional narratives tend to represent identities as closed concepts. The different genres appeal to different audiences. Whereas all of the six texts are contributions to the black gay political discourse of the 1980s and 1990s, they need not be seen as solely addressed at a black gay audience.

From the Harlem Renaissance until today, the intended readership of black literature has changed. Initially, black writers wrote for a white Euro-American audience in order to raise acceptance for black people. Consequently, their texts made formal contributions to literary forms that were used by white writers and could be understood easily by a white audience. In the context of the Civil Rights movement and other black liberation movements, the role of black literature changed and the implied readership with it. Since the 1960s, many African American writers have addressed the black community in their writings and thereby started and contributed to a dialogue among black people.[719] In her 1984 essay, "Rootedness: The Ancestor as Foundation" Morrison has a black readership in mind when she delineates one function of the novel for African-Americans as a means of passing on information from one generation to the next. She uses the terms "village" and "community" to define the readers her novels are aimed at.[720]

The texts collected in *In the Life* and *Brother to Brother* have to be seen in this context and are clearly directed at a black audience. Their aim is to start a discussion about homosexuality among the black community. The same is true for Dixon's and Kenan's novels. Both of them refer to black cultural traditions, such as black southern folk traditions and jazz, which are immediately decipherable by a black audience. The writers combine these elements with a black gay narrative to start a discussion about homosexuality among the larger black community. Corbin seems to have a black heterosexual and a white gay and lesbian readership in mind because *No Easy Place to Be* contains didactic elements to educate white gay men and lesbians about black history and to educate a black heterosexual audience about queer culture. Julien's film and Delany's writings have a different status. It can be argued that *Looking for Langston* raises questions concerning black and gay identities but does not

---

719 Diedrich 1994, 420–21.

720 Toni Morrison, "Rootedness: The Ancestor as Foundation," *What Moves at the Margins: Selected Nonfiction*, ed. Carolyn C. Denard, Jackson: UP of Mississippi, 2008. 56–64, 64.

provide answers. Julien's combination of a black gay subject matter with an avant-garde form addresses a black gay audience, white queer communities, the larger black community, as well as an academic audience familiar with the theoretical concepts the film refers to. The implied readership of Delany's writings is even less clearly defined. He does not seem to solely address the black community, but he has all those in mind who interrogate the way identities are constructed through social and political power relations.

With the exception of Delany's texts, all of the longer texts analyzed in this study clearly signify on writings by Bruce Nugent or James Baldwin. These texts are examples of what Gates calls "unmotivated signifying" or "pastiche" because they embrace the writings of the earlier black homosexual writers. Delany's signifying strategies do not refer solely to texts by black or black homosexual writers. They explicitly refer to texts often regarded as constitutive of white traditions, such as Hart Crane's modernist poem *The Bridge*. Delany's humorous and ironic comments on texts such as Wright's *Native Son* and his irony concerning black tropes such as the passing narrative and the migration narrative are examples of what Gates calls "motivated signifying" or "parody."

In contrast to Delany's texts, the texts by Julien, Corbin, Kenan, and Dixon are similar in their alteration of those elements from Nugent's and Baldwin's texts contradicting the political agenda of black gay men in the 1980s and 90s. For example, in appropriating Nugent's "Smoke, Lilies, and Jade," Julien and Corbin alter the race of the white man Beauty to that of a black character, and they make the sexuality of its black protagonist less ambiguous by changing his bisexuality into homosexuality. The homosexuality of John Grimes, which Baldwin only suggests in *Go Tell It on the Mountain*, is fully elaborated in the representation of the black gay protagonist Horace Cross in Kenan's *A Visitation of Spirits*. In Dixon's *Vanishing Rooms*, which signifies on Baldwin's *Giovanni's Room*, the relationship of the two white men David and Giovanni in Paris is transferred to New York City and depicted as an interracial relationship between the black man Jesse and the white man Metro.

These appropriations diminish the racial and sexual ambiguity of the texts they signify on, an effect which can be explained in the light of critical debates in the 1980s regarding the dominance of white men within the gay community. Even though black gay men and black transgendered persons actively participated in the social movements of the 1960s, they had a difficult position in the black liberation movements and have been marginalized in the course of the emergence of a more visible gay community since the 1970s. Black gay cultural activists reacted to this situation in their politics by formulating an autonomous political agenda. Consequently, the writings by black gay men published in the early black gay anthologies critically address interracial desire and reveal racist attitudes within the white-dominated gay community. The texts by Julien, Corbin, Kenan, and Dixon take up these debates and represent white gay characters who perpetuate racist stereotypes of black masculinity. Supporting an afrocentric gay agenda, they suggest that intraracial relationships between black gay men are the only way out of this situation.[721]

Delany's approach is different. Throughout his texts, he shows that racism is a social structure that is linked to class. It is not merely represented as a personal attitude held by white persons. Instead of depicting "black men loving black men," he frequently represents inter-racial desire and directs the reader's attention to class as an important axis of difference. The way he depicts sex between white and black men who come from different class backgrounds shows the rewarding and subversive effects of what in *Times Square Red, Times Square Blue* he has also theoretically reflected on as "interclass contact." Delany does not formulate a negative critique of the politics of the black gay movement. His critique is put forward with the use of humor and irony as well as his use of metafictional devices. He explicitly reflects on his own role in the construction of his autobiographical memoir, and he frequently points out and analyzes the role of discourse for social formations.

My juxtaposition of the texts of Corbin, Julien, Kenan, and Dixon to those written by Delany should not be understood as the claim that Corbin, Julien, Kenan, and Dixon form a homogenous group. I have shown in my analysis that these texts, though rooted in the debates of the black gay movement, differ widely from one another.

---

721 Julien's later films follow a different political and aesthetic paradigm.

I have argued that Corbin's historical novel *No Easy Place to Be* consolidates black gay identity and combines the quest of its two black homosexual protagonists with the didactic aim of raising tolerance for black gay men and lesbians and of empowering black gay and lesbian readers. It represents black gay identity as a static concept that, at all times, has been connected with the same conflicts, problems, and rewards. Choosing the genre of historical novel, Corbin paradigmatically and didactically visualizes the quest of its black gay protagonist Rudy, whose coming out as a black gay man is represented as a development from a state of innocence and social constraints to one of knowledge and freedom. Because of the novel's didacticism in showing the reactions of Rudy and Miriam's black families and friends to their sexual orientation, I have argued that it is mainly addressed at the black community. The novel also formulates a critique of the black community in showing the exclusionary politics of black political organizations, and showing the arrogant way the black female writer Velma is treated by her black male colleagues. The novel depicts the boundaries between blackness and whiteness as impermeable, a strategy which is most clearly shown in the failure of Louise's attempt at passing for white. Consequently, as there are no representations of homosexual relationships between black and white persons, the novel tends to support a 1980s gay afrocentric agenda. In contrast to Julien in *Looking for Langston* and Delany in "Atlantis: Model 1924," Corbin does not use devices that reflect the influence of his own position as a black gay man in the 1980s on the construction of the Harlem Renaissance as a place for black homosexual men and women. He does not employ any postmodern elements of historiographic metafiction because these would contradict the aim of consolidating black gay identity as a closed and unambiguous concept.

In my analysis of Julien's avant-gardist film essay *Looking for Langston*, I have shown that he employs the stylistic devices of experimental cinema as a way of fusing different epochs and locations specific to black gay culture into a single space of simultaneity. Influenced by black British Cultural Studies and the concept of hybridity, Julien's film points at the limitations of traditional concepts of identity. It directly connects the situation of black gay men in the 1980s to the historical footage of the 1920s. I have shown that Julien also visualizes an awareness of his own agency in the process of constructing a black gay lineage. The experimental form of *Looking for Langston* challenges the viewing habits of the audience of mainstream cinema, but the film is nevertheless the most popular of the six longer texts. Julien's film meditates on black gay identity by experimentally fusing the Harlem Renaissance, the Protest Era, and the 1980s. This experimental device has two effects. On the one hand, it empowers black gay viewers whose identity is legitimized by this direct connection to earlier black cultural traditions. On the other hand, the experimental form makes transparent the very process of constructing this black gay lineage, for example, by including the filmmaker Isaac Julien embodying the dead Langston Hughes in the beginning of the film. The critique of white dominance within the gay community is also linked to earlier cultural productions. By directly alluding to the white homosexual photographers Carl Van Vechten, George Platt Lynes, and Robert Mapplethorpe, all of whom have been criticized for objectifying black male bodies, Julien connects 1980s discussions about white gay racism to a critique of the dominance of the white male homosexual gaze within the history of the visual arts. By making this process of objectification transparent in showing the white homosexual character Karl among projections of images of Mapplethorpe, the film empowers black gay viewers and gives them a new position from which to look at Mapplethorpe's photographs. This process is one example of what Muñoz calls disidentification.

I have analyzed how Kenan's novel *A Visitation of Spirits* refers to black rural culture and southern traditions. The postmodern narrative experimentally draws on disparate cultural sources, such as southern Gothicism, popular culture, and black magic to juxtapose these elements with the matter-of-fact description of the suicide of the black gay adolescent Horace. In doing so, the novel shows the very real and material limits of the postmodern understanding of identity as an open concept under constant negotiation. Horace's suicide represents the ultimate failure of the Tims Creek community, which is characterized by a lack of solidarity for the black gay adolescent. Alluding to Alice Walker's concept of womanism, which is grounded in the solidarity among black women, including black lesbians, the novel deals with a lack of solidarity even between two generations of black gay men. Another criticism is directed at the normative construction of gayness as a white identity. In order to live a gay life, Horace literally has to put on a white mask.

In my reading of Dixon's novel *Vanishing Rooms*, I have focused on how a homophobic hate crime affects the lives of three persons who occupy different positions regarding race, class, gender, and sexual orientation. I have analyzed this particular construction of characters by means of Crenshaw's theoretical concept of representational intersectionality. By shifting the narrative center of the novel among three protagonists, Dixon makes transparent the way various lines of difference intersect. The form of *Vanishing Rooms* de-centers the white male perspective of Baldwin's *Giovanni's Room* and asserts that questions of guilt and innocence cannot easily be answered on the grounds of the characters' sexual orientation, gender, or race alone. The political black community, represented for example by a group of politically active students at the campus where Jesse is studying, is criticized for not accepting Jesse's gayness. The novel examines the debate around interracial sexuality and cautiously propagates an afrocentric black gay agenda. Because of the critique of the white dominated gay community, I have referred to hooks's analysis of representations of whiteness in the black imagination and argued that gay whiteness is represented as terror. Black gay readers are ultimately empowered by the depiction of love among two black men as a way out of a situation determined by black homophobia and white gay racism.

Kenan's and Dixon's novels represent different facets of black gay identity. In contrast to the way *No Easy Place to Be* depicts only one model of being black and gay, the difficult but successful coming out process as a black gay man, *A Visitation of Spirits* and *Vanishing Rooms* depict different possibilities of living as black gay men. The critique of black homophobia and white gay racism contained in these novels is directed at both the white and the black communities. In contrast to the traditional narrative mode of *No Easy Place to Be*, both novels contain postmodern narrative elements that depict the complexity of an identity determined by various lines of difference.

Against the background of the other texts analyzed in my study, both of Delany's texts are exceptional. In my reading of "Atlantis: Model 1924," I have argued that it can be regarded as a work of historiographic metafiction because it displays an awareness of the process of depicting an earlier historical period and because of its extensive references to disparate cultural traditions. In analyzing *The Motion of Light in Water*, I have shown that it contains such metafictional elements as the self-reflexivity of the author as both subject and object of his autobiographical memoir, and the transparency of the role of fictional elements in autobiographical writings. Delany's two experimental texts assert that identity is a concept under constant negotiation. Referring to the epoch of the Harlem Renaissance, "Atlantis: Model 1924" deliberately constructs an historical lineage that refers to modernism and takes the white writer Hart Crane as a literary forebear. *The Motion of Light in Water* evokes expectations of African American and gay literary traditions, such as the genre of black autobiography, the quest motif, and the coming-out narrative, but it does not fulfill these expectations. Owing to the experimental form of the texts, their use of humor and irony, and the multiple cultural sources they refer to, they are postmodern texts that resist closure.

Delany's readership is probably as diverse as the genres he writes in. His experimental texts and the humorous critique directed at the form of identity politics employed by black gay men in the 1980s and 1990s do not aim at being completely decipherable by members of any particular community. Nonetheless, the black gay community has embraced Delany as a pioneer of black gay literature, he has received awards both for his Science Fiction and for his gay writings, and the inclusion of parts of "Atlantis: Model 1924" in the *Norton Anthology of African American Literature* secures his place as a canonical writer of black literature.

Since the mid-1990s, the work of the first wave of black gay cultural activists has been in danger of being forgotten. During the 1980s, there were a lot of black gay groups, writers' collectives, magazines, editors, and publishers. This lively scene would probably have produced more work and become visible on a larger scale. But because of the devastating consequences of the AIDS epidemic, this first wave of black gay cultural activists ended in the mid-1990s. Today, their texts are met with growing interest within black studies, queer studies, and black queer studies. A new generation of black gay cultural activists has emerged, but these black gay men do not form a cohesive community with its own infrastructure. Currently, black gay men work in different genres of cultural production. For example, the commercially successful sequels to novels by E. Lynn Harris and James Earl Hardy depict black gay life. Rodney Evans's film *Brother to Brother* once again visualizes the importance of the Harlem Renaissance and Baldwin for the young protagonist's quest and coming out as a black gay man. The homohop of black gay hip-hop groups like deepdickollective shows an awareness of the work black gay men started in the 1980s. Black gay hip-hop artists challenge the heteronormativity and homophobia that can be found in hip-hop culture, as well as the racism in the white dominated gay community. All of these writers, filmmakers, artists, and activists are empowered by and actively remember the black gay cultural activists of the 1980s and 1990s.

Works Cited

Ajanaku, Oye Apeji. "Discharge USN '63." *In the Life: A Black Gay Anthology*. Ed. Joseph Beam. Boston: Alyson, 1986. 114–115.

Althusser, Louis. "Ideology and Ideological State Apparatusses." *Lenin and Philosophy, and Other Essays*. London: New Left Books, 1971. 121–173.

Arroyo, José. "The Films of Isaac Julien: Look Back and Talk Black." *Cinemas of the Black Diaspora: Diversity, Dependence, and Oppositionality*. Ed. Michael T. Martin. Detroit: Wayne State UP, 1995. 318–339.

Baldwin, James. *Giovanni's Room*. New York: Delta, 1956.

———. *Another Country*. New York: Vintage, 1993. (1962)

———. "Preservation of Innocence." *Collected Essays*. New York: Library of America, 1998. 594–600. (1942)

———. "The Male Prison." *Collected Essays*. New York: Library of America, 1998. 231–235. (1952)

———. "Everybody's Protest Novel." *Collected Essays*. New York: Library of America, 1998. 11–18. (1949)

———. "Many Thousands Gone." *Collected Essays*. New York: Library of America, 1998. 19–34. (1951)

———. "Alas, Poor Richard." *Collected Essays*. New York: Library of America, 1998. 247–268. (1961)

———. "The Black Boy Looks at the White Boy." *Collected Essays*. New York: Library of America, 1998. 269–285. (1961)

———. "No Name in the Street." *Collected Essays*. New York: Library of America, 1998. 349–476. (1972)

———. *Go Tell It on the Mountain*. New York: Dial, 2005. (1953)

Baraka, Amiri (LeRoi Jones). "American Sexual Reference: Black Male." *Home: Social Essays*. New York: Morrow, 1966. 216–234.

———. "Brief Reflection on Two Hot Shots." *Home: Social Essays*. New York: Morrow, 1966. 116–121.

Barthes, Roland. "The Reality Effect." *The Novel: An Anthology of Criticim and Theory 1900–2000*. Ed. Dorothy J. Hale. Malden MA and Oxford UK: Blackwell, 2006, 229–234. (1967)

Beam, Joseph, Barbara Smith, Cheryl Clarke, and Phil Robinson. "Speaking of Baldwin." *Au Courant* 6.6 (1987).

Beam, Joseph. "Black Men Loving Black Men: The Revoulutionary Act of the 1980s." *Gay Community News* (1985): 5.

———. Ed. *In the Life: A Black Gay Anthology*. Boston: Alyson, 1986.

———. "Introduction." *In the Life: A Black Gay Anthology*. Ed. Joseph Beam. Boston: Alyson, 1986. 13–18.

———. "Brother to Brother: Words From the Heart." *Brother to Brother: New Writings by Black Gay Men*. Ed. Essex Hemphill. Boston: Alyson, 1991. 230–242.

———. "James Baldwin: Not a Bad Legacy, Brother." *Brother to Brother: New Writings by Black Gay Men*. Ed. Essex Hemphill. Boston: Alyson, 1991. 184–186.

Beavers, Herman. "Finding Common Ground: Ralph Ellison and James Baldwin." *The Cambridge Companion to the African American Novel*. Ed. Maryemma Graham. Cambridge: Cambridge UP, 2004. 189–202.

Belton, Don. "Gay Voices, Gay Lives: Black Gay Men Speak Out in an Anthology – Celebrating and Defining Their World." *The Philadelphia Inquirer* Aug. 25 (1991): 1c-2c.

Benjamin, Walter. *Illuminations*. London: Fontana, 1973.

Bérubé, Allan. "How Gay Stays White and What Kind of White It Stays." *The Making and Unmaking of Whiteness*. Ed. Birgit Brander Rasmussen. Durham: Duke UP, 2001. 234–256.

Black, Carlyle R. "James Baldwin (1924–1987)." *Brother to Brother: New Writings by Black Gay Men*. Ed. Essex Hemphill. Boston: Alyson, 1991. 187–188.

Bodziock, Joseph. "Richard Wright and Afro-American Gothic." *Richard Wright: Myths and Realities*. Ed. James Trotman. New York: Garland, 1988. 27–42.

Boone, Joseph Allen. *Libidinal Currents: Sexuality and the Shaping of Modernism*. Chicago: U of Chicago P, 1998.

Boykin, Keith. *One More River to Cross: Black and Gay in America*. New York: Doubleday, 1996.

Brinkley, Sidney. *Making History. NCBLG – 25 Years Ago a Small Group of Black Lesbians and Gay Men Formed the First National Black Gay Organization*. <http://www.blacklightonline.com/ncblg.html>, accessed Oct. 7, 2006.

———. *The Complete Blacklight*. <http://www.blacklightonline.com>, accessed October 7, 2007.

British Film Institute. "Biographies." "Looking for Langston:" *A Film by Isaac Julien* [DVD Booklet]. Ed. British Film Institute. London: BFI, 2006. 37–41.

Brody, Jennifer DeVere and Dwight A. McBride, eds. "Plum Nelly: New Essays in Black Queer Studies." *Callaloo* 23.1 (2000): Special Edition.

Bronski, Michael. "Reading Through *Brother to Brother. New Writings By Black Gay Men* (Between the Lines with Michael Bronski: Books in Review)." *The Guide* July (1991): n.p.

Bryant, Cedric Gael. "'The Soul has Bandaged Moments': Reading the African American Gothic in Wright's 'Big Boy Leaves Home,' Morrison's *Beloved*, and Gomez's *Gilda*." *African American Review*. 39.4 (2005), 541–553.

Butler, Judith. *Bodies that Matter: On the Discursive Limits of 'Sex.'* New York: Routledge, 1993.

Campt, Tina. *Other Germans: Black Germans and the Politics of Race, Gender, and Memory in the Third Reich*. Ann Arbor: U of Michigan P, 2005.

Carbado, Devon W., Dwight A. McBride, Donald Weise, and Evelyn C. White, eds. *Black Like Us: A Century of Lesbian, Gay, and Bisexual African American Fiction*. San Francisco: Cleis, 2002.

Carby, Hazel. *Race Men*. Cambridge Mass. and London: Harvard UP, 1998.

Chaucer, Geoffrey. "The Knight's Tale." *Canterbury Tales*. London: Penguin, 1969. 37–103.

Chauncey, George. *Gay New York: Gender, Urban Culture, and the Making of the Gay World, 1890–1940*. New York: Basic Books, 1994.

Chlada, Marvin. *Heterotopie und Erfahrung*. Aschaffenburg: Alibri, 2005.

Cleaver, Eldridge. "Notes on a Native Son." *Soul on Ice*. New York: Delta, 1992. 122–138. (1966)

Cohen, Cathy J. *The Boundaries of Blackness: AIDS and the Breakdown of Black Politics*. Chicago: U of Chicago P, 1999.

Cohen, William A. "Liberalism, Libido, Liberation: Baldwin's *Another Country*." *Genders* 12 (1991): 1–21.

Combahee River Collective, The. "A Black Feminist Statement." *Social Perspectives in Lesbian and Gay Studies*. Eds. Peter M. Nardi and Beth E. Schneider. London: Routledge, 1998. 521–522. (1977)

Constantine-Simms, Delroy. Ed. *The Greatest Taboo: Homosexuality in Black Communities*. Los Angeles, CA: Alyson, 2001.

Corber, Robert J. *In the Name of National Security: Hitchcock, Homophobia, and the Political Construction of Gender in Postwar America*. Durham: Duke UP, 1993.

_____. *Homosexuality in Cold War America: Resistance and the Crisis of Masculinity*. Durham: Duke UP, 1997.

Corbin, Steven. *No Easy Place to Be*. New York: Simon and Schuster, 1989.

Crane, Hart and Ute Eisinger. *Die Brücke/The Bridge*. Salzburg: Jung und Jung, 2004.

Crenshaw, Kimberlé Williams. "Mapping the Margins: Intersectionality, Identity Politics, and Violence Against Women of Color." *Stanford Law Review* 43 (1991): 1241–1299.

_____. "Beyond Racism and Misogyny: Black Feminism and 2 Live Crew." *Words that Wound: Critical Race Theory, Assaultive Speech, and the First Amendment*. Ed. Mari J. Matsuda. Boulder: Westview, 1993. 111–132.

Dais, Stephen Lee. "Don't Turn Your Back On Me." *In the Life: A Black Gay Anthology*. Ed. Joseph Beam. Boston: Alyson, 1986. 60–62.

Davis, Angela Y. "Reflection on the Black Women's Role in the Community of Slaves." *Black Scholar* 4 (1971): 2–15.

Deepdickollective. *On Some Other.* Oakland: Sugartruck, 2007, CD.

Delany, Samuel R. *The Mad Man.* New York: Richard Kasak, 1994.

———."Sword & Sorcery, S/M, and the Economics of Inadequation: The Camera Obscura Interview." *Silent Interviews: On Language, Race, Sex, Science Fiction, and Some Comics.* Hanover, NH: Wesleyan UP, 1994. 127–163.

———. *Silent Interviews: On Language, Race, Sex, Science Fiction, and Some Comics.* Hanover, NH: Wesleyan UP, 1994.

———."Introduction: Reading and the Written Interview." *Silent Interviews: On Language, Race, Sex, Science Fiction, and Some Comics.* Hanover, NH: Wesleyan UP, 1994. 1–17.

———."Atlantis: Model 1924." *Atlantis: Three Tales.* Middletown, CT: Wesleyan UP, 1995. 1–121.

———."Atlantis Rose. Some Notes on Hart Crane." *Longer Views: Extended Essays.* Hanover, NH: UP of New England, 1996. 174–250.

———. *Times Square Red, Times Square Blue.* New York: New York UP, 1999.

———."Some Queer Notions About Race." *Dangerous Liaisons: Blacks and Gays and the Struggle for Equality.* Ed. Eric Brandt. New York: New Press, 1999. 259–289.

———."Coming/Out." *Shorter Views: Queer Thoughts and the Politics of the Paraliterary.* Hanover, NH: Wesleyan UP, 1999. 67–97.

———."The Paradoxa Interview: Inside and Outside the Canon." *Shorter Views: Queer Thoughts and the Politics of the Paraliterary.* Hanover, NH: Wesleyan UP, 1999. 186–217.

———. *Shorter Views: Queer Thoughts and the Politics of the Paraliterary.* Hanover, NH: Wesleyan UP, 1999.

———. *The Motion of Light in Water: Sex and Science Fiction Writing in the East Village.* Minneapolis: U of Minnesota P, 2004.

_____. *Phallos*. Whitmore Lake, MI: Bamberger, 2004.

_____. *About Writing: Seven Essays, Four Letters, and Five Interviews*. Middletown, CT: Wesleyan UP, 2005.

_____. *Dark Reflections*. New York: Caroll & Graf, 2007.

Delany, Sarah Louise, Annie Elizabeth Delany, and Amy Hill Hearth. *Having Our Say: The Delany Sistsers' First 100 Years*. New York: Kodansha International, 1993.

Diawara, Manthia. "The Absent One: The Avant-Garde and the Black Imaginary in *Looking for Langston*." *Representing Black Men*. Eds. Marcellus Blount and George P. Cunningham. New York and London: Routledge, 1996. 205–224.

Diedrich, Maria. *Ausbruch aus der Knechtschaft: Das Amerikanische Slave Narrative Zwischen Unabhängigkeitserklärung und Bürgerkrieg*. Stuttgart: Steiner, 1986.

_____."James A. Baldwin – Obituaries for a Black Ishmael." *James Baldwin: His Place in American Literary History and His Reception in Europe*. Ed. Jakob Kollhöfer. Frankfurt a.M.: Peter Lang, 1991. 129–140.

_____."Afro-amerikanische Literatur." *Amerikanische Literaturgeschichte*. Ed. Hubert Zapf. Stuttgart: Metzler, 1996. 402–426.

Diedrichsen, Diedrich. „Verloren Unter Sternen: Das Mothership und Andere Alternativen zur Erde und Ihren Territorialien." *Loving the Alien: Science Fiction, Diaspora, Multikultur*. Ed. Diedrich Diedrichsen. Berlin: ID Verlag, 1998. 105–133.

Dixon, Melvin. *Vanishing Rooms*. New York: Cleis, 1991.

Doyle, JD. *Queer Music Heritage*. <www.queermusicheritage.us/nov2001.html>, accessed February 27, 2008.

Duberman, Martin B. "On Contemporary Gay Male Literature in the United States. A Symposium with Christopher Bram, Dennis Cooper, Michael Cunningham, Dale Peck, Robert Reid-Pharr, and Assotto Saint." *Queer Representations. Reading Lives, Reading Cultures: A Center for Gay and Lesbian Studies Book*. Ed. Martin B. Duberman. New York: New York UP, 1997. 371–377.

Duplechan, Larry. „Interview with Steven Corbin." *BLK: The National Black Gay and Lesbian Newsmagazine* 4.1 (1992): 11–25.

Dyer, Richard. *White.* London: Routledge, 1997.

Edition Salzgeber. Ed. *Begleitheft zu Isaac Juliens* "Looking for Langston." Berlin: Salzgeber, 1989.

Edwards, Brent Hayes. "The Uses of Diaspora." *Social Text* 66 (2001): 45–73.

Elbert, Monika. "Gothicism." *The Toni Morrison Encyclopedia.* Ed. Elizabeth Ann Beaulieu. Westport, Conneticut and London: Greenwood, 2003. 144–147.

Eldrege, Charles C. „Calla Moderna: 'Such a Strange Flower'." *Georgia O'Keeffe and the Calla Lily in American Art, 1860–1940.* Eds. Barbara Buhler Lynes and Georgia O'Keeffe. New Haven: Yale UP, 2002. 4–37.

Epstein, Steven. "Gay Politics, Ethnic Identity: The Limits of Social Constructionism." *Social Perspectives in Lesbian and Gay Studies.* Eds. Peter M. Nardi and Beth E. Schneider. London: Routledge, 1998. 134–160.

Evans, Rodney, dir. *Brother to Brother.* San Jose CA: Wolfe, 2004, DVD.

Ferguson, Roderick A. "The Parvenu Baldwin and the Other Side of Redemption." *James Baldwin Now.* Ed. Dwight A. McBride. New York: New York UP, 1999. 233–261.

———.*Aberrations in Black: Toward a Queer of Color Critique.* Minneapolis: U of Minnesota P, 2004.

Field, Douglas. "Looking for Jimmy Baldwin." *Callaloo* 27.2 (2004): 457–480.

Fluck, Winfried. *Inszenierte Wirklichkeit. Der Amerikanische Realismus 1865–1900.* München: Fink, 1992.

———."Surface Knowledge and 'Deep' Knowledge: The New Realism In American Fiction." *Neo-Realism in Contemporary American Fiction.* Ed. Kristiaan Versluys. Amsterdam and Atlanta: Rodopi, 1992. 65–85.

Foucault, Michel. *History of Sexuality: The Will to Knowledge.* London: Penguin, 1990. (1976)

———."Different Spaces." *Aesthetics, Method, and Epistemology.* Eds. Michel Foucault and James D. Faubion. New York: New Press, 1998. 175–185. (1967)

Frankenberg, Ruth. *White Women, Race Matters: The Social Construction of Whiteness.* Minneapolis: U of Minnesota P, 1993.

Fuller, Charles Henry. "The Jazz Singer." *Brother to Brother: New Writings by Black Gay Men.* Ed. Essex Hemphill. Boston: Alyson, 1991. 3–6.

Fullwood, Steven G. *Black Gay and Lesbian Archive.* <http://bgla.stevenfullwood.org>, accessed September 2, 2005.

Garber, Eric. "A Spectacle in Color: The Lesbian and Gay Subculture of Jazz Age Harlem." *Hidden from History: Reclaiming the Gay and Lesbian Past.* Eds. Martin B. Duberman, Martha Vicinus, and George Chauncey. New York: New American Library, 1989. 318–331.

Gates Jr., Henry Louis. *The Signifying Monkey: A Theory of Afro-American Literary Criticism.* New York: Oxford UP, 1988.

_____."The Black Man's Burden." *Fear of a Queer Planet: Queer Politics and Social Theory.* Ed. Michael Warner. Minneapolis: U of Minnesota P, 1993. 230–238.

_____."Looking for Modernism." *Black American Cinema.* Ed. Manthia Diawara. New York: Routledge, 1993. 200–207.

_____. *Thirteen Ways of Looking at a Black Man.* New York: Random House, 1997.

Gerima, Haile. *Sankofa.* <http://sankofastore.com/catalog/homepage.php>, accessed May 1, 2007.

Gilroy, Paul. *The Black Atlantic: Modernity and Double Consciousness.* Cambridge, Mass: Harvard UP, 1993.

Glick, Elisa F. "Harlem's Queer Dandy: African-American Modernism and the Artifice of Blackness." *MFS Modern Fiction Studies* 49.3 (2003): 414–442.

Goethe, Johann Wolfgang von. "Dichtung und Wahrheit." *Poetische Werke.* Vol. 8. Essen: Phaidon, 1999. 9–536.

Goddu, Teresa A. *Gothic America. Narrative, History, and Nation.* New York: Columbia UP, 1997.

Gubar, Susan. *Racechanges: White Skin, Black Face in American Culture.* New York: Oxford UP, 1997.

Gutterman, David S. "Postmodernism and the Interrogation of Masculinity." *Theorizing Masculinities*. Eds. Harry Brod, and Michael Kaufman. Vol. 5. Thousand Oaks: Sage, 1994. 219–238.

Halberstam, Judith. "Shame and White Gay Masculinity." *Social Text* 84–85.23 (2005): 219–233.

Hall, Stuart. "New Ethnicities." *Black Film, British Cinema*. Ed. ICA. London: Institute of Contemporary Arts, 1988. 27–30.

Halperin, David M. *One Hundred Years of Homosexuality*. New York: Routledge, 1990.

Hardy, James Earl. *B-Boy Blues*. Boston: Alyson, 1994.

Hare, Nathan and Julia Hare. *The Endangered Black Family: Coping with the Unisexualization and Coming Extinction of the Black Race*. San Francisco: Black Think Tank, 1984.

Harper, Phillip Brian. *Private Affairs: Critical Ventures in the Culture of Social Relations*. New York: New York UP, 1999.

Harris, Craig G. "Cut Off From Among Their People." *In the Life: A Black Gay Anthology*. Ed. Joseph Beam. Boston: Alyson, 1986. 63–69.

———. "State of Grace." *Sojourner: Black Gay Voices in the Age of Aids*. Ed. Michael B. Hunter. New York: Other Countries, 1993. 151 -152.

Harris, Trudier. *Black Women in the Fiction of James Baldwin*. Knoxville: U of Tennessee P, 1985.

Hemphill, Essex. "Introduction." *Brother to Brother: New Writings by Black Gay Men*. Ed. Essex Hemphill. Boston: Alyson, 1991. xv-xxxi.

———. "When My Brother Fell." *Brother to Brother: New Writings by Black Gay Men*. Ed. Essex Hemphill. Boston: Alyson, 1991. 110–112.

———. "Does Your Mama Know About Me." *Ceremonies: Prose and Poetry*. San Francisco: Cleis, 1992. 41–47.

———. "If His Name Were Mandingo." *Ceremonies: Prose and Poetry*. San Francisco: Cleis, 1992. 156.

_____."Heavy Breathing." *Ceremonies: Prose and Poetry*. San Francisco: Cleis, 1992. 4–21.

Henderson, Mae G. "Notes." *Passing* by Nella Larsen. New York: The Modern Library, 2002. 183–204.

_____."James Baldwin's *Giovanni's Room*: Expatriation, 'Racial Drag,' and Homosexual Panic." *Black Queer Studies: A Critical Anthology*. Eds. E. Patrick Johnson and Mae G. Henderson. Durham, NC: Duke UP, 2005. 298–322.

Holland, Sharon P. "(Pro)Creating Imaginative Spaces and Other Queer Acts." *James Baldwin Now*. Ed. Dwight A. McBride. New York: New York UP, 1999. 265–288.

hooks, bell. "Seductive Sexualities: Representing in Poetry and on Screen." *Yearning: Race, Gender, and Cultural Politics*. Boston: South End, 1990. 193–201.

_____."Revolutionary Black Women." *Black Looks: Race and Representation*. Boston: South End Press, 1992. 41–60.

_____."Representing Whiteness in the Black Imagination." *Displacing Whiteness: Essays in Social and Cultural Criticism*. Ed. Ruth Frankenberg. Durham: Duke UP, 1997. 165–179.

Hornung, Alfred. "Postmoderne bis zur Gegenwart." *Amerikanische Literaturgeschichte*. Ed. Hubert Zapf. Stuttgart and Weimar: Metzler, 1994. 304–375.

Howe, Irving. "James Baldwin: At Ease in Apocalypse." *James Baldwin: A Collection of Critical Essays*. Ed. Keneth Kinnamon. Englewood Cliffs, N.J.: Prentice Hall, 1974. 96–108.

Hughes, Langston. "The Negro Artist and the Racial Mountain." *The Nation* June 23 (1926).

_____."Poem [2]." *The Collected Poems of Langston Hughes*. Eds. Langston Hughes, Arnold Rampersad, and David E. Roessel. New York: Knopf, 1995. 52.

_____."Café: 3 a.m." *The Collected Poems of Langston Hughes*. Eds. Langston Hughes, Arnold Rampersad, and David E. Roessel. New York: Knopf, 1995. 406.

Humphries, Martin. Ed. *Tongues Untied*. London: Gay Men's Press, 1987.

———. "Introduction." *Tongues Untied*. Ed. Martin, Ed Humphries. London: Gay Men's Press, 1987. 5–10.

Hunter, Michael B. "Introduction." *Sojourner: Black Gay Voices in the Age of Aids*. Ed. Michael B. Hunter. New York: Other Countries, 1993. xiii–xiv.

Hutcheon, Linda. *A Poetics of Postmodernism*. New York: Routledge, 1988.

Hutchinson, George. *The Harlem Renaissance in Black and White*. Cambridge, Mass: Belknap-Harvard UP, 1995.

ICA. Ed. *Black Film, British Cinema*. London: Institute of Contemporary Arts, 1988.

Jackson, Isaac. "Review of Black Men/White Men." *Blackheart* 2 (1984): 48–50.

Jeanmarie, Redvers. "An Interview with Bayard Rustin." *Other Countries: Black Gay Voices*. Ed. Other Countries. New York: Other Countries, 1988. 3–16.

Joachimsthaler, Jürgen. "'the spaces between the columns'. Die Text-Räume und Raum-Texte des Samuel R. Delany." *Zeitschrift für Anglistik und Amerikanistik* 55 (2007): 395–416.

Johnson, Brad. "Protest Poem." *In the Life: A Black Gay Anthology*. Ed. Joseph Beam. Boston: Alyson, 1986. 116.

Johnson, Cary Alan. "Morning After Blues." *Other Countries: Black Gay Voices*. Ed. Other Countries. New York: Other Countries, 1988. 63–82.

Johnson, E. Patrick. "SNAP! Culture: A Different Kind of 'Reading'." *Text and Performance Quarterly* 15 (1995): 122–142.

———. "'Quare' Studies, or (Almost) Everything I Know About Queer Studies I Learned from My Grandmother." *Black Queer Studies: A Critical Anthology*. Eds. E. Patrick Johnson and Mae G. Henderson. Durham: Duke UP, 2005. 124–157.

Julien, Isaac and Kobena Mercer. "Race, Sexual Politics, and Masculinity: A Dossier." *Male Order: Unwrapping Masculinity*. Eds. Rowena Chapman and Jonathan Rutherford. London: Lawrence and Wishart, 1988. 97–165.

_____."True Confessions: A Discourse on Images of Black Male Sexuality." *Brother to Brother: New Writings by Black Gay Men.* Ed. Essex Hemphill. Boston: Alyson Publications, 1991. 167–173.

Julien, Isaac, *Diary of a Young Soul Rebel.* London: BFI, 1991.

_____."Confessions of a Snow Queen: Notes on Making The Attendant." *The Film Art of Isaac Julien.* Ed. Amada Cruz. Annandale-on-Hudson: Center for Curatorial Studies, 2000. 79–83.

_____.dir. *Looking for Langston.* London: BFI, 2006, DVD. (1989)

Katz, Jonathan. *Gay American History.* New York: Harper and Row, 1976.

_____. *Gay/Lesbian Almanac.* New York: Harper and Row, 1983.

Kenan, Randall. *A Visitation of Spirits.* New York: Vintage, 1989.

_____."Wash Me." *Shade: An Anthology of Fiction by Gay Men of African Descent.* Eds. Bruce Morrow and Charles H. Rowell. New York: Avon, 1996. 260–272.

Ketchin, Susan. "Interview with Randall Kenan." *The Christ-haunted Landscape: Faith and Doubt in Southern Fiction.* Ed. Susan Ketchin. Jackson: UP of Mississippi, 1994. 277–302.

Learning Center WEB DuBois. *The Meaning of the Symbolism of the Sankofa Bird.* <http://duboislc.net/SankofaMeaning.html>, accessed May 5, 2007.

Leddick, David. *George Platt Lynes 1907–1955.* Köln: Taschen, 2000.

Lee, A. Robert. "The South in Contemporary African-American Fiction." *A Companion to the Literature and Culture of the American South.* Eds. Richard J. Gray and Owen Robinson. Malden, MA: Blackwell, 2004. 552–570.

Levine, Lawrence W. *Black Culture and Black Consciousness: Afro-American Folk Thought from Slavery to Freedom.* New York: Oxford UP, 1977.

Lewis, David L. *When Harlem was In Vogue.* New York: Knopf, 1981.

Locke, Alain. Ed. *The New Negro.* New York: Touchstone, 1997.

Löbbermann, Dorothea. "Looking for Harlem: (Re)Konstruktionen Harlems als 'queer mecca' 1925–1995." *Amerikastudien/American Studies* 46 (2001): 55–69.

———. *Memories of Harlem: Literarische (Re)Konstruktionen eines Mythos der Zwanziger Jahre*. Frankfurt am Main: Campus, 2002.

Mailer, Norman. *Advertisements for Myself*. New York: Putnam, 1959.

Mance, Ajuan Maria. "Magical Realism." *The Toni Morrison Encyclopedia*. Ed. Elizabeth Ann Beaulieu. Westport, Conneticut and London: Greenwood, 2003. 197–201.

Marriott, David. "Reading Black Masculinities." *Understanding Masculinities: Social Relations and Cultural Arenas*. Ed. Mairtin Mac an Ghaill. Buckingham: Open UP, 1996. 185–201.

May, Vivian M. "Reading Melvin Dixon's Vanishing Rooms: Experiencing 'the ordinary rope that can change in a second to a lyncher's noose or a rescue line'." *Callaloo* 23.1 (2000): 366–381.

McBride, Dwight A. "Straight Black Studies: On African American Studies, James Baldwin, and Black Queer Studies." *Black Queer Studies: A Critical Anthology*. Eds. E. Patrick Johnson and Mae G. Henderson. Durham: Duke UP, 2005. 68–89.

McKay, Claude. *Home to Harlem*. Boston: Northeastern UP, 1987. (1928)

McKoy, Sheila Smith. "Rescuing the Black Homosexual Lambs: Randall Kenan and the Reconstruction of Southern Gay Masculinity." *Contemporary Black Men's Fiction and Drama*. Ed. Keith Clark. Urbana 2001. 15–36.

McRuer, Robert. *The Queer Renaissance: Contemporary American Literature and the Reinvention of Lesbian and Gay Identities*. New York: New York UP, 1997.

Mercer, Kobena. "Dark and Lovely: Black Gay Image Making." *Welcome to the Jungle: New Positions in Black Cultural Studies*. New York: Routledge, 1994. 221–232.

———. "Reading Racial Fetishism: The Photographs of Robert Mapplethorpe." *Welcome to the Jungle: New Positions in Black Cultural Studies*. New York: Routledge, 1994. 171–220.

Micheler, Stefan and Jakob Michelsen. "Von der 'Schwulen Ahnengalerie' zur Queer Theory. Geschichtsforschung und Identitätsstiftung." *Jenseits der Geschlechtergrenzen: Sexualitäten, Identitäten und Körper in Perspektiven von Queer Studies.* Ed. Ulf Heidel. Hamburg: MännerschwarmSkript, 2001. 127–143.

Moglen, Seth. "Modernism in the Black Diaspora: Langston Hughes and the Broken Cubes of Picasso." *Callaloo* 25.4 (2002): 1189–1205.

Moraga, Cherríe and Gloria Anzaldúa, eds. *This Bridge Called My Back: Writings by Radical Women of Color.* New York: Kitchen Table Women of Color Press, 1983.

Morrison, Toni. *Playing in the Dark: Whiteness and the Literary Imagination.* Cambridge, Mass: Harvard UP, 1992.

_____."Rootedness: The Ancestor as Foundation." *What Moves at the Margins: Selected Nonfiction.* Ed. Carolyn C. Denard. Jackson: UP of Mississippi. 2008. 56–64. (1984)

Moynihan, Daniel. *The Negro Family: The Case for National Action.* Washington: US Department of Labor, 1965.

Muñoz, José Esteban. *Disidentifications: Queers of Color and the Performance of Politics.* Minneapolis: U of Minnesota P, 1999.

_____."Photographs of Mourning: Melancholia and Ambivalence in Van der Zee, Mapplethorpe, and *Looking for Langston.*" *Disidentifications: Queers of Color and the Performance of Politics.* Minneapolis: U of Minnesota P, 1999. 57–74.

Mvuyekure, Pierre-Damien. "American Neo-HooDooism." *The Cambridge Companion to the African American Novel.* Ed. Maryemma Graham. Cambridge, UK: Cambridge UP, 2004. 203–220.

Nash, Mark. "Langston in Retrospect." *"Looking for Langston:" A Film by Isaac Julien* [DVD Booklet]. Ed. British Film Institute. London: BFI, 2006. 4–6.

Nelson, Emmanuel S. "The Novels of James Baldwin: Struggles of Self-Acceptance." *Journal of American Culture* 8.4 (1985): 11–16.

———."African-American Literature: Gay Male." *GLBTQ: An Encycopledia of Gay, Lesbian, and Queer Culture.* <www.glbtq.com/literature/African_am_lit_gay.html>, accessed June 26, 2005.

Nero, Charles I. "Toward a Black Gay Aesthetic: Signifying in Contemporary Black Gay Literature." *Brother to Brother: New Writings by Black Gay Men.* Ed. Essex Hemphill. Boston: Alyson, 1991. 229–252.

———."Fixing Ceremonies: An Introduction." *Ceremonies: Prose and Poetry.* Essex Hemphill. San Francisco: Cleis, 1992. xi-xxiii.

———."Black Gay Men and White Gay Men: A Less Than Perfect Union." *Out in the South.* Eds. Carlos L. Dews and Carolyn Leste Law. Philadelphia: Temple UP, 2001. 115–126.

———."Why are Gay Ghettoes White?" *Black Queer Studies: A Critical Anthology.* Eds. E. Patrick Johnson and Mae G. Henderson. Durham: Duke UP, 2005. 228–245.

Newton, Huey. "A Letter from Huey to the Revolutionary Brothers and Sisters About the Women's Liberation and Gay Liberation Movements." *We Are Everywhwere: A Historical Sourcebook of Gay and Lesbian Politics.* Eds. Mark Blasius and Shane Phelan. New York and London: Routledge, 1997. 404–406.

Nugent, Richard Bruce. "Smoke, Lilies and Jade." *Fire!!.* Ed. Wallace Thurman. Metuchen, N.J: Fire!! Press, 1982. 33–39. (1926)

Omi, Michael and Howard Winant. *Racial Formation in the United States: From the 1960s to the 1990s.* New York: Routledge, 1994.

Other Countries Collective. "Introduction." *Other Countries: Black Gay Voices.* Ed. Other Countries. New York: Other Countries, 1988. 1.

Parks, Noel. *Magazines for Gays of Color.* <www.blacklightonline.com/gcn.html>, accessed October 7, 2006.

Phoenix, Ann and Pamela Pattynama, eds. "Special Issue on Intersectionality." *European Journal of Women's Studies* 13.3 (2006).

Podhoretz, Norman. "In Defense of James Baldwin." *Five Black Writers: Essays on Wright, Ellison, Baldwin, Hughes, and Le Roi Jones.* Ed. Donald B. Gibson. New York: New York UP, 1970. 143–148.

Posnock, Ross. *Color and Culture: Black Writers and the Making of the Modern Intellectual.* Cambridge, Mass: Harvard UP, 1998.

Ra, Sun and his Astro-Infinity Arkestra. *Atlantis.* New York: Saturn (ESR 507 Intergalactic Series II) LP, 1969.

Rampersad, Arnold. "Introduction." *The New Negro.* Ed. Alain LeRoy Locke. New York: Touchstone, 1997. ix-xxiii.

Reichert, Klaus. "Zu Hart Cranes The Bridge." *Die Brücke/The Bridge.* Eds. Hart Crane and Ute Eisinger. Salzburg: Jung und Jung, 2004. 161–167.

Reid-Pharr, Robert. "Books, Journals, and Periodicals by Black Gay Authors and Publishers." *Brother to Brother: New Writings by Black Gay Men.* Ed. Essex Hemphill. Boston: Alyson, 1991. 263–269.

_____."Dinge." *Black Gay Man.* New York: New York UP, 2001. 85–98.

_____.-*Black Gay Man.* New York: New York UP, 2001.

Riggs, Marlon. "Tongues Untied." *Brother to Brother: New Writings by Black Gay Men.* Ed. Essex Hemphill. Boston: Alyson, 1991. 200–205.

Roediger, David R. *The Wages of Whiteness: Race and the Making of the American Working Class.* London: Verso, 2007.

Rosenblatt, Roger. "Black Autobiography." *Autobiography: Essays Theoretical and Critical.* Ed. James Olney. Princeton, N.J: Princeton UP, 1980. 169–180.

Ross, Marlon B. "White Fantasies of Desire." *James Baldwin Now.* Ed. Dwight A. McBride. New York: New York UP, 1999. 13–55.

Ruff, Shawn Stewart. Ed. *Go the Way Your Blood Beats: An Anthology of Lesbian and Gay Fiction by African-American Writers.* New York: H. Holt, 1996.

Saint, Asotto. Ed. *The Road Before Us: 100 Gay Black Poets.* New York: Galiens, 1991.

_____.Ed. "Risin' to the Love We Need." *Spells of a Voodoo Doll.* New York: Masquerade, 1996. 321–380.

————."Why I Write." *Spells of a Voodoo Doll*. New York: Masquerade, 1996. 3–8.

Saint-Aubin, Arthur Flannigan. "Black Gay Male Discourse: Reading Race and Sexuality between the Lines." *Journal of the History of Sexuality* 3.3 (1993): 468–490.

Schwarz, A. B. Christa. *Gay Voices of the Harlem Renaissance*. Bloomington: Indiana UP, 2003.

Sandler, Joseph, Ethel Spector Person, and Peter Fonagy, eds. *Freud's "On Narcissism: An Introduction."* New Haven: Yale UP, 1991.

Scott, Darieck. "Jungle Fever? Black Gay Identity Politics, White Dick, and the Utopian Bedroom." *GLQ* 1 (1994): 299–321.

Segal, Lynne. *Slow Motion: Changing Masculinities, Changing Men*. New Brunswick, N.J: Rutgers UP, 1990.

Seymour, Craig. "Envisioning Lives: Homosexuality and Black Popular Literature." *The Greatest Taboo: Homosexuality in Black Communities*. Ed. Delroy Constantine-Simms. Los Angeles: Alyson, 2001. 362–383.

Shaw, George Bernard. *An Autobiography 1856–1898: Selected from his Writings by Stanley Weintraub*. London, Sydney, Toronto: Max Reinhardt, 1970.

Shechner, Mark. "American Realisms, American Realities." *Neo-Realism in Contemporary American Fiction*. Ed. Kristiaan Versluys. Amsterdam and Atlanta: Rodopi, 1992. 27–50.

Shinat, Molly. "Black History and Desire." *"Looking for Langston:" A Film by Isaac Julien* [DVD Booklet]. Ed. British Film Institute. London: BFI, 2006. 14–19.

Shively, Charley. "Smoke, Lilies, and Jade: Black Gay Poetry as an Act of Revolution." *Gay Community News* (1987): 7–10.

Silberman, Seth Clark. "Lighting the Harlem Renaissance AFire!!: Embodying Richard Bruce Nugent's Bohemian Politic." *The Greatest Taboo: Homosexuality in Black Communities*. Ed. Delroy Constantine-Simms. Los Angeles: Alyson, 2001. 254–273.

Simmons, Ron. "Some Thoughts on the Challenges Facing Black Gay Intellectuals." *Brother to Brother: New Writings by Black Gay Men*. Ed. Essex Hemphill. Boston: Alyson, 1991. 211–228.

Sinfield, Alan. *On Sexuality and Power*. New York: Columbia UP, 2004.

Smith, Barbara. Ed. *Home Girls: A Black Feminist Anthology*. New York: Kitchen Table Women of Color Press, 1983.

Smith, Charles Michael. "Bruce Nugent: Bohemian of the Harlem Renaissance." *In the Life: A Black Gay Anthology*. Ed. Joseph Beam. Boston: Alyson, 1986. 209–220.

Smith, Max C. "By the Year 2000." *In the Life: A Black Gay Anthology*. Ed. Joseph Beam. Boston: Alyson, 1986. 224–229.

Smith, Michael J. Ed. *Black Men/White Men: A Gay Anthology*. San Francisco: Gay Sunshine Press, 1983.

Smith, Stephanie A. "A Most Ambiguous Citizen: Samuel R. 'Chip' Delany." *American Literary History* 19 (2007): 557–570.

Smitherman, Geneva. *Talkin and Testifyin: The Language of Black America*. Detroit: Wayne State UP, 1986.

Somerville, Siobhan B. *Queering the Color Line: Race and the Invention of Homosexuality in American Culture*. Durham: Duke UP, 2000.

Spurlin, William J. "Rhetorical Hermeneutics and Gay Identity Politics: Rethinking American Cultural Studies." *Reconceptualizing American Literary/Cultural Studies: Rhetoric, History, and Politics in the Humanities*. Ed. William E. Cain. New York: Garland, 1996. 169–185.

———. "Culture, Rhetoric, and Queer Identity." *James Baldwin Now*. Ed. Dwight A. McBride. New York: New York UP, 1999. 103–121.

Stanford, Adrian. *Black and Queer*. Boston: Good Gay Poets Press, 1977.

Terry, Jill. "Oral Culture and Southern Fiction." *A Companion to the Literature and Culture of the American South*. Eds. Richard J Gray and Owen Robinson. Malden, MA: Blackwell, 2004. 518–535.

Thomas, Anthony. "The House the Kids Built: The Gay Black Imprint on American Dance Music." *The Greatest Taboo: Homosexuality in Black Communities.* Ed. Delroy Constantine-Simms. Los Angeles: Alyson, 2001. 327–336.

Threadgold, Terry. "Text." *New Keywords: A Revised Vocabulary of Culture and Society.* Eds. Tony Bennett, Lawrence Grossberg, and Meaghan Morris. Malden, MA and Oxford, 2005. 345–347.

Thurman, Wallace. *Infants of the Spring.* Boston: Northeastern UP, 1992. (1932)

Tinney, James S. "James Baldwin 'Comes Out' at Gay Forum." *Blacklight* 3.5 (1982): 4.

Tongson, Karen. "Metronormativity and Gay Globalization." *Quer Durch die Geisteswissenschaften: Perspektiven der Queer Theory.* Eds. Elahe Haschemi Yekani and Beatrice Michaelis. Berlin: Querverlag, 2005. 40–52.

Tucker, Jeffrey A. *A Sense of Wonder: Samuel R. Delany, Race, Identity, and Difference.* Middletown, CT: Wesleyan UP, 2004.

Tucker, Lindsey. "Gay Identity, Conjure, and the Uses of Postmodern Ethnography in the Fictions of Randall Kenan." *MFS Modern Fiction Studies* 49.2 (2003): 277–302.

Vance, Carole S. "Social Construction Theory: Problems in the History of Sexuality." *Social Perspectives in Lesbian and Gay Studies.* Eds. Peter M. Nardi, and Beth E. Schneider. London: Routledge, 1998. 160–173.

Walcott, Rinaldo. "Somewhere Out There: The New Black Queer Theory." *Blackness and Sexualities.* Eds. Michelle M. Wright, and Antje Schuhmann. Berlin: Lit, 2007. 29–40.

Walker, Alice. "Looking for Zora." *In Search of Our Mothers' Gardens: Womanist Prose.* San Diego: Harcourt Brace Jovanovich, 1983. 93–116.

Wallace, Michele. *Black Macho and the Myth of the Superwoman.* London: John Calder, 1978.

Watson, Steven. *The Harlem Renaissance: Hub of African-American Culture, 1920–1930.* New York: Pantheon, 1995.

PS
153
.G38
D53
2011

West, Cornel. "The New Cultural Politics of Difference." *The Cultural Studies Reader*. Ed. Simon During. London: Routledge, 1999. 256–271.

Whitaker, Rick. "Telling Politics." *City Pages* Dec. 6 (1991): 50–51.

White, Hayden V. *Metahistory: The Historical Imagination in Nineteenth-Century Europe*. Baltimore: John Hopkins UP, 1973.

Whitman, Walt. "Crossing Brooklyn Ferry." *Leaves of Grass*. New York: Signet, 1954. 144–149. (1856)

Williams, John Alfred. *Clifford's Blues*. Minneapolis: Coffee House, 1998.

Williamson, Judith. "Two Kinds of Otherness." *Black Film, British Cinema*. Ed. ICA. London: Institute of Contemporary Arts, 1988. 33–37.

Wilson, Arthur T. and Assotto Saint, eds. *Here to Dare: 10 Gay Black Poets*. New York: Galiens, 1992.

Wirth, Thomas H. "Introduction." *Gay Rebel of the Harlem Renaissance: Selections from the Work of Richard Bruce Nugent*. Eds. Bruce Nugent and Thomas H. Wirth. Durham: Duke UP, 2002. 1–61.

Woltersdorff, Volker. *Coming Out: Die Inszenierung Schwuler Identitäten Zwischen Auflehnung und Anpassung*. Frankfurt a.M.: Campus, 2005.

Woods, Gregory. "Gay Re-Readings of the Harlem Renaissance Poets." *Critical Essays: Gay and Lesbian Writers of Color*. Ed. Emmanuel S. Nelson. New York: Haworth, 1993. 127–142.

Wright, Michelle M. *Becoming Black: Creating Identity in the African Diaspora*. Durham: Duke UP, 2004.

Wright, Richard. "How Bigger was Born." *Native Son*. New York: Perennial Classics, 1998. 431–462. (1940)